FUNDAMENTALS
of
POLICE
ADMINISTRATION

Charles D. Hale

PUBLIC ADMINISTRATION
SERVICE

Holbrook Press, Inc.

Boston

Printed in the United States of America

Library of Congress Cataloging in Publication Data

Hale, Charles D.
    Fundamentals of police administration.

    Bibliography: p.
    Includes index.
    1. Police administration—United States.   I. Title.
HV7935.H32   350'.74'0973   76-41266
ISBN 0-205-05688-1

Contents

Preface

Police administration is a field that has increased in both complexity and importance in recent years. As a result, the role of the police administrator in the community has changed, as have the skills and aptitudes that are required of a successful police administrator.

Historically, police chiefs have been skilled police practitioners first and adept administrators and managers second, if at all. Seniority, as much as anything else, has been the primary consideration when appointing chiefs of police; and, with rare exceptions, the chief of police is almost always selected from within the department.

Consequently, police departments in the United States today, especially small and medium-sized ones, are generally poorly organized, improperly managed, and badly administered.

One of the reasons for this sorry state of affairs is that, historically, police administration has been viewed as a field unlike any other, with characteristics and subtleties which can only be understood by those who have come up through the ranks and who are intimately familiar with the intricacies of police work. Adding to the problem is the fact that few police administrators have attempted to apply the principles developed in the social sciences to the problems of police administration, even in the face of ample proof of relevance and applicability.

This book is intended to be read by students and practitioners, particularly in small and medium-sized departments, of police administration. It does not pretend to offer a totally new approach to the subject. Indeed, some academicians may be critical of this text in that many of the subjects discussed are "old hat," long ago discarded by modern theorists. But this book is not about theory; rather, it is aimed at reality. My experience as a consultant to a good number of police organizations (mostly small and medium-sized) leads me to the conclusion that, while theories have a place in the classroom, too often they are not grounded in the reality of day-to-day police operations. For this reason, if for no other, I believe this book will suitably meet the needs of hundreds and thousands of police practitioners who continue to toil with the routine problems of police organization, administration, and management.

This book borrows heavily from the traditional literature of public administration in an attempt to make the police practitioner aware that the problems he or she faces in the everyday affairs of the police organization are not unlike those faced by the manager of any small business. At the same time, I am acutely aware of the peculiarities of the police organization, and I have attempted to address them in sufficient detail.

I have dwelt heavily upon personnel issues in this book, and I have devoted three entire chapters—nearly a third of the total volume—to specific personnel problems. This is for good reason; I am convinced that the quality of personnel determines the caliber of services that a police department will provide to its community. In addition, the field of public personnel administration, owing particularly to the impact of affirmative action/equal employment opportunity guidelines and related factors, has gained tremendous importance in the last decade. No other book on general police administration of which I am aware focuses as much attention on the subject, which I believe to be of paramount importance to the police practitioner.

This book is unique in other ways as well. For example, the issue of police productivity is a relatively recent one, and one that has not yet been addressed in substantial detail. I have not attempted to cover the entire field of police productivity, for this would require a book in itself; but, I hope that the treatment given herein will inspire police administrators to become sufficiently interested to study the topic further.

Few books—perhaps none—can cover the entire field of police administration in depth. I have not tried to do so, for this would be a herculean task beyond my capabilities. I have, however, attempted to cover in sufficient detail the basic issues that I have found to be of paramount importance to police managers in small and medium-sized departments. In so doing, I have drawn generously upon the literature of the field, supporting my conclusions, wherever possible, with substantiation that may lead the reader to further inquiry.

If this book is to be used as a basic text in college courses on police administration (as I hope it will), it should necessarily be supplemented with other texts that cover specific subject areas, such as operations research, management by objectives, and police records administration.

Finally, it is my hope that this book will make some contribution—however small—to our understanding of and appreciation for the field of police administration. If so, I shall have succeeded doing what I intended originally.

C.D.H.

Acknowledgements

A text such as this is the result of a collaborative effort, combining the energies and resources of many people. The author is merely the instrument through which an abstract idea becomes solid reality, although he alone must assume the consequences for the final product.

I have been fortunate to receive the counsel and assistance of many persons and organizations in assembling the materials that are presented in these pages. I do not claim original insight into the ideas contained in this text. For the most part, they are a reflection of my own learning process (which, I hope, will continue beyond the publication of this book) beginning with my initiation into the police service several years ago and which has been sharpened considerably through my association with Public Administration Service.

As a staff member with Public Administration Service, I have been privileged to have been associated with several professional public administrators whose generous (and patient) counsel and guidance have enabled me to develop more fully my own appreciation for contemporary principles of management and administration. I am truly indebted to them, and I hope that this book will bring them no discredit.

I am also indebted to the administrators and practitioners with whom I have had the opportunity to work during the past three years in my role as consultant with Public Administration Service. My exposure to a variety of organizational settings, management practices, and operational philosophies has considerably expanded my own understanding of the significant and unique role played by police organizations in the delivery of public services at the local level.

I have also been fortunate to have much assistance provided to me in collecting the reference materials from which many of the ideas contained in this book were drawn. The staff of the Joint Reference Library at the Public Administration Center in Chicago has been most generous and helpful in this respect. In addition, a number of individuals and police agencies have been kind enough to provide me with the photographs which appear in the book. To them I am also most grateful.

Finally, I must acknowledge the debt I owe to my family. Although at times strained, their patience and understanding have allowed me to devote the time and energy necessary for the completion of this book. I sincerely hope that they will recognize the significance of their contribution.

C.D.H.

To my parents

Consulting Editors for the Holbrook Press
Criminal Justice Series

Vern L. Folley

Chief of Police
Bismarck, North Dakota

Donald T. Shanahan

Associate Director, Southern Police Institute
and University of Louisville

William J. Bopp

Director, Criminal Justice Program
Florida Atlantic University

FUNDAMENTALS
of
POLICE
ADMINISTRATION

ONE

Police Administration and the Democratic Process

General
Observations . . .

Police administration does not take place in a vacuum—police agencies are public institutions that are created by law and exist within a complex administrative system designed to carry out the law. In a democracy police agencies are charged with the difficult task of enforcing laws and protecting lives and property. Yet, they must guard against infringing upon those individual rights that are protected under a democratic form of government. At times, these duties and responsibilities seem to conflict. Therefore, it is essential that the student of police administration understands the fundamentals of the democratic process and the administrative system within which the police operate.

Administration is the process by which certain activities are carried out in a logical, orderly, and efficient manner. Nearly all organized activities with which we are familiar are administered by someone in some fashion. Military units, supermarkets, and manufacturing plants all have administrative components. While the nature of these organizations is drastically different, the administrative processes by which their responsibilities are carried out are strikingly similar.

Police administration is that field of endeavor by which the duties and responsibilities of the police are fulfilled. Since the police are but one element of a greater governmental system, the administration of police has much in common with the administration of other public institutions, such as schools, hospitals, and welfare agencies. Accordingly, the study of police administration involves not only an inquiry into the nature and substance of police operations, but also requires a basic familiarity with those theories, concepts, and principles that comprise the broader field of public administration. This chapter discusses the nature of the police function in a democratic society and the evolution of the administrative process as an inherent element of government.

Police Administration in a Democratic Society

The Beginning   In the beginning, there were no police. There were no specialized organizations whose duty it was to maintain social control and to protect the innocent from transgressors. In the beginning, people were their own police. Standards of conduct were agreed upon casually and enforced informally through peer pressure and mutual consent. Mores and customs defined acceptable and expected conduct. With the advent of primitive organized societies, tribal leaders ascended to positions of power and leadership. Tribal chieftans performed the duties of decision maker, law enforcer, administrator, and arbiter. The growth and development of social organizations was accompanied by the emergence of administrative processes designed to serve the needs of society. Food had to be obtained and distributed; enemies had to be guarded against and fought off; hunting and farming instruments were fashioned and placed in selected hands. These functions, and many more, were basic administrative processes.

As societies grew and developed, the responsibility of administering to the needs of the people became more complex and demanding. Rules of conduct became more formalized, and penalties were prescribed for those who violated the rules. Concurrently, a system of administering the rules and carrying out punishments came into being.

Two thousand years before the birth of Christ, the first recorded criminal code was developed in Babylon under King Hammurabi. This code defined the responsibilities of individuals to each other and to society as a whole. Certain individuals were delegated authority to enforce the code and to exact punishments from those who failed to abide by it. A few centuries later, Egypt established a system of courts and judges to administer the laws of the land. Most of the laws at that time were quite primitive and dealt with such offenses as murder, theft, and adultery. Still later, more advanced legal codes and administrative systems were developed in Persia, Greece, and Rome. In each succeeding civilization, the emergence of a legal system was accompanied by an administrative process designed to facilitate the fulfillment of the law.

The Concept of Democracy

In a democratic society, consensus of the governed with regard to the laws by which they are governed is essential. When consensus is eroded, public confidence in government is weakened and governmental effectiveness suffers accordingly. Total consensus, however, is rare in any social or political setting. There will always be differences of opinion among people, even in the smallest group. This is a human trait that is inescapable. Otherwise, there would be no need for formal laws and regulations, nor would there be any need for institutions (i.e., police, courts, prisons) to enforce and administer the laws.

Police forces were created, through a long process of development, in recognition of the need by society to have available some means of enforcing rules of conduct and protecting the innocent from those who would transgress against them.[1] The police, then, evolved as society recognized the fact that

Source: Radio Times Hulton Picture Library, London

Mid-Eighteenth-Century Watchmen

total consensus of the governed, and thus, complete compliance with the law, is not possible in an organized society. The duties and powers of the police and their importance as a social force increase as societal consensus and observance of laws decline.

In theory, the ideal form of government embraces the concept of total self-government—people governing themselves in a manner that reflects their own best interests. In fact, true democracy as a pure form of social control is not practical in a large, heterogeneous society in which people have different interests, customs, beliefs, and life styles. In the United States, the closest thing to true democracy that still exists are the town meetings of New England in which all citizens are invited to take an active part in the affairs of their community government.

Despite its idealistic attractiveness, true democracy suffers from many imperfections and limitations insofar as large, complex societies are concerned. In all but the most simple societies, it is not feasible for all citizens to take an active part in the affairs of government. Crises arise at a moment's notice and immediate action may be required. Each member of the community cannot be polled every time a decision must be made regarding government's response to a particular problem. Efficient government requires a level of continuity and stability that is not possible under the true form of democracy. Unique problems require the attention of persons with specialized skills and training that may be lacking among the members of the general populace. For these reasons, and many more, we live under what may be described as a "representative" democracy, rather than a pure democracy.

Representative Democracy

A representative democracy is one step removed from the true form of democracy. In a representative democracy, members of society are elected to represent the interests of their fellow citizens, or constituents. This form of government, although less democratic than a true democracy, is more efficient. In a representative democracy, all citizens do not take an active role in government; rather, they delegate certain powers and responsibilities to persons of their choosing. This increases efficiency because it concentrates the affairs of government in the hands of a small number of people who can act in a more deliberate and intelligent manner on behalf of their fellow citizens.

The concept of pure democracy is further weakened when elected officials select and appoint others to carry out the administrative affairs of government. While this further diminishes popular control over governmental activities, it increases efficiency. Appointed officials, insulated from political pressures and granted broad administrative powers, are able to devote their specialized skills to the complex problems of government. Usually, due to their technical training and experience, they are much more qualified to manage the administrative affairs of government, allowing elected officials to devote their time to more general policy matters.[2]

Further decreases in democratic control over governmental activities occur when appointed officials seek to delegate certain responsibilities to their subordinates. These officials, in turn, may delegate a share of their responsibilities to other subordinates, and so on down the line. The process of delegation of authority and responsibility may continue through several levels within the governmental hierarchy. As each administrative level becomes further removed from popular control, the concept of democracy is further weakened. At the same time, as the affairs of government become more and more the responsibility of administrative specialists, efficiency is further increased.[3]

In our society, we elect representatives (congressmen, mayors, county supervisors) to conduct the affairs of government. This representative form of government frees us from duties that we have neither the time nor the technical competence to perform and ensures that the affairs of government will be properly attended to by persons who have the authority and time to deal with them.

Our elected officials have the power to select and appoint a variety of officials to whom are delegated many administrative duties. City managers, for example, are appointed by elected representatives to conduct the administrative affairs of city governments. While broad policy matters, such as tax increases, zoning changes, and the adoption of city ordinances, are a prerogative of elected officials, administrative officers play a key role in advising legislators on policy matters. A city manager, for example, with the help of a planning staff, may advise the city council as to what actions regarding zoning changes would be in the best interests of the city. The final decision on such matters, however, rests with the policy-making body.

In larger communities, the chief administrative officer may have a staff of several specialists to assist in technical

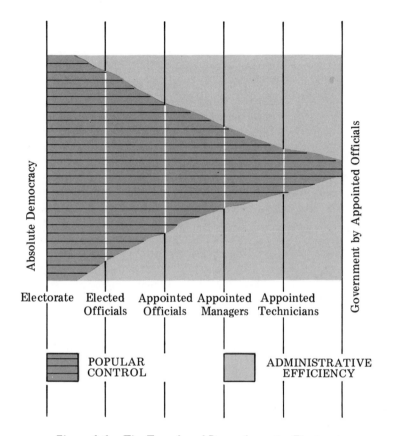

Figure 1-1. The Transfer of Power from the Electorate to Appointed Officials.

matters. A city manager may appoint several department heads, such as a chief of police, a finance director, and a personnel officer, to assist in conducting the city government. The city manager usually will have the power, depending upon the form of city government, to appoint and dismiss these officials as he sees fit.

Department heads may be allowed to select specific subordinates to assist them in carrying out their duties and responsibilities. In some cases, however, the power of a department head to choose his own assistant may be circumscribed by inflexible civil service procedures. In any event, assistants will be appointed to assume part of the department head's duties. In the police department, for example, the chief of police will be assisted by commanding officers who will be responsible for overseeing the operations of various bureaus and divisions.

Thus, as the burdens of government become heavier and as the tasks required to fulfill public obligations become more complex, the powers once possessed by the governed are transferred, first to elected officials, and eventually to lower-ranking administrative officials, over whom the people have no direct control. This problem is fundamental to the system of representative democracy under which we live. It is particularly critical with respect to the police.

> The accretion of specialization and of technological and social complexity seems to be an irreversible trend, one that leads to increasing dependence upon the protected, appointive public service, thrice removed from direct democracy. Herein lies the central and underlying problem . . . how can a public service so constituted be made to operate in a manner compatible with democracy?[4]

This is a question that confronts all police administrators as they attempt to serve the interests of the people in the most efficient and effective manner possible.

The Nature of Public Administration

The Origin of Public Administration

Public Administration, as an inherent element of the process of government, has existed for thousands of years. Indeed, it is as old as government itself. From the time that men began to formulate laws and the means to enforce them, public administration has existed. But as a separate and distinct field of endeavor, complete with its own theories and principles, public administration is less than 100 years old. The first authoritative effort to define the scope and nature of the field of public administration was Woodrow Wilson's "The Study of Administration" published in 1887.[5] A few years later, Frank J. Goodnow's *Politics and Administration* generated further interest in the study of administration in government.[6]

From its earliest days, public administration was viewed as a separate discipline within the more general field of political science, and was believed to be concerned with the execution, rather than the formulation, of policy. This approach to the study of public administration, with its emphasis on techniques, processes, and procedures, has been commonly referred to as the "institutional approach."[7] There is, however, no clear line of demarkation between the development and implementation of policy in the arena of government. Administration is an integral part of the governmental process. Government and administration are inseparable. Without a sound administrative force, government could not function properly, nor could it fulfill its obligations effectively. Laws have little value if there exists no provision for enforcing them. State and local governments would be unable to conduct vital affairs without trained, professional administrators. The Congress could not enact a federal budget if there were not skilled administrative staff available to tend to the laborious technical details of budget preparation. Woodrow Wilson fully recognized the important role of the administrative process in the conduct of governmental affairs:

> Administration is the most obvious part of government; it is government in action; it is the executive, the operative, the most visible side of government, and is of course as old as government itself. [8]

Public Administration as a Science

There has always been some controversy as to whether or not public administration can be considered a science. The full thrust of these arguments is beyond the scope of the present discussion, but a few general observations may underscore the ramifications of the issue in the minds of the student.

First, those who would argue that public administration is an art rather than a science, point out that from the earliest days of government, administration was reserved for those of high social status and prestige, and those who were presumed to be more gifted. Typically, administrators were descended from the aristocratic class. Hence developed the notion of the born administrator.[9]

Modern public administration, however, is no longer the privileged function of the wealthy, but rather, it has evolved into a highly technical and specialized element of government that requires intelligence, good judgement, professional training, and practical experience. The days of the born administrator are gone forever. Today, the field of public administration is a highly complex one in which only the most skilled and dedicated professionals can adequately perform. Nevertheless, the question remains: Is public administration an art or a science? It is the premise of this text, and the author's belief, that public administration is in fact a science, although it may lack some of the qualities and characteristics normally attributed to a scientific field of endeavor.

In some minds, public administration is categorized, along with other fields of inquiry, such as psychology and sociology, as a "quasi-science." The reason for this is that such disciplines, unlike many of the "hard" sciences, such as physics and chemistry, cannot rely upon simple formulae and mathematical relationships to predict the outcome of future events. Rather, it is the task of the social sciences, of which public administration is one, to derive sense and logic from the complex and nonsensible world of human beings. As a result, the challenge to the social scientist is much greater than that which confronts the physical scientist.

> Natural science, after all, has undertaken the comparatively simple and easy task of understanding the mechanistic and mathematical relationships of the physical world and has left to philosophy, ethics, religion, education, sociology, political science, and other social sciences the truly difficult and the truly important aspects of life and knowledge.[10]

While physical scientists may boast of the great accuracy with which they can predict the outcome of the experiments they undertake in the sterile and controlled environment of their laboratories, social scientists cannot. While physical scientists may concern themselves solely with inanimate objects and physical matter whose properties are well known and clearly defined, social scientists must deal instead with a wide range of humanistic phenomena that are difficult to predict and explain. Moreover, most of the physical sciences are thousands of years old, while few of the social sciences have been in existence more than a century.

Another criticism that physical scientists often make of their counterparts in the social sciences is that the latter field of endeavor is "value laden." That is, in the social sciences, certain judgements may be made about the moral virtue of a predictable phenomenon. Certain events and activities are seen as either good or bad, desirable or undesirable. Social scientists endeavor to "correct" deviant behavior, or to develop means to "cure" alcoholism. Physical scientists, on the other hand, do not place values on the subjects under their control. To them, there are no good or bad effects, but merely results. If hydrogen, under certain conditions, combines with oxygen to form water, the result is not to be evaluated in a moral context, but is merely recognized as a physical fact. Thus, while both physical and social scientists are problem oriented, the nature of the problems with which they are concerned differs greatly.

The whole intent of the social sciences is to develop a greater sense of awareness and understanding of the social, political, and cultural environment in which we live in order to improve our ability to coexist in a social milieu. While the physical sciences, through the development of improved technology and expanded material resources, have certainly contributed to a more enjoyable way of life, their efforts would be for naught if the social sciences were not available to increase our ability to survive in a social setting.

Values are fundamental to the social sciences. If the social scientist is to improve the quality of life, then certain values must be established as goals that will help to define whether one social condition is more acceptable than another. In other words, the "goods" must be distinguished from the "bads." While there are no universal values, general agreement can be reached on a number of issues. For example, stability is preferred to instability; efficiency is more desirable than inefficiency; pleasure is preferred to discomfort; peace is more acceptable than conflict, and so on. It is against such a panorama of values that the social scientist must endeavor to seek knowledge that will improve the quality of our lives.

The physical scientist has one great advantage over the social scientist. The physical scientist has at his disposal an almost unlimited variety and number of raw materials with which to conduct experiments. He can analyze, dissect, and manipulate these materials in the sterile vacuum of the laboratory under perfectly controlled conditions. The physical scientist has a wide assortment of sophisticated instruments—telescopes, microscopes, and powerful electronic gadgets of all shapes and sizes—with which to conduct experiments.

The social scientist, on the other hand, must work in the uncontrollable environment of the real world. The social scientist's subjects are human beings; and, they cannot be controlled or manipulated as easily as tiny particles in a test tube. Moreover, human beings are unique, no two are alike, and no two react the same under similar conditions. Social experimentation is more difficult to control than the laboratory experiments conducted by the physical scientist in a laboratory.

Physical and social scientists share their effort to develop an advanced state of knowledge that will add to our understanding of, and make easier our struggles to cope with, the world in which we live. Public administration, as an element of the broader field of political science, is a respectable member of the social science family. As such, it has available to it a wide range of scientific techniques—observation, measurement, analysis, prediction, and explanation—which will provide man with a better understanding of, and the means to improve, the governmental process. Through scientific inquiry and the development and application of modern principles of administration, the process of government may become more responsive to the needs of citizens.

Public versus Private Administration

Public administration is a process that is common to nearly every level of government and one that may be found in nearly every type of government activity.[11] In fact, it is difficult to visualize any government function in which public administration is not involved. Libraries, hospitals, police stations, university classrooms, and city halls are all included in the realm of the public administrator. The list of activities in which the public administrator might become involved is virtually endless.

Private administration, on the other hand, is concerned with nongovernmental endeavors. Private administrators are engaged in a wide variety of enterprises that form the private sector of our economy. As in government, it is difficult to imagine any private business activity in which administration does not play an important role. Steel mills, canning factories, supermarkets, gas stations, movie theaters, and a host of other business activities are subject to some form of administration. Despite the fact that administration is common to both private and public enterprises, there are several basic differences between the two types of administration; these will be briefly explored. Finally, the commonalities between private and public administration will be presented.

The Differences

The primary objective of government is to provide a service to the public. Public services are provided on an "as needed" basis, at no direct cost to the consumer. In general, everybody pays for public services, such as law enforcement and fire prevention, even though they may not have the occasion to use them. Homeowners, for example, may pay property taxes that help to support public schools, even though they may have no children in school. There is no direct relationship between the amount of taxes a citizen pays to support the government and the amount of public services received. People who pay lesser taxes are entitled to the same level of public services as those who pay more.

Private businesses are not supported by public funds, but operate on a profit motive, whereby there is a direct relationship between the amount of money expended for the goods received. Only those persons who can afford the services or products are eligible to receive them. As a result, private enterprise is competetive in nature, while government is not. Commercial businesses must strive to maintain a profitable balance between the cost of producing goods and services and the money received for them. Failure to maintain this profit margin may result in the loss of the market to a competitor. Public agencies do not have this problem.

Public institutions are usually the "sole source" for a particular service. That is, they provide a service that no one else has to offer. Citizens do not "shop around" to obtain the best possible police service or fire protection they can get. They take what is available.[12] Thus, public institutions do not compete with each other to gain a corner on the market.

Another important distinction between private and public administration is that the activities of public agencies are open to a greater deal of public scrutiny than are those of private firms.[13] As Felix Nigro points out, public officials, unlike their counterparts in private industry, operate in a "fishbowl."[14] Since the expenditure of public funds is involved, citizens have a right to know how their tax dollars are being spent and what accomplishments are being gained from those expenditures. Since public policy is involved, citizens have a legitimate interest in knowing how those policies affect their lives. Since public services are directly tied to the welfare and safety of citizens, they have a right to know whether those services are being provided in an equitable and efficient manner.

Private corporations are not exposed to the same rigors of public scrutiny. Although they must strive to develop and maintain an adequate market for their services and an acceptable margin of profit, they are not obliged to inform the consumer about their operations. So long as they can provide a reasonably good product at a reasonable cost to the consumer, it is unlikely that the average citizen will be concerned very much about such matters.

Citizens can exert a great deal of control when they want to over the affairs of public agencies. Citizens' lobbying groups, for example, can bring pressure to bear upon public officials that will have a significant impact upon public agencies. New laws may be passed, old ones may be more rigorously enforced (or not enforced at all), new policies and procedures may be adopted, and public officials may be replaced if enough pressure can be generated by citizens' groups. The civil rights marches and antiwar demonstrations of the 1960s clearly illustrate how effective such tactics can be in bringing about changes in public institutions and policies.

Consumers, on the other hand, are not nearly as effective in bringing their demands before private corporations. The only pressure they can bring to bear is through their own buying power, or the withdrawal of it. Except in a few rare instances, consumer groups have not been successful in changing the policies and procedures of private businesses. In those cases where they have succeeded in affecting change, it has usually been with the assistance of government intervention, as in the case of environmental protection. In general, however, consumers have no reasonable expectation that their demands will have a direct or immediate effect on private business.

Public agencies, unlike private firms, are created by law, and their affairs are regulated by statutory authority derived, ultimately, from the electorate. The manner in which their officers are selected, the way in which they conduct their affairs, and their responsibilities to the public are carefully defined by law. In this respect, citizens have direct control over their activities.

Private corporations, however, operate with almost unlimited freedom from government regulation and intervention. While certain of their activities are subject to government review and control by such agencies as the Federal Communications Commission, the Interstate Commerce Commission, and the Federal Trade Commission, private businesses are generally free to conduct their affairs as they see fit. Compared to public agencies, private businesses are relatively free from public control.

The Similarities
If private and public institutions are dissimilar in the context in which they operate, they are quite alike in their administrative processes. For example, they draw from a common body of knowledge concerning the most efficient way in which to achieve their goals and objectives. The problems and frustrations that confront the manager of a department store are not unlike those faced by the chief executive officer of a municipality. Vacancies in the organization must be filled by competent people. New employees must be given adequate training and on-the-job supervision. Meager budgets must be wisely administered. Property and equipment must be ordered, accounted for, and properly utilized. Individuals and operating units must be evaluated and held accountable for their actions. Strategies for accomplishing goals and objectives must be devised and implemented. The list of similarities goes on and on. The important thing to keep in mind is that while the *substance* of public administration may differ from that of private administration, the processes of the two are alike in many ways.

> While there are differences of objectives and emphasis, it is now clear that these are superficial, and that the underlying facts of experience are similar and complementary. It is therefore highly probable that public administration and private administration are part of a single broad science of administration.[15]

Does this mean that managing the operations of a police agency is no different than running a department store, a bank, or some other type of private business? Of course not! Police agencies have many unique characteristics not found in other types of organizations, and the police administrator must be particularly sensitive to them. But a police chief is an administrator and what he lacks in knowledge of police operations he must make up for in administrative ability.

Public Administration and the Political Process
Public administration may be defined as the process of carrying out the policies of political decision makers. It is the responsibility of the public administrator to interpret and implement the decisions of elected officials. The purpose of public administration is to transform policy decisions into actions and to perform those duties and responsibilities that will en-

sure that the goals and objectives that have been established through the political process will be accomplished. Woodrow Wilson characterized the distinction between policy making and administration in the following manner:

> Public administration is detailed and systematic execution of public law. Every particular application of public law is an act of administration. The assessment and raising of taxes, for instance, the hanging of a criminal, the transportation and delivery of the mails, the equipment and recruiting of the army and navy, etc., are all obviously acts of administration; but the general laws which direct those things to be done are as obviously outside of and above administration. The broad plans of governmental action are not administrative; the detailed execution of such plans is administrative.[16]

Theoretically, then, there is a clear distinction between the making of policy and the administration of it; but, in practice this distinction sometimes becomes blurred. In some cases, it is difficult to distinguish between the making of policy and the implementation of it.

The Public Administrator as Policy Maker

In practical terms, public administration encompasses those duties and responsibilities performed by the executive branch of government. Policy making, on the other hand, is the responsibility of the legislative branch. At the local level, the legislative branch may be the village board of trustees, the city council, or the county board of supervisors, while the executive branch may consist of the town administrator, the city manager, the county administrative officer and their respective staffs.

The distinction between the duties of the legislative and executive branches of government is embodied in the principle of separation of powers that is fundamental to the Constitution of the United States and to the constitutions of each of the fifty states. The dichotomy between administration and policy making, however, is less marked in practice than in theory. This is due to the fact that public administration is carried out in a politically charged environment. Few decisions made by public administrators, whether they be chiefs of police or city managers, are without political implications.

Since it is nearly impossible for law makers to envisage every circumstance in which the laws they enact may apply, nor to anticipate fully the ultimate consequences of those laws, public administrators are often required to make decisions concerning the implementation of policies that are fully as important as the law itself. In addition, since the legislative branch of government does not always possess sufficient expertise concerning the laws they enact, or the policies they make, they must frequently rely upon administrators who, with the support of their own technical staffs, are able to advise legislators on such matters.

Legislators also rely upon administrators to oversee the machinery of government necessary to accomplish the goals and objectives established by law. As the legislative branch relinquishes a part of its authority to the executive branch, it gives greater policy-making power to the public administrator. As the public administrator transposes policy into action, he has the opportunity to invoke personal values into the policy set forth by the legislative branch.

Thus, as the burden of government becomes more complex and cumbersome, and as law makers are faced with more difficult decisions in the course of their duties, much of the authority inherent in their positions is transferred to the public administrator. As a result, the public administrator has become more than ever a policy maker.[17]

Administrative Discretion

As public power is transferred from the legislative to the executive branch of government, the public administrator becomes entrusted with more and more discretion in the manner in which he performs his duties. Discretion is necessary in order for the public administrator to successfully translate policy into action. In many cases, the decisions made by administrators have the same effect as the law itself. Administrative discretion thus becomes a very important part of the governmental process.

Administrative discretion is particularly important where the police are concerned. Law enforcement officers can never hope to enforce all the laws in the manner originally intended by the legislative branch. It thus must be left to the police to determine which laws to enforce and in what manner. Should all drunk drivers go to jail, for instance, or should they be sent home in a taxi cab? The law does not answer this question. It merely says that drunk drivers are *subject* to arrest. Whether or not they will actually be arrested is left to the discretion of the individual police officer.

In some departments, written policy substitutes for individual discretion. Policies may specify under what condition drunk drivers will be arrested and under what conditions they will not. Such policies are not an exception to the law, but rather an amplification of it. In addition, they are an expression of administrative discretion on the part of the chief of police. Such decisions, both at the level of execution and at the administrative level, are indispensible to law enforcement and many other public endeavors as well. Administrative discretion, however, must have certain limits. When those limits are exceeded, the public good is placed in jeopardy.[18]

There are several advantages to be gained by allowing public officials discretion in their duties. For example:

1. Administrative discretion conserves time and allows decisions to be made more rapidly.
2. Decisions made by public administrators are removed from the political arena and thus are less subject to political bias.
3. Public administrators can bring personal expertise and technical know-how to bear on a wide range of subjects, thus improving the quality of the decision-making process.
4. Decisions made by technically qualified administrators are often more effective than those made by politically sensitive legislators.
5. Since public officials are closer to the practical problems of government, they are often in a better position to know what impact their decisions will have on public affairs.

Discretion may be exercised by public administrators in a variety of situations. These may be generally categorized as:

Routine. Administrative discretion is frequently exercised during the day-to-day operations of a public agency. A police chief, for example, may decide how many officers to assign to security duty for a rock concert. A public works director may need to decide whether to schedule street repairs before or after a busy holiday season. A finance director may be required to judge whether or not the current budget will allow for the purchase of additional items of requisitioned equipment. These are rather routine and low-key decisions that reflect administrative discretion in its lowest form.

Emergency. In emergency situations, speed is the primary consideration when administrative discretion is being exercised. Quick decisions must be made, often based upon only scant facts. Time does not permit the leisurely review of alternatives and their possible consequences. A public health officer, for example, may be required to decide whether to quarantine a school where an outbreak of a contagious disease has occurred. A police chief may have to decide whether to request state police assistance in quelling a riot or providing security at the scene of a natural disaster. The impact of these decisions may have far-reaching political implications.

Control. A common form of administrative discretion is that exercised when a public official is faced with decisions that regulate private enterprise. Such decisions are made when licensing businesses, approving requests for special permits (e.g., parades, demonstrations, and the like), conducting fire and safety inspections, and so on. In such instances, the decisions made by the public official may be challenged by persons who have a vested interest in the matter if the decision goes against them.

Controlling Public Administrators

Despite the growing power and autonomy of public administrators, there are many ways in which their activities can be controlled.[19]

1. *Legal restrictions.* The duties and salaries of public administrators, the number of departments they will oversee, the number and type of employees they will supervise, and the budgets they will administer, are frequently specified by laws enacted by the legislative branch.
2. *Budgetary controls.* The legislative branch may also impose restrictions on administrators through the budgetary process. The budget not only determines how much money an administrator will have to spend, but may also dictate how many employees will be hired and what programs will be retained or instituted. The legislature thereby may use the budgetary process as an extension of its policy-making authority.
3. *Administrative audits.* If a legislative body feels that its policy is being improperly interpreted, or that the executive branch is misusing its authority, it may call for an

audit of the administrative practices of the government. An administrative audit serves to objectively review the administrative practices of a unit of government and to discover weaknesses and propose remedial actions. At the local level, a city council may hire a management consulting firm, an accounting firm, or some similar agency to inspect and prepare a report on the administrative practices of the executive branch and to make recommendations for improvement, if necessary. At the federal level, Congress has its own watchdog agency to oversee various government activities—the General Accounting Office (GAO).

4. *Rules and Regulations.* Carefully devised rules of procedure for administrative officials can help to ensure that the limits of administrative discretion are not exceeded. Such rules should be neither vague nor ambiguous; neither should they be so specific and rigorous that they unnecessarily inhibit the discretionary powers of the administrator. Wisely applied, limited discretion is necessary if the public administrator is to be able to perform his or her duties effectively.

Summary

In this first chapter, we have discussed the concept of democracy and the administrative process. We have tried to show that police administrators have much in common with administrators of other public and private agencies. We have stressed the idea that managing the affairs of a police organization requires more than a knowledge of police operations. It requires a sensitivity to the broader and complex problems of administration, management, and organization theory. These subjects will be discussed in greater detail in the following chapters.

Discussion Questions

1. *What is meant by the statement that police administration does not take place in a vacuum?*

2. *Define the term* administration. *How does police administration differ from other forms of public administration? How are they similar?*

3. *Why were police forces created?*

4. *Give several reasons why true democracy, as defined in the text, is impractical in a large, heterogeneous society.*

5. *What is meant by the institutional approach to public administration?*

6. *Do you agree that public administration is more a science than an art? Give several reasons to support your opinion.*

7. *Describe several ways in which public administration differs from private administration. Discuss several ways in which they are similar.*

8. *Discuss in detail the distinction between policy making and administration.*

9. *In what repects does a public administrator become a policy maker? Give specific examples.*

10. *What is administrative discretion? Why is it essential to a public administrator?*

References

1. For a cogent discussion of the development of criminal law and the legal process, see William J. Chambliss, ed., *Crime and the Legal Process* (New York: McGraw-Hill Book Company, 1969), pp. 1–32; A. C. Germann, Frank D. Day, and Robert R. J. Gallati, *Introduction to Law Enforcement and Criminal Justice*, Rev. 19th Printing (Springfield, Illinois: Charles C. Thomas, Publisher, 1973), pp. 43–58.

2. The relationship between democracy and administration is explored at length in Emmette S. Redford, *Democracy in the Administrative State* (New York: Oxford University Press, 1969).

3. Frederick C. Mosher, *Democracy and the Public Service* (New York: Oxford University Press, 1968), pp. 2–3.

4. Ibid., p. 3.

5. *Political Science Quarterly*, 2 (June, 1887), pp. 197–222.

6. Frank J. Goodnow, *Politics and Administration* (New York: The Macmillan Company, 1900).

7. David M. Levitan, "Political Ends and Administrative Means," in Louis C. Gawthrop, ed., *The Administrative Process and Democratic Theory* (Boston: Houghton Mifflin Company, 1970), p. 428. For a discussion

of several other approaches to the study of public administration, see Marshall E. Dimock, "The Meaning and Scope of Public Administration," in John M. Gaus, Leonard D. White, and Marshall E. Dimock, *The Frontiers of Public Administration* (Chicago: University of Chicago Press, 1936), pp. 1–12.

8. Woodrow Wilson, "The Study of Administration," as reprinted in Gawthrop, *The Administrative Process and Democratic Theory*, p. 77.

9. E. N. Gladden, *The Essentials of Public Administration* (London: Staples Press, 1953), p. 19.

10. Luther Gulick, "Science, Values, and Public Administration," in Luther Gulick and Lyndall F. Urwick, eds., *Papers on the Science of Administration* (New York: Institute of Public Administration, 1937), p. 191.

11. H. A. Simon, D. W. Smithburg, and V. A. Thompson, "The Universality of Administration," in Donald C. Rowat, ed., *Basic Issues in Public Administration* (New York: The Macmillan Company, 1961), pp. 18–23; Robert Macgregor Dowson, "The Civil Service is Different," in Rowat, *Basic Issues*, pp. 23–26. See also, Raymond J. Barrett, "Management in the Public Sector," *New Jersey Municipalities*, 52 (December, 1975), pp. 8–9, ff.

12. There are exceptions to this rule, however, such as those people who choose to send their children to private schools rather than public ones, and those businesses that employ private security forces either as a supplement to or in lieu of public police protection.

13. Not all activities of public agencies are open to public inspection, of course. Private citizens, for example, cannot gain access legally to classified military information, nor can they routinely inspect the confidential files of investigative agencies.

14. Felix A. Nigro, *Modern Public Administration*, 2d ed. (New York: Harper & Row, Publishers, 1970), pp. 17–18.

15. Luther Gulick, "Next Steps in Public Administration," *Public Administration Review*, 15 (Spring, 1955), p. 74.

16. Wilson, "The Study of Administration," as reprinted in Rowat, *Basic Issues*, p. 36.

17. For an excellent discussion of the policy-making role of the public administrator at the local level, see Ronald O. Loveridge, *City Managers in Legislative Politics* (Indianapolis: Bobbs-Merrill, 1971).

18. The subject of police discretion, its uses, and abuses, is covered more thoroughly in Jerome H. Skolnick, *Justice Without Trial: Law Enforcement in Democratic Society* (New York: John Wiley, 1966).

19. Paul C. Bartholomew, *Public Administration*, 3d. ed. (Totowa, N.J.: Littlefield, Adams & Co., 1972), pp. 33–43.

Organizations

General
Observations . . .

In the last chapter it was pointed out that police administration is similar in many respects to other forms of administration. One reason is that police departments, although unique in many ways, exhibit many of the same characteristics found in other types of organizations. Consequently, many of the principles that apply to other types of organizations are equally true of police departments. To really understand organizations, we must concentrate on their essential characteristics rather than on outward appearances.

Organizations are an integral part of our society. However, most people pay little attention to the nature, purpose, or characteristics of the organizations that surround them and shape their lives. Indeed, few people give much thought at all to the important role that organizations play in their lives.

Most of us are totally involved in some form of organization, to a greater or lesser degree, from the day we are born until the day we die.[1] Nevertheless, our knowledge of organizations and our ability to maximize their potential for the purpose of accomplishing stated goals remains scant. As Lewis E. Lloyd has observed:

> The problem of how best to organize the efforts of a group of people is an ancient one—dating back to the most rudimentary beginnings of society. Many theories have been proposed and tried. Vogues spring up and are later superseded. Skill at organization remains more an art than a science; in fact, organization remains one of society's major unsolved problems.[2]

It would therefore appear necessary that we begin to expand our knowledge of organizations in order that we may make more productive use of their potential in society. In this chapter, the nature and purposes of organizations will be examined, along with fundamental theories of organization. It is hoped that this discussion will enable the police manager to better understand the organization under his command, to assess its strengths and weaknesses, and to develop methods by which its efficiency and effectiveness can be improved.

What Is an Organization?

What is an organization, and for what purpose was it created? Too often, we tend to think of an organization as merely a collection of individuals working in unison toward some common goal. This is but a superficial analysis of the true nature of an organization. An organization transcends the parameters of its component elements and is more than the sum of its separate parts. It is an entity unto itself, with its own unique characteristics, capabilities, and limitations.

When an individual becomes a member of an organization, he assumes a common identity with other members of the organization. Instead of being just Citizen X, he becomes something more—a member of the track team, an employee of XYZ Canning Co., or a police officer. Whatever the situation, the individual becomes something more than before, and the organization assimilates him into its being.

While no two organizations are exactly alike, they all share one feature: they are composed of individual members. The individual, even though he loses some identity in the organizational structure, remains the key ingredient of the organization. Thus, individuals—their behavior, their capabilities, and their limitations—play an important role, determining the outcome of organizational endeavors.

Psychologist Edgar H. Schein has defined an organization:

> An organization is the rational coordination of the activities of a number of people for the achievement of some common explicit purpose or goal, through division of labor and function, and through a hierarchy of authority and responsibility.[3]

An organization, therefore, may be thought of as the logical and systematic arrangement of resources in a manner that will most efficiently achieve specific purposes. The resources available to an organization may include raw materials, personnel, facilities, and finances. If we were to dissect a typical organization, we would likely find the following components.

1. *Several people.* Organizations commonly consist of two or more members.
2. *Logical Arrangement.* The term organization implies that the elements are arranged systematically, with some consideration given to overall structure and ease of coordination. Groups of people are not organizations because they have no definite structure and their efforts are not coordinated.
3. *A Common Goal.* Organizations exist for a purpose. Without definite goals, an organization has no reason for being.
4. *Hierarchy of Authority.* If an organization is to function effectively, it must have a leader—someone who will take charge and assume responsibility for its actions. The concept of hierarchy of authority will be discussed at greater length later in this chapter.
5. *Division of Tasks.* In most organizations, jobs are divided among members in order to improve efficiency and to capitalize on individual skills and interests. According to Luther L. Gulick, there are a number of good reasons for dividing work among members of an organization:

- Because men differ in nature, capacity, and skill, and gain greatly in dexterity by specialization;
- Because the same man cannot be at two places at the same time;
- Because one man cannot do two things at the same time;
- Because the range of knowledge and skill is so great that a man cannot within his life-span know more than a small fraction of it. In other words, it is a question of human nature, time, and space.[4]

Organizing work is both a physical and a mental process.[5] As a physical process, organizing involves the systematic ordering of separate parts into a logical arrangement that will best suit the needs of the structure and most effectively accomplish its goals. As a mental process, organizing requires the creation of a mental image of exactly how component elements may be joined together in the most efficient manner. The process of organizing requires a combination of practical knowledge and experience, and it is facilitated by a thorough understanding of the basic principles of organizational theory.

The Purpose of Organization

Organizations are not natural institutions, nor do they develop spontaneously; they are created by man to serve specific purposes. Organizations are the logical outgrowth of man's acquired knowledge and they represent the idea that collective activity is more effective than individual effort. "Organizations come into being," according to Chris Argyris, "when goals to be achieved are too complex for any one individual."[6]

As gifted as man may be, he is a frail creature, and is severely limited in mental, physical, and psychological capacities. For this reason, he has traditionallly joined with others to accomplish those tasks which lie beyond individual capabilities. In this manner have organizations been created, and for this reason they have continued to flourish and grow throughout history.

It would appear that man first organized in order to protect himself from natural enemies and to enhance chances for survival in the struggle with the elements. As Robert Michels has noted, organizations are based upon the principle of least effort and are the weapon of the weak in their struggle with the strong.[7] The presence in our society of modern armies and navies serves as a reminder that collective and well organized effort is still essential for survival. Fortunately, more constructive uses for organizations have developed since man first learned the advantages of collective effort.

Today, organizations dominate our lives, for better or for worse. We are engaged in continuous interaction with a multitude of organizations that serve a wide range of purposes. There are religious organizations to meet our spiritual needs; social organizations, in which we may enjoy the pleasure of interpersonal contact; political organizations, through which we gain and dispense power; and work organizations, in which we participate in order to sustain ourselves financially. Of these, work organizations probably dominate our lives more completely than all others.

The Police Organization

Police forces in the United States today follow a general pattern that first evolved in England, where the first regular police force was organized by Sir Robert Peel, the British Home Secretary in 1829.[8] Unfortunately, many police forces in the United States have grown and developed with little attention to sound organization principles. As a consequence, they have become unwieldy, outmoded, and unable to perform their obligations in an efficient manner.

The proper management of police resources depends upon a fundamental knowledge of what organizations are, how they operate, and what can be done to improve them. If police administrators are to effectively serve the interest of their communities and to make the most efficient use of the resources at their disposal, they must be thoroughly acquainted with the basic principles of organization. In the following section, a few basic principles of organization will be discussed.

Organization Principles

There are no absolutes in the study of police organization and management. Unique situations require tailored solutions. While some techniques may work well in some cases, they may fail in others. Similarly, organization principles cannot be applied universally. The principles discussed in this section are not concrete laws, but rather they are offered as guides to be used sparingly in the management of police organizations. It is recognized that, today, the field of police administration and the nature of police organizations are changing rapidly. As changes occur, new ways of thinking about police organization and management will emerge. What has been accepted in the past as vital will become obsolete.

The following discussion offers no revelations to the police administrator of the future. Rather, the principles of organization examined here are relevant to the police organization as it exists today, not as it may exist sometime in the future. Although change is healthy and although it is recognized that change must inevitably come to all things, nevertheless, police organizations have a way of resisting change more successfully than most organizations. Thus, if this book is to have any practical value at all, it must concern itself with assisting prospective police adminstrators to cope with their organizations as they will likely find them today, not as they may see them some years in the future.

The Hierarchy of Authority

Hierarchy of authority refers to the arrangement, in ascending and descending order, of different classes of positions, accompanied by proportionate levels of authority. To better understand the principle of hierarchy of authority, an organization may be viewed as a pyramidal structure, consisting of a series of levels of authority. Authority is commensurate with one's position within the hierarchy. Authority increases as one travels up the hierarchial ladder. As one nears the top of the pyramid, the number of positions is decreased while the level of authority is increased. This idea is represented in Figure 2-1.

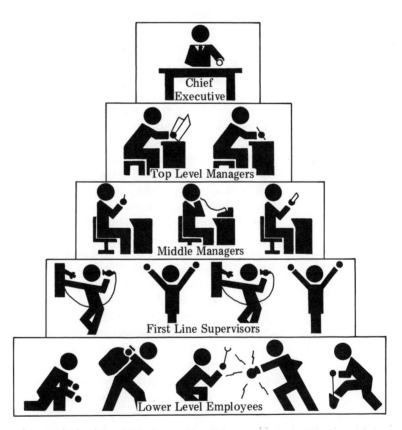

Figure 2-1. Typical Organization Structure Representing Concept of Hierarchy of Authority.

The principle of hierarchy of authority is based on the theory that authority is most effective when applied sparingly within the organization and when vested in a few carefully selected individuals. Obviously, if all members of an organization exercised equal authority, control and discipline would be hard to maintain.

Authority flows from the top of the organization downward. In the police organization, the chief of police represents the pinnacle of authority—the top of the organizational pyramid. The chief of police derives authority from legal sources that created the police organization and delineated its duties and responsibilities. Authority in the police organization is vested in the chief of police who delegates it to subordinates. At each successive descending level of the pyramid, individuals exercise authority over those subordinate to them.

In the police organization, as in the military, authority is sometimes commensurate with rank. A sergeant, for example, has more authority than a patrolman, while a lieutenant has more authority than a sergeant. Authority may also be vested in positions within the organization. For example, the commander of a division (e.g., the Field Services Division) will have more authority than the commander of a bureau (e.g., the Traffic Bureau), regardless of the rank held by the two individuals. Moreover, two division commanders (e.g., Field Operations Division and Administrative Division) may have equal authority, even though their respective ranks are unequal. Therefore, authority may be commensurate with either rank or position. In some cases rank will correspeond with position, while in others it will not.

Authority may be defined as "legal or rightful power, a right to command or act."[9] As Koontz and O'Donnell have indicated, authority "is the basis for responsibility and the binding force in organization."[10] Formal authority is vested in the chief executive officer of an organization (e.g., chief of police) and is derived from the sources that created the organization and enable it to operate. For authority to be meaningful in an organization, it must be accepted by the members of the organization. Acceptance of authority by subordinates legitimizes the authority of superiors. For subordinates to accept authority, they must recognize the basis for such authority and must submit to it.

The classical definition of authority was devised by Weber, who distinguished between three different bases of authority: traditional, rational-legal, and charismatic.[11] **Traditional authority** is that which has always been accepted as a matter of custom. In a monarchy, for example, the authority of the king or queen was accepted as a matter of divine right. In the family, the right of the parents to govern the conduct of children is accepted as a matter of tradition and custom. **Rational-legal authority** is that type which is found in most modern organizations. Such authority is based on the notion that authority must be formally assigned to individuals on the basis of some rational criteria and should be governed by formal laws or contracts. Individuals are elevated to positions of authority on the basis of demonstrated competence and willingness to accept responsibility. **Charismatic authority** may also be found in the formal organization, but usually lies beyond formally delegated authority. Charismatic authority is vested in those persons who demonstrate a magnetic personality and who are able to influence others as a result.

Authority is usually accompanied by responsibility. Those in whom authority is vested must be held accountable for their actions. In the formal organization, authority and responsibility are two parts of the same whole. As Henri Fayol observed—

> Authority is the right to give orders and the power to exact obedience . . . Responsibility is a corollary of authority, it is its natural consequence and essential counterpart, and wheresoever authority is exercised, responsibility arises. [12]

Not all scholars, however, agree that responsibility is commensurate with authority. Mason Haire, for example, challenges what he perceives to be the "myth" of organizational theory that responsibility must be attached to authority. He suggests that by specifically relating responsibility to authority, we impose a special meaning on both terms and thereby defeat the purpose of individual commitment to organizational goals.

> If by responsibility one means that the incumbent is completely answerable for the success or failure of an operation, then he must, to protect himself, limit his responsibility to those things over which he has a direct and immediate control. This kind of sense of responsibility must surely work against the general goals of the organization. We want him to feel the broadest possible responsibility for the objectives and activities of the firm. [13]

In the police organization, however, it is in the interest of efficient management and effective control to ensure that responsibilities, and the authority required to fulfill them, are carefully and systematically apportioned among members of the organization. By delegating authority, accountability for specific actions will be ensured.

The maintenance of authority is essential to the proper functioning of the police organization. When authority is ignored or denied, loss of control may occur, and the organization will fail to function effectively. Denial of authority threatens the internal stability of the organization and reflects unfavorably upon organizational morale and efficiency. Most members of an organization support the goals of the organization and will submit to authority if they believe it to be in the best interests of the organization. Those who willfully defy authority that is considered legitimate by other members of the organization will receive little support from their peers.

In the police organization, formal authority (rational, legal) and informal authority (charismatic) are to be found. Of the two, formal authority is the most evident, although both types exert considerable influence on the operations of the organization. Formal authority is the most evident in the police organization due to the traditional reliance on formal rank structures, military-like uniforms, and the use of prominent symbols of rank, such as badges, chevrons, insignia, and the like.

In the police organization, as in other organizations, informal authority plays an important role. Persons with little or no authority may exercise a great deal of power and influence over the affairs of the department merely because of their personal prestige, or charisma. Since promotions are relatively scarce in most police organizations, there are inevitably a number of veteran officers who never rise above the rank of patrolman. Due to their experience, age, and street know-how, these individuals are often held in high esteem by other members of the organization and wield considerable influence over the actions of their peers. For instance, the veteran police officer who is assigned to "break in" a rookie officer may have more influence upon the future actions of the new officers than all the instructors in recruit training school. In some cases, personal authority may be more pervasive in the police organization than formal authority. Many times, those who occupy positions of formal authority may submit to persons subordinate to them merely due to their recognized personal influence. A young patrol sergeant, for example, may rely heavily upon an experienced patrolman for suggestions concerning a particular problem that he is unable to solve.

Delegation of Authority   In an organization, authority emanates from the chief executive and is passed down through the hierarchy of command. Each level of management in the organization must be delegated authority in order to perform its proper function. The extent to which authority may or should be delegated, however, poses a central management problem.

Traditionally, lower-level managers have been entrusted only with that degree of authority required for them to carry out their responsibilities as directed. All other authority has been reserved for top management. Thus, in such cases, the sphere of authority of a lower-level manager or supervisor is carefully circumscribed. However, contemporary management theorists suggest that the traditional notion of authority delegation is counter-productive and should be reversed. Drucker, for example, describes a situation in which all authority not specifically reserved for top management is delegated to lower-level managers. Peter Drucker defends this distribution of authority, contending that these "firing line" managers, as he calls them, are closer to the day-to-day operations of the organization and, thus, are called upon to make more important decisions than higher management.[14]

Furthermore, as Drucker points out, there are reasonable limits to the authority of any manager.[15] A single manager or supervisor can only make those decisions that affect the operations directly under his control. A patrol sergeant, for example, must have the authority to assign subordinates to those areas where they are most needed and to require them to perform functions most likely to produce the desired results. He does not, however, have the authority to determine the level of pay to which his subordinates are entitled, or whether they will be assigned to rotating or permanent shifts. These are decisions which, because they affect more than one group within the organization, are reserved for higher management. Similarly, a detective sergeant can dictate to the personnel under his command the manner in which a particular case is to be investigated, but he has no authority, unless it is specifically delegated to him, to assign or direct the activities of patrol officers in the field. (Refer to the section concerning *unity of command* in this chapter.)

Authority must be balanced with responsibility. A person should not be held responsible for actions over which he has no authority. Conversely, once given authority, a person must be held accountable for his actions. This is a fundamental principle of management, articulated many years ago by L. Urwick.

To hold a group or individual accountable for activities of any kind without assigning to him or them the necessary authority to discharge that responsibility is manifestly both unsatisfactory and inequitable. It is of great importance to smooth working that all levels of authority should be coterminous and coequal.[16]

Delegation of authority is important in an organization for a number of reasons. First, in all but the smallest organization, a single individual cannot manage alone. Every manager usually needs help of some kind. Unfortunately, some executives refuse to delegate authority and attempt to carry the entire burden of management themselves. In most cases, this will lead to grave consequences for the manager and for his organization.

> One of the tragedies of human experience is the frequency with which men, always efficient in anything they personally do, will finally fail under the weight of accumulated duties that they do not know and cannot learn to delegate.[17]

Second, delegation of authority encourages lower-ranking members of the organization to assume responsibility for their own acts and helps to develop leadership potential. The manager who is reluctant to delegate authority will likely leave office, when the time comes, with no one prepared to succeed him. On the other hand, the successful manager is the one who can turn over the management of the department to a subordinate, fully confident that the affairs of the organization will continue to be managed in a competent manner.

Third, delegation of authority stimulates greater interest in and enthusiasm for the operations of the organization by its members. On the other hand, lower-level managers and supervisors who are not given proper authority cannot function up to their capacities and will become discouraged and disillusioned. (Refer to the section concerning *participative management* in Chapter 3.)

Span of Control   Span of control refers to the number of subordinates one person is expected to be able to supervise with a reasonable degree of effectiveness. This principle is based on the belief that if a person's span of control is too wide—that is, if he has too many people to supervise—he will be unable to supervise them properly. On the other hand, if a span of control is too limited, a supervisor is not being used to his fullest capacity.

Authorities do not agree upon what the optimum span of control should be. Various numbers have been suggested, but there is really no magic formula for determining the maximum number of individuals one person can effectively supervise. A number of factors must be considered when determining span of control. These include the nature of the work being performed, its level of complexity, the degree of specialization, the competence of subordinates, and the degree to which responsibility must be delegated. In general, the more difficult or complex the nature of work being performed, the smaller should be the span of control. For example, it is more difficult to supervise a number of laboratory technicians performing highly specialized and technical operations, than it is to oversee the work of a number of assembly line workers performing routine, identical tasks.

In the police organization, the span of control may vary with the type of work being performed. The span of control in the detective division, for instance, may be different from that of the patrol division, due to the nature of the work. In addition, the experience and skill of the supervisor may also affect his span of control. Older, more experienced supervisors may be able to control the activities more effectively than younger, newer supervisors.

Realistically, the span of control in most police departments will range from four to eight. A patrol supervisor may have as many as ten patrol officers to supervise, but rarely more. Although there is no precise way of determining what the exact span of control should be in all situations, the police administrator should carefully examine the span of control of each of his subordinates in terms of their overall operating efficiency, making adjustments accordingly.

There are a number of considerations to keep in mind when determining an optimum span of control.

1. A short span of control creates a tall (as opposed to a short) organizational structure, thus increasing the levels of supervision required and making more difficult the task of overall management and control.
2. Increased levels of authority in the organization also increase administrative expenses by adding costs for executive salaries, offices, and administrative expenses.
3. A shorter span of control distorts the communication flow within the organization by adding more supervisory levels through which information must pass.

4. A short span of control dilutes the influence of senior executives by giving more power and authority to a greater number of subordinates.
5. Finally, a short span of control increases the complexity of the decision-making process by increasing the number of persons who must participate in decisions.

A span of control that is too wide creates just as many problems as one that is too narrow. If a span of control is too wide, the supervisor simply will not be able to exercise effective control over subordinates. The difference bewteen a wide and a narrow span of control is shown in Figure 2-2. In general, the shorter span of control is to be preferred over one that is too wide.

Chain of Command

In large, complex organizations, there must be some way in which orders, directives, and other sorts of communications can be transmitted from one level or part of the organization, to another. Moreover, there should be some logical and orderly manner of supervising and controlling the actions of individuals and units within the organization. In some organizations—including most police agencies—these objectives are achieved by establishing and maintaining an effective chain of command.

A chain of command may be defined as that linkage of authority and responsibility that joins one level of an organization to another. Under the principle of chain of command, each person in the organization has an immediate superior to whom he is responsible and through whom all authority, communications, orders, and directives must pass. Thus, the chain of command is employed to uniformly channel information, authority, and responsibility throughout the organizational structure.

That the chain of command must be firmly established and that it should not be violated is a basic principle of police organization. The integrity of the chain of command is essential to the well-being and proper functioning of the police organization.

Because supervisors are charged with the responsibility of always being aware of and accountable for the actions of their subordinates, it is important that the chain of command not be violated purposely. Frequent violations of the chain of command will erode the control that a supervisor must exer-

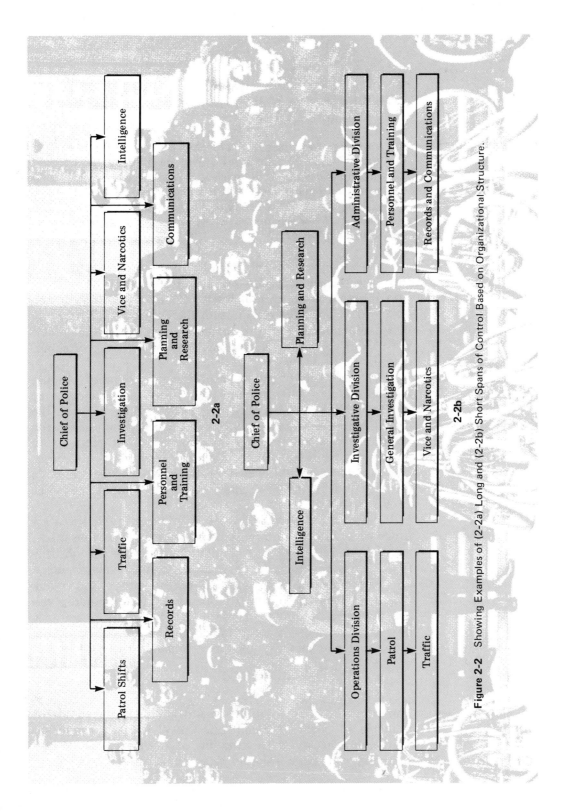

Figure 2-2 Showing Examples of (2-2a) Long and (2-2b) Short Spans of Control Based on Organizational Structure.

cise over subordinates, and will prove detrimental to the overall effectiveness of the organization. This point was emphasized by Wilson and McLaren.

> Diverting orders, directives, or reports around a level of command usually has disastrous effects on efficiency of the organization if the level which is bypassed is ordinarily capable and responsible. The bypassed supervisor has no official knowledge of the nature of a directive going downward. Since he is unaware of a directive, he can hardly be responsible for enforcing it.[18]

An effective and well maintained chain of command ensures the orderly transmission and dissemination of information throughout the various levels of the organization. It also serves to balance the distribution of authority and responsibility among members of the department. Finally, it facilitates the task of controlling and supervising the activities of subordinates.

The principle of the chain of command, however, should be applied with restraint and reason, and should not be so rigidly enforced that it impedes, rather than facilitates, the operations of the organization. For example, there may arise situations in which it is not only expedient but necessary to bypass one or more levels of authority in the organization to meet a particular need. This is particularly true when time is a critical factor, as it is in so many situations in which the police are involved.

Since much of police work is crisis oriented, there are times when information must be transmitted, decisions made, and actions taken, all with a minimum of delay and obstruction. Too strict compliance with the chain of command in such cases may disrupt the efficient performance of the organization. In such cases, it may be necessary to temporarily violate the chain of command. In routine, day-to-day operations, however, the chain of command should be closely observed in order that the integrity of the command structure be preserved.

Unity of Command   The principle of unity of command is closely linked to the principle of chain of command. Unity of command means simply that in any given situation, at any particular point in time, only one person should be responsible for the affairs of other persons. To put it another way, any one individual in an organization should have only one supervisor at any one time; and, each command situation should be supervised by one person only.

The principle of unity of command minimizes confusion in work situations and ensures more efficient operations. If a person is faced with a dilemma of trying to choose between the orders of two or more supervisors continually, he will undoubtedly become confused and frustrated; and, his performance will suffer accordingly.

The principle of unity of command was first articulated by the French industrialist, Henri Fayol, who wrote—

> For any actions whatsoever, an employee should receive orders from one supervisor only. Such is the rule of unity of command, arising from general and ever-present necessity and wielding an influence on the conduct of affairs, which to my way of thinking, is at least equal to any other principle whatsoever.[19]

In the police organization, the principle of unity of command enhances efficiency in the working relationships among members of individual units. To give an example, a patrol officer assigned to field duty is usually supervised by a patrol supervisor, frequently a sergeant. The sergeant, in turn, may be supervised by a lieutenant, who may be in command of a patrol shift or a sector of the city. Within this relationship, orders and information are passed to the patrolman from the lieutenant through the sergeant. If a supervisor in another unit (for example, a lieutenant of detectives) were to issue instructions to a uniformed patrol officer, he would be violating the principle of unity of command. The patrol officer may be placed in jeopardy if he ignores those orders, even though he may know they should have not been issued. As a result, he may become confused and unsure of what action to take.

The principle of unity of command ensures that all members of the organization know who they are responsible to and that, given an order, it must be obeyed. The principle of unity of command must be obeyed, by supervisors and subordinates alike, if the operations of the organiation are to be conducted with a minimum of confusion.

Like the principle of chain of command, the principle of unity of command must be applied reasonably and with good judgement. It must also be flexible and adaptable to different situations. It should not be so strictly interpreted that it obstructs operations unnecessarily. The principle of unity of command should not prohibit members of one organizational unit from working with members of other units or from taking orders from someone other than their normal supervisor, under exceptional circumstances.

For example, in the police organization, it is common for members of a patrol unit to work closely with members of a detective unit in conducting raids, maintaining surveillance activities, and so forth. In such cases, the patrol officers may be placed under the command of the detective responsible for the operations. This temporary transfer of authority and responsibility does not violate the principle of unity of command, since the details of the operation have been carefully planned in advance and lines of authority and responsibility have been well established for the purpose of the operation. On the other hand, it would be wrong for a supervisor in one unit to arbitrarily assume responsibility for the actions of members of another unit, or to issue them orders without receiving advance permission from their regular supervisor.

In some cases, the principle of unity of command may be set aside for special or emergency reasons, such as at the scene of a major crime or natural disaster. At such times, the senior officer present may temporarily assume command of all police operations, regardless of his normal responibilities, until such time as the situation can be normalized.

The principle of unity of command is intended to simplify the task of direction and control, to avoid confusion and duplication of efforts, to facilitate coordination among organizational units, and to provide for a more systematic and orderly method of accomplishing the goals of the organization. If observed and practiced with flexibility and good judgement, the principle of unity of command will enhance the overall effectiveness of the police operation.

Specialization   A basic organizational principle dictates that similar tasks and functions should be combined and performed by particular units within the organization. In an organization in which a number of highly specialized activities are to be performed, it is common practice for those activities to be divided among a number of individuals or units, each specializing in one particular type of activity. This is especially true in police organizations consisting of more than a few individuals. Because of the highly diversified nature of the police function, it is necessary to divide work by function and to distribute work to various units having a particular orientation or capability. As a police organization grows larger and the nature of its responsibilities becomes more complex, it will become even more specialized. Where there once may have been a small detective unit, there now may be a number of specialized units, each concentrating on a particular type of investigation, such as homicide, burglary, or robbery.

The purpose of dividing tasks among individuals or units is to increase the overall efficiency of the organization. Because individuals are limited in the number of skills they can master, it seems appropriate to apportion work among several individuals, each specializing in a particular type of activity. An illustration of this principle is a large automobile manufacturing plant. Some workers are assigned to do nothing but install headlights, while others may place the engine on the chassis, while others may apply the finished coat of paint. Each of these individuals is proficient in his own sector of responsibility. This assembly-line approach to manufacturing has greatly enhanced the productivity of such endeavors.

Although police agencies cannot be compared to assembly lines, it is true that specialization does increase the level of efficiency in police work. Even though most police officers are required to have basic knowledge of many subjects, including criminal law, traffic investigation, criminal investigation, human psychology, and patrol procedures, to name a few, they cannot be expected to become proficient in all these subjects. Therefore, it becomes necessary to divide these diverse functions among a number of specialists who can become proficient in particular areas. Patrol officers, for example, may become very adept at spotting unusual activities or suspicious circumstances, but may have neither the training nor the technical experience required to conduct a sophisticated crime scene investigation.

Specialization in law enforcement first occurred in London in 1843, when a detective squad was organized in the Metropolitan Police Department. When the Boston Police Department was first organized, it also assigned a number of its personnel to detective duties. Later, in 1920, with the advent of the automobile, traffic enforcement became another specialized police function. Today, specialization has become an accepted principle in most police organizations.

As a police organization grows and develops new responsibilities, the opportunities for specialization become manifest. It is virtually impossible, today, for a police officer with only basic police training to perform all of the highly technical skills required of the police profession. Today, more than ever before, police agencies must acquire new technical skills in order to provide the level of service required of them. New and emerging fields, such as crime prevention, community relations, and juvenile care, require the careful attention that only a trained specialist can provide.

There are a number of advantages to be gained from specialization. First, specialization ensures that persons to whom tasks are assigned are proficient in their duties due to advanced training or extensive experience. An investigator who has been thoroughly trained in the art of crime scene investigation will be more thorough in his work than a patrolman who has been given only the most rudimentary training in such matters. Second, the person who has a specialized assignment will normally take much more interest in his work. Many police officers may not care for traffic enforcement duties; but, officers who are assigned to such duties usually want them and because they have received specialized training. Specialization enables officers with particular interests and abilities to be assigned to those duties to which they are most suited. Third, specialization allows for the orderly and rational distribution of work in the organization. Certain functions are assigned to certain individuals or units; as new needs arise, new units may be created to account for them. In this way, specialization ensures that all work will be performed as required.

Specialization is not without its drawbacks, however. (Refer to the section concerning *specialized police operations* in Chapter 5.) First of all, too much specialization limits the usefulness of the individual police officer. Although a crime scene technician may be an expert at collecting physical evidence, he will be of little value otherwise. If the work of the organization does not justify such specialization, personnel resources may be wasted. Specialization should only be used when the need can be justified. There is little reason for creating a specialized traffic unit in a small police department if such duties can be effectively performed by patrol officers.

Second, specialization tends to narrow the focus of individual officers with the result that they become more interested in their own particular jobs and less concerned about the goals of the organization. Detectives, for example, may be only interested in solving the cases assigned to them, attaching more importance to their duties than to the overall efficiency of the police operation.

Third, specialization can lead to an unhealthy rivalry causing friction between separate units within the organization. Members of one specialized unit may place the interests of their own unit above other units or those of the entire organization. This may lead to a disruption in organizational operation and may debilitate the harmonious relationship that must be maintained if efficiency of operations is to be achieved.

Fourth, too much emphasis on specialization in the police organization may place an unnecessary burden on the resources of the patrol force, which is commonly recognized as the basic unit of operation. Rarely, if ever, does the police executive have the necessary resources to support both specialized units and the patrol force to the extent believed justified. He must sometimes choose between the two. If too much reliance is placed on specialized units, the patrol force may suffer, and the basic services of the department may be jeopardized.

Fifth, specialization in the police organization may place a greater burden upon the police supervisor to ensure proper coordination among the various units of the organization. Increased specialization results in problems of both control and coordination with a subsequent decrease in efficiency of operations.

> As specialists and specialized units are created or expanded, the police chief executive may find that both his operational flexibility and his overall control are diminished. The greater the specialization, the more inflexible the operation becomes.[20]

Finally, when specialization occurs within an organization, it places limits on the authority of other units, often resulting in wasted manpower and decreased efficiency. For example, policy may dictate that patrol officers turn all narcotic investigations over to a specialized unit although the patrol officer may be entirely capable of conducting the preliminary investigation himself. When this occurs, the authority of individuals within the organization may be unnecessarily restricted. Conflict, frustration, and bitterness may result, to the detriment of the overall police operation. Thus, it is essential that the police administrator be cognizant of the problems created by specialization and that he attempt to utilize specialized units sparingly. While specialization is inevitable in the police organization, many of the problems discussed can be avoided if careful thought and attention are given to them by persons in places of responsibility.

Line-Staff Relationships

In most police organizations, there exist two classes of positions—line and staff. **Line positions** are those which are directly involved in the operational activities of the organization. Typical police line functions include patrol, traffic, and criminal investigation. **Staff functions** are those positions that supplement or support line operations. In the police organization, staff functions may include planning and research, personnel, and training. In the police nomenclature, staff functions may also be known as auxiliary or support services.

According to Keith Davis, staff services may fall into one of three categories of activities: advisory, service, and control.[21] The **advisory staff** serves to provide counsel to the chief executive. The advisory staff has no authority to compel others to take their advice, and the chief executive may either accept or reject the counsel offered. In the police organization, a planning and research officer may provide the chief of police with alternative methods of accomplishing organizational goals, but the decision of which alternative to take rests with the chief of police. Such is an example of an advisory staff position.

Service staff functions are those that exist to facilitate the job of members of line activities by providing some service to them. In most organizations, line activities depend rather heavily upon service staff support, and could not function effectively without such support. In the police organization, a communications section provides support services to the line operations. Without communications, the line operations could not function.

Control staff functions are those that exercise some degree of control over line activities. Control staffs do have the power to exert authority over line operations. In a police department, for instance, an inspection unit may compel other members of the organization to adhere to certain procedures and directives, and may take corrective action if compliance is not maintained.

Staff assistance can be invaluable to a police organization if it is properly used and if the duties, responsibilities, and relationships of the staff positions are clearly delineated by departmental policy and identified in organizational charts. In some police organizations, there is no clear distinction between line and staff responsibilities. Such ambiguity results in confusion, impeding the efficient management of the police organization. An example of such a police organization is shown in Figure 2–3a on page 46. The same organization, with line and staff responsibilities clearly identified, is shown in Figure 2–3b, also on page 46.

Conflicts between line and staff units sometimes arise in police organizations. These conflicts can usually be avoided if careful thought and attention are given to clarifying the specific duties and responsibilities of staff units. Common sources of conflict that may arise between line and staff units in the police organization include the following:[22]

1. Line and staff officers may compete with one another for authority. Conversely, they may fail to recognize the limits of their own respective spheres of authority.
2. Staff officers are sometimes eager to develop new policies and procedures for line units, but they are not held accountable for the results.
3. Line and staff officers sometimes fail to exchange information that would make their activities more useful and complementary to the organization as a whole.
4. Staff officers may attempt to take credit for successful actions initiated by them, placing the blame for failures on line personnel.
5. Line officers may feel that staff officers do not understand the day-to-day problems of line units, that they are too far removed from the practicalities of line operations, and thus, that they are not qualified to make decisions affecting line units.
6. Line officers may fail to take advantage of the special skills of staff personnel, may resist new ideas proposed by staff units, and may prefer to rely upon traditional methods rather than accept advice from staff units.

An efficient and well managed police organization will be characterized by a proper balance between line and staff duties and responsibilities. The police executive must clearly delineate the roles and relationships of line and staff units, endeavoring to facilitate a harmonious working relationship between the two. Failure to do so may result in conflict, confusion and a loss of organizational efficiency.

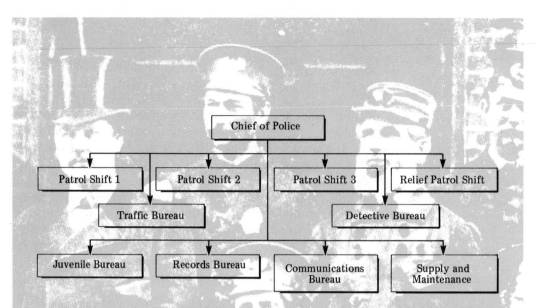

Figure 2-3a. Example of a Poorly Organized Police Organization, with no Balance Between Line and Staff Functions.

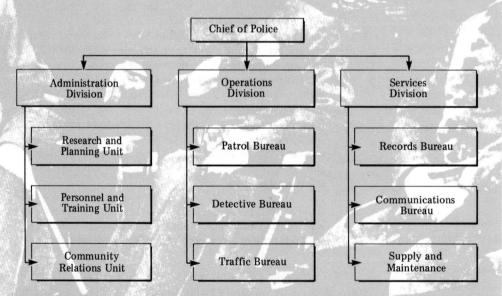

Figure 2-3b. Example of a Well-Organized Police Department, Observing Proper and Well-Defined Line-Staff Relationships.

Types of Organizations

Organizations are products and reflections of the social, political, economic, and cultural environment in which they operate. Accordingly, organizations are not static entities, but are continuously evolving and assuming new shapes and forms. Organizations represent man's attempt to achieve specified goals (political, economic, religious, etc.) in an orderly and efficient manner. Organizations are shaped by the changing conditions around them and are subject to a number of influences. In one sense, the changing nature of organizations reflects the evolution of man's way of thinking about himself and his fellow man. Organizations are structured and managed according to our assumptions about human behavior and interpersonal relationships. As our assumptions about human behavior change, and as our thinking about human relationships evolves, organizations undergo the same processes.

Keith Davis has traced the evolution of organizations through history and has identified four basic types of organizations that have emerged during the past seventy-five years. [23] While the following four models by Davis may not be entirely representative of any one type of organization, they do serve as useful guides for thinking about organizations, reflecting the historical trend of organizational thought and practice.

The Autocratic Model   The autocratic model dominated organizational thought at the beginning of the twentieth century. In the autocratic model, control is maintained through the exercise of formal authority and power. Orders are given and followed without question. Workers are motivated, not through individual commitment to the goals of the organization, but by fear of losing their jobs or suffering economic reprisal. As a result, workers perform only as much as is required. Productivity is increased in the autocratic organization by improving physical working conditions and eliminating waste, rather than by developing the potential of the individual employees.

The Custodial Model   The custodial model of organization emerged during the 1920s and 1930s. It reflected a growing awareness among managers and scholars that frustrated, insecure employees were a detriment to organizational efficiency and that something ought to be done to improve the condition of the individual worker. Psychologists and industrial relations specialists were hired to study organizations. They concluded that the needs of employees must be reckoned with if they were to produce at their maximum capacities. Economic rewards, in the form of increased salaries, pensions, and additional fringe benefits were the chief tools used by managers to enhance employee satisfaction with their jobs. Although economic rewards did produce more satisfied workers, they failed to engender a greater commitment by the individual employee to the organization and its goals. Moreover, the rewards did little to improve individual performance. As a result, new organizational models were sought.

The Supportive Model

In the supportive model of organization emphasis shifted from economic to psychological support of employee needs. The supportive model depends upon leadership rather than on power or economic incentives to develop and maintain individual commitment to the organization. The employee is encouraged to become involved in the organization and to develop a sense of participation in organizational activities. The manager in the supportive model plays a key role, fostering a climate in which personal growth and self-fulfillment are the dominating interests.

The Collegial Model

The collegial model, which is still evolving in our society, is merely an extension and refinement of the supportive model. In the collegial model, even greater emphasis is placed upon developing a sense of mutual participation and involvement among employees. Managers are no longer seen as bosses, but rather as joint participants in the activities of the organization. Employees develop a sense of ego-satisfaction by an awareness that they are contributing something to the overall success of the organization. Teamwork is stressed in the accomplishment of organizational goals. Employees receive and accept a greater sense of responsibility for their work, thus becoming more inclined to increase their own efficiency and productivity.

It may be reasoned that organizations will continue to evolve and assume new forms and characteristics as our knowledge and understanding of human behavior increases. In addition, it should be recognized that any single type of organization may not be best for all circumstances, and that one style of organization may work well in one situation, but may be inappropriate for another. Organizations are rarely purely one type or another. The typology developed by Davis is merely a useful way of thinking about organizations that may exhibit characteristics common to one of the models discussed.

Police organizations are generally characteristic of the autocratic model due to their emphasis upon strict discipline and rigid compliance with rules and regulations. Still, there is evidence that police organizations are on the verge of change and that some departments (admittedly, very few) have already undergone significant change in response to a growing awareness of the limitations of traditional organizational styles. More emphasis is being placed upon developing organizational models in which members are encouraged to commit themselves to organizational goals and in which they receive a greater sense of responsibility for individual accomplishments.

Due to their unique characteristics and responsibilities, police organizations will evolve at a much slower rate than other types of organizations, but they will continue to change. It will be the task of the police executive of the future to encourage organizational change and to develop and maintain an organizational climate that maximizes the potential of the individual employee.[24]

The Informal Organization

In most work settings, two elements exist: the formal organization and the informal organization. The **formal organization** is that structure which is portrayed by the organization chart and which is reflected in the formal roles, positions, and relationships that have been established by rules, regulations, and operational procedures. The formal organization, however, is somewhat artificial, because it fails to reflect the human qualities of the organization.

The **informal organization,** on the other hand, directly reflects the human qualities of the members of the organization: their needs, emotions, feelings, and personal attributes. The informal organization may operate independently of the formal organization, and may possess its own system of communication, its own behavior pattern, and its own norms and

standards of conduct.[25] Informal organizations, if not recognized and properly treated, can create problems in the management of the organization. Conflicts may develop between the
formal and the informal organization with respect to desired
or established goals and the methods for achieving them. Informal organizations may have leaders different from those
recognized by the formal organization. Moreover, the standards of conduct observed by the informal organization may
be at variance with those recognized by the formal organization. As a result, internal conflict may erupt between the informal and formal organization, thereby detracting from the
overall effectiveness of the formal organization.

While informal organizations may be detrimental to the
well being of the formal organization, the opposite may also
hold true. According to Phillip Selznick, informal organizations "may also function to widen the available resources of
executive control and thus contribute to rather than hinder
the achievement of the stated objectives of the organization."[26]

In addition, Keith Davis has described a number of ways
in which the informal organization can contribute to the functional well being of the formal organization.[27]

1. Informal organizations blend with the formal organization
   to produce a workable system for getting work done.
2. Informal organizations can relieve the manager of some of
   his responsibilities and can stimulate higher productivity
   and efficiency.
3. The informal organization can provide an element of job
   satisfaction that may be missing in the formal organization.
4. The informal organization provides a check and balance
   on the power of the manager, thus forcing him to act
   more judiciously and prudently in his managerial responsibilities.
5. The informal organization provides for increased communication that is conducive to the efficient operation of
   the organization.

Effective communication among members and units of an
organization is vital to operational efficiency. The formal organization, which relies almost exclusively on the formal chain
of command to carry its messages and directives, does not
always achieve a smooth flow of communication and a complete dissemination of information throughout the organiza-

tion. In fact, too strict reliance upon the chain of command may actually impede the effective flow of information and thus jeopardize the efficiency of the operation.

The informal organization, on the other hand, facilitates information flow. Not bound by structural rigidities imposed in the formal organization, the informal organization provides the setting for a freer and more complete exchange of information among members and between subordinate units. As shown in Figures 2–4a and 2–4b, the information networks in the formal and informal organization differ considerably. In Figure 2–4a, communications follow the hierarchial structure of the formal organization. Cross-communication between members and subordinate units is channeled and quite limited. In the formal organization, as depicted in Figure 2–4b, information flows freely, following no set pattern, handicapped by no set structure. The result is a more effective exchange of information.

The task of the chief executive is to recognize the existence of the informal organization, to maximize its potential in achieving the goals of the organization, and to eliminate sources of conflict that may arise between the formal and the informal organization. If properly utilized, the informal organization can be a valuable asset to the formal organizational structure.

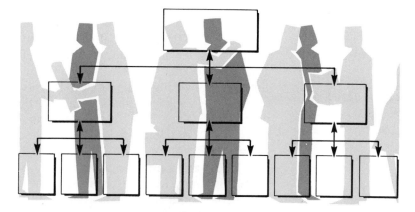

Figure 2-4a.   Lines of Communication in Formal Organization.

One-way communication

Two-way communication

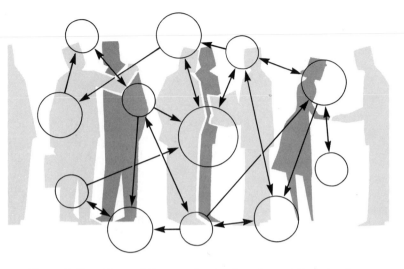

Figure 2-4b.   Lines of Communication in Informal Organization.

One-way communication

Two-way communication

Organizational Conflict

Conflict is inherent in organizations. In some cases, conflict in organizations is healthy, because it is an indication of change. But, conflict can be, and often is, detrimental to the organization as well. Organizational conflict can produce unnecessary tensions among individual members and between subordinate units in the organization. It can reduce organizational efficiency by diverting the energies and resources of the organization from established goals. In addition, conflict may disrupt internal solidarity and consensus among members of the organization and contribute to lower morale and decreased productivity.

There are a number of sources of organizational conflict. While they may not all exist in any one organization, the chief executive should be alert to them and take remedial action to correct them or minimize their adverse consequences, if possible. Among the sources of organizational conflict which may be susceptible to corrective action are the following:[28]

1. *Jurisdictional Ambiguity.* Jurisdictional ambiguity may arise in an organization when there is a lack of clear un-

derstanding and agreement between subordinate units and individuals in an organization regarding respective responsibilities and duties. Proper delineation of authority and responsibility relationships by management can eliminate or reduce the negative consequences of this source of conflict.

2. *Conflict of Interests.* The pursuit of goals by one unit in the organization at the expense of other units or to the detriment of the organization as a whole may lead to conflict of interests. In a police organization, top management should work to ensure that the goals and objectives of subordinate units are in harmony with each other and that they all contribute to the overall objectives of the organization.

3. *Lack of Communication.* Physical and organizational barriers may impede or inhibit the flow of communication which is necessary for efficient operations. This may be overcome by designing and implementing improved systems of information processing and transmission and by developing an organizational structure that facilitates the free flow of information throughout the organization.

There are a number of factors commonly found in organizations which do not readily lend themselves to remedial measures. These include:[29]

1. *Structural Differentiation.*   Structural differentiation may occur in several forms.

   • Specialization denotes the extent to which work within an organization is performed by specialists rather than by generalists. The greater the degree of specialization within the organization, the higher the level of structural differentiation, and the more likely the possibility of internal conflict.
   • The more levels of authority that an organization has, the greater will be its structural differentiation, and the more likely it will be to experience organizational conflict.
   • Organizational complexity refers to the extent to which the functions of an organization are distributed among a number of interdependent units and levels of authority. In organizations with greater complexity of operations, the chances for internal conflict are increased.

2. *Participation in the Authority System.*   In general, there will be less conflict in an organization in which the members of the organization are provided with an opportunity

to participate in the decision-making process and to determine how the organization will be run. Highly autocratic structures, in which authority is concentrated at the upper levels of the organization, are more likely to experience internal conflict.

3. *Regulating Procedures.* Regulating procedures may also contribute to organizational conflict in the following manner:

- Standardization of Procedures refers to the extent to which the activities of the organization are standardized by formal procedures. Too much standardization, or too little, may result in increased organizational conflict.
- Emphasis on Rules means the degree to which an organization relies upon formal rules of conduct to regulate individual behavior in the organization. While rules of conduct are often necessary to ensure proper behavior of members, too much reliance on such rules, or too strict an interpretation of them, may have adverse effects on internal solidarity.
- Close Supervision of a worker by his supervisor may be related to organizational conflict. Too close supervision may create resentment and frustration on the part of the employee.

4. *Heterogeneity.* Heterogeneity refers to the extent to which members of the organization hold divergent values and perceptions of the organization. In theory, at least, the greater the degree of heterogeneity, the less consensus there will be among members, and the more likely the chance for conflict. Total homogeneity (the opposite of heterogeneity), however, is rarely possible in large organizations.

5. *Instability.* Instability is the extent to which the organization is subjected to frequent turnover in personnel (attrition) and the influx of new members. The fewer people that enter or leave an organization, the more stable it will become, and less conflict will be experienced.

As noted earlier, not all conflict in an organization is bad, and some degree of conflict is to be expected in an organization. The role of the chief executive is to identify possible sources of harmful conflict and minimize the extent to which they can have detrimental effects on the operational stability of the organization.

Individual Needs and the Organization

Organizations share one common, underlying characteristic: they are composed of human beings. But, why does an individual belong to an organization? The answer is that the organization satisfies certain needs for the individual. It is this drive for "need satisfaction" that keeps an individual in an organization. Once an organization ceases to satisfy the needs of its members, they will no longer remain part of it.

Organizations satisfy several different types or levels of individual needs. Abraham Maslow, a psychologist, identified five levels of human need that are commonly satisfied by organizations. He ordered them into a hierarchy of needs beginning with the most basic and ascending to the highest order of need.[30]

At the lowest level of the hierarchy are the **physiological needs** such as hunger, thirst, shelter, and so on. Man works in an organization in order to make money to satisfy these needs. The second level of needs represents man's desire for **safety and security.** Again, a weekly paycheck, fringe benefits, and a retirement plan satisfy this need.

The third level of needs consists of man's **social needs**— the need to belong to a group and to feel wanted. The social structure of an organization (i.e., the informal organization discussed earlier) satisfies this need. The fourth level of need includes man's **egoistic needs,** which relate to the longing to receive recognition from peers for competence and skill in his profession. At the top of the needs hierarchy are the needs for **self-fulfillment** that reflect man's desire to prove to himself that he is performing an essential and meaningful task in a competent manner.

Maslow suggested that as each need level is satisfied, the individual begins to seek to satisfy the next higher level, and that he will never be completely fulfilled until all needs are satisfied. These needs are not mutually exclusive, however. Some needs may be satisfied simultaneously. Moreover, it is unlikely that two individuals will have precisely the same order of needs. Some may place greater value on satisfying security and safety needs, while others may be more interested in gaining recognition and self-acceptance.

Needs serve as human motivators. In an organization, man performs the duties expected of him in return for the satisfaction of his own needs. So long as he seeks to fulfill those needs, he will continue to perform as required. Once needs have been satisfied, however, they will cease to serve as motivating factors. This is an important thought to keep in mind in the management of organizations.

Humanism in the Police Organization

As we have shown earlier in this chapter, there has developed in recent years a growing body of evidence to suggest that traditional concepts of organization are no longer relevant to today's changing society. There is an increasing demand for change, innovation, and flexibility in organizations. Traditional models of organization, it seems, are simply not capable of coping with the stresses and pressures of our rapidly evolving society.

One of the chief critics of traditional organization models is Chris Argyris, who has argued that such principles as span of control, chain of command, and task specialization tend to make employees feel dependent, subordinate, and passive—feelings that are contrary to human nature, and which ultimately destroy human dignity and decrease the value of employees to the organization.

> This type of situation may create frustration, conflict, and failure for the employee. He may react by regressing, decreasing his efficiency, and creating informal systems against management.[31]

This shift away from traditional organization structures toward work situations reflecting a concern for employee needs and satisfaction may be regarded as a shift toward humanism in organization management. This trend has been recognized in the police community as well, and many authorities have written of the need for a more democratic and humanistic perspective in the management of police organizations. A British police executive described the need for humanism in the police organization in the following words.

> In our increasingly mechanical world, with its obsession with science and technology, with its fallacious belief that every-

thing can be weighed, measured, and reduced to formulae, with its pathetic delusion that human individuality can be authoritatively reduced to type and predictability, one might think that humanism had little place. But it is precisely *because* there is so much mechanism in life today that humanism is needed. It is needed most of all by those who have power over their fellowmen. They need it because it can give them vision, insight, judgement, and intellectual strength, because it can create imagination and creativity.[32]

These thoughts are echoed by George Berkley.

A democratic police force cannot hope to function in a manner consistent with a democratic society if its internal operations deviate from society's norms and values.[33]

Writing on the need to democratize the police, Berkley goes on to say that what constitutes democratic police administration is not really clear. Nevertheless, it is becoming increasingly evident that the management of police forces must undergo a dramatic change in coming years if the police are to achieve and maintain the support of the communities in which they operate.

Traditional police organizations, for a variety of reasons, are not capable of providing the type of working environment which is conducive to creative thought, individual initiative, professional conduct, and democratic processes, all of which are essential to the police function. Among the prominent weaknesses of the traditional police organizational structure are the following:[34]

1. Organizational goals and objectives are frequently in conflict with individual (employee) needs and aspirations.
2. Highly structured systems, which are characteristic of many police agencies, inhibit personal incentive and initiative, are not conducive to individual growth and professional development, and suppress individual instincts and motivations.
3. Traditional police organizations are not capable of coping with environmental change and evolving societal complexity.

There are a number of ways that police administrators can make their organizations more receptive to new ideas, more adaptable to change, and more conducive to individual growth and development.[35] Several ways of accomplishing these objectives are—

1. recruiting police personnel from outside the immediate geographic area to reduce or minimize police provincialism.
2. supporting tolerance within the police organization by removing artificial and arbitrary obstacles to individuality and personal initiative.
3. reducing organizational rigidity by fostering adaptability and flexibility in rules, values, and customs that are characteristic of traditional police organizations.
4. opening channels of communication within the organization by reducing physical and psychological obstacles to the smooth flow of information and the free exchange of ideas. Such obstacles include formal rank structures, complex and rigid chains of command, confused and vague communication networks.
5. reducing reliance on formal authority by minimizing the need for close supervision and autocratic methods of control and emphasizing participative decision-making, persuasion, and negotiation.

There is, unfortunately, no precise formula for making police organizations more democratic and humanistic. What is needed is a more pronounced recognition by police administrators of the individual worth and professional capabilities of subordinates and a demonstrated concern by police managers for the welfare and satisfaction of their employees. It has been stated that one of the highest sources of occupational stress and tension among police officers is the feeling that members of the police management team do not fully understand or appreciate the problems of their subordinates.[36] This feeling, of course, creates additional difficulties for individual police officers, who already face a demanding job.

The task of policing has evolved from one in which the primary incentives to enter the profession were job security and a modest income, to one in which more substantial benefits have become important. Now, more than ever, the individual police officer is concerned about the management policies that affect him and his profession. He feels an intense need to participate in those decisions that pertain to his job, and he wants to become a part of the management team.[37] If police organizations are to develop in a manner that will foster a spirit of professionalism, the police manager must strive to develop an organizational climate that encourages individual initiative and recognizes the principles of democratic and humanistic management processes.

Summary

Organizations play an important role in our society. Most of us work in organizational settings and attempt to derive some sense of satisfaction from them. Organizations influence our lives in many ways. It is important, therefore, that we understand them in order to better cope with them and derive the maximum benefit from them. Although police organizations are unique, they share many features that are common to other organizations. That they are comprised of individuals, all of whom have aspirations, needs, and motivations that must be met is their most significant common feature.

In this chapter we have focused on the nature of organizations, the functions they perform, and some of the problems inherent in organizational behavior. It is important that the police administrator become familiar with basic principles of organization and be able to apply them, where appropriate, to work settings. Police administrators must also be constantly alert for weaknesses in the organization of their departments and eliminate or minimize defects whenever they appear. They must also improve their ability to manage complex human organizations. This subject is addressed in the next chapter.

Discussion Questions

1. *Name several organizations in which you are involved. How are they different? How are they similar?*

2. *Briefly describe several purposes of organizations.*

3. *Briefly define the following terms and give axamples of each:*

   a. *Hierarchy of authority*
   b. *Span of control*

c. *Chain of command*
d. *Task specialization*

4. *Give several advantages and disadvantages of organizational specialization.*

5. *Discuss briefly the distinction between line and staff operations. Give examples of each.*

6. *Define the informal organization and contrast it with the formal organization.*

7. *Discuss several advantages and disadvantages of the informal organization.*

8. *In your own words, describe several sources of organizational conflict.*

9. *Describe Maslow's hierarchy of needs and its importance to organizational behavior.*

10. *List several ways in which the management of police organizations may become more democratic and humanistic.*

References

1. Amitai Etzioni, *Modern Organizations* (Englewood Cliffs, N.J.: Prentice-Hall, 1964), p. 1.

2. Lewis E. Lloyd, "Origins and Objectives of Organizations," in Mason Haire, ed., *Organization Theory in Industrial Practice* (New York: John Wiley & Sons, 1962), p. 28.

3. Edgar H. Schein, *Organizational Psychology* (Englewood Cliffs, N.J.: Prentice-Hall, 1965), p. 8.

4. Luther L. Gulick and L. Urwick, eds., *Papers on the Science of Administration* (New York: Institute of Public Administration, 1937), p. 3.

5. Andrew F. Sikula, *Management and Administration* (Columbus, Ohio: Charles F. Merrill, 1973), pp. 81–110.

6. Chris Argyris, "Personality and Organization Theory Revisited," *Administrative Science Quarterly*, 18 (June, 1973), p. 141.

7. Robert Michels, "Oligarchy," in Oscar Grusky and George A. Miller, eds., *The Sociology of Organizations* (New York: The Free Press, 1970), p. 25.

8. President's Commission on Law Enforcement and Administration of Justice, *Task Force Report: The Police* (Washington, D.C.: U.S. Government Printing Office, 1967), pp. 4–5.

9. Harold Koontz and Cyril O'Donnell, *Principles of Management: An Analysis of Managerial Functions*, 4th ed. (New York: McGraw-Hill, 1968), p. 59.

10. Ibid.

11. Schein, *Organizational Psychology*, pp. 12–13.

12. Henri Fayol, *General and Industrial Management*, trans. Constance Storrs (London: Sir Isaac Pitman and Sons, 1949), p. 21.

13. Haire, *Organization Theory*, p. 3.

14. Peter F. Drucker, *Management: Tasks, Responsibilities, Practices* (New York: Harper & Row, 1973), pp. 415–17.

15. Ibid.

16. L. Urwick, *The Elements of Administration* (New York: Harper & Brothers, 1943), p. 46.

17. James D. Mooney, *The Principles of Organization*, rev. ed. (New York: Harper & Row, 1947), p. 20.

18. O. W. Wilson and Roy C. McLaren, *Police Administration*, 3d. ed. (New York: McGraw-Hill, 1972), p. 66.

19. Fayol, *General and Industrial Management*, p. 24.

20. National Advisory Commission on Criminal Justice Standards and Goals, *Police* (Washington, D.C.: U.S. Government Printing Office, 1973), p. 207.

21. Keith Davis, *Human Relations at Work: The Dynamics of Organizational Behavior*, 3d ed. (New York: McGraw-Hill, 1967), pp. 175–76.

22. Melville Dalton, "Conflict Between Staff and Line Managerial Officers," in Amitai Etzioni, ed., *Complex Organizations: A Sociological Reader* (New York: Holt, Rinehart and Winston, 1961), pp. 212–21.

23. Keith Davis, "Evolving Models of Organizational Behavior," *Academy of Management Journal*, 11 (March, 1968), pp. 27–38.

24. *See also* the discussion of "Humanism in the Police Organization," in this chapter.

25. Norman C. Kassoff, *Organizational Concepts* (Washington, D.C.: International Association of Chiefs of Police, 1967), p. 16. *See also*, Peter M. Blau and W. Richard Scott, *Formal Organizations* (San Francisco: Chandler, 1962), pp. 1–8.

26. Phillip Selznick, "Foundations of the Theory of Organization," in Amitai Etzioni, ed., *Complex Organizations: A Sociological Reader* (New York: Holt, Rinehart and Winston, 1961), p. 22.

27. Keith Davis, *Human Relations at Work: The Dynamics of Organizational Behavior*, 3d. ed. (New York: McGraw-Hill, 1967), pp. 218–19.

28. Richard E. Walton, John M. Dutton, and Thomas P. Cafferty, "Organizational Context and Interdepartmental Conflict," *Administrative Science Quarterly*, 14 (December, 1969), pp. 522–42. *See also*, Fred Luthans, *Organizational Behavior: A Modern Behavioral Approach to Management* (New York: McGraw-Hill, 1973), pp. 461–77.

29. Ronald G. Corwin, "Patterns of Organizational Conflict," *Administrative Science Quarterly*, 14 (December, 1969), pp. 507–20.

30. Abraham H. Maslow, *Motivation and Personality*, 2d. ed. (New York: Harper & Row, 1970). *See also*, Philip B. Applewhite, *Organizational Behavior* (Englewood Cliffs, N.J.: Prentice-Hall, 1965), pp. 6–35.

31. Chris Argyris, "The Individual and Organization: Some Problems of Mutual Adjustment," *Administrative Science Quarterly*, 2 (June, 1957), p. 1.

32. Phillip John Stead, "Humanism of Command," *The Police Chief*, 41 (January, 1974), pp. 26–27.

33. George E. Berkley, *The Democratic Policeman* (Boston: Beacon Press, 1969), p. 29.

34. John E. Angell, "Toward an Alternative to the Classical Police Organizational Arrangement: A Democratic Model," *Criminology*, 9 (August-November, 1971), pp. 185–206.

35. Robert M. Igleburger, John E. Angell, and Gary Pence, "Changing Urban Police: Practitioners' Views," *Criminal Justice Monograph: Innovations in Law Enforcement* (Washington, D.C.: National Institute of Law Enforcement and Criminal Justice, Law Enforcement Assistance Administration, U.S. Department of Justice, 1973), pp. 99–104.

36. William H. Kroes, Bruce L. Margolis, and Joseph H. Hurrell, Jr., "Job Stress in Policemen," *Journal of Police Science and Administration*, 2 (June, 1974), pp. 145–55.

37. Martin Reiser, "Some Occupational Stresses on Policemen," *Journal of Police Science and Administration*, 2 (June, 1974), pp. 156–59.

The Task
of
Management

General
Observations . . .

In Chapter 2 we examined the nature, structure, and functions of organizations. We also discussed several ways by which the effectiveness of organizations could be improved. But, organizations are only as effective as those who manage them. In this chapter we will look at the task of management, exploring some of the ways in which police administrators can manage the resources at their disposal more effectively.

Essentially, management is the task of creating and maintaining an environment in which members of an organization can work together in harmony to achieve specified goals and objectives with a maximum degree of efficiency.[1] Management is a complex and difficult task requiring a broad range of skills and experiences. Henri Fayol, an early authority on the management process, defined management in the following terms.

> To manage is to forecast and plan, to organize, to command, to co-ordinate and to control. To foresee and provide means examining the future and drawing up the plan of action. To organize means building up the dual structure, material and human, of the undertaking. To command means maintaining activity among the personnel. To co-ordinate means binding together, unifying and harmonizing all activity and effort. To control means seeing that everything occurs in conformity with established rules and expressed command.[2]

Management is not an exact science, nor is it a mechanical process that can be mastered by applying precise formulae to particular situations. The key to successful management, perhaps more than anything else, is the understanding of people and their behavior in an organizational setting. Moreover, a successful manager must learn to develop a "feel" for the people over whom he exercises control. He must have a keen insight into their individual characteristics, problems, attitudes, capabilities, and interests. And, he must attempt to integrate them totally—both physically and psychologically—into the organization. He must also stimulate their interest in the goals and objectives of the organization.

Management is the process of controlling human behavior in an organizational setting. According to Douglas McGregor:

> Every managerial decision has behavioral consequences. Successful management depends—not alone, but significantly—upon the ability to predict and control human behavior.[3]

McGregor, who taught psychology at the Massachusetts Institute of Technology in the late 1930s and 1940s, emphasized that managers control people, not organizations, and that understanding and coping successfully with human problems in an organization is the key to effective management. McGregor challenged many of the traditional notions of management theory, and while he acknowledged that they comprise a logically persuasive set of assumptions which have had a profound influence upon managerial behavior, he labeled them merely the result of "armchair speculation" because they were not based on empirical studies. It should be noted, however, that McGregor's own contributions to management theory were not based on empirical research either, but were essentially a set of assumptions based upon intuitive deductions.

Over the years, a number of management theories have evolved that have attempted to define the most appropriate means of maximizing the potential of the individual worker in an organizational setting. This evolution is still in process.

Evolving Trends in Management Thought

Scientific Management   The roots of management theory date back to biblical times, and various writers have traced the rudiments of modern management principles as far back as the ancient Romans and Egyptians.[4] However, it was not until the twentieth century that a truly scientific approach to the task of management was developed. This occurred in 1911, with the publication of Frederick W. Taylor's historic work, *The Principles of Scien-*

tific Management.[5] Taylor's landmark work provided the stimulus for a wave of study and research into this formerly neglected field, and earned him the title "Father of Scientific Management."[6]

Taylor's principal contribution to the study of management was his devotion to the idea that traditional rule-of-thumb approaches to management should be replaced with scientific methods. Taylor held firm the belief that "the best management is a true science, resting upon clearly defined laws, rules, and principles, as a foundation."[7]

Increased efficiency—obtaining the maximum possible result from the least possible effort—was the underlying theme of Taylor's approach to management. His ideas created a wave of efficiency experts who, with stopwatches, measuring tapes, and clipboards in hand, invaded the workshops and factories of America, searching for new and better ways of doing things.[8]

Despite the recognized importance of Taylor's work, his efforts did not escape criticism. In his attempt to maximize efficiency, Taylor was accused of neglecting the human qualities of the working man and of exploiting labor. However, in his writings, Taylor made it quite clear that the principles which he espoused in no way neglected or infringed upon the interests of the worker. "The principal object of management," he wrote, "should be to secure maximum prosperity for the employer, coupled with the maximum prosperity for each employé."[9]

In fact, Taylor criticized those who believed that the fundamental interests of individual workers and employers were diametrically opposed to each other. According to Taylor's way of thinking, scientific management

> ... has for its very foundation the firm conviction that the true interests of the two are one and the same; that prosperity for the employer cannot exist through a long term of years unless it is accomplished by prosperity for the employee, and *vice versa* . . . .[10]

So intense were some of the feelings against Taylor's ideas, however, that a special committee of the United States House of Representatives was formed to investigate the man and his work. Taylor appeared before the committee in January 1912 and vigorously defended the concepts he had developed. Today, despite many attacks upon the credibility of his work, Taylor is remembered as a pioneer in the development of the scientific approach to management.

Even before Frederick Taylor made the study of management popular, Henri Fayol had been actively engaged in developing his own set of theories concerning the management of organizations. Fayol's principal work, *Administration Industrielle et Generale,* was published in 1916, although it was not until 1929 that it was translated into English. His work was not published in the United States until twenty years later. Today, Fayol is recognized as one of the most important contributors to the evolving theory of management. Whereas Taylor's interest was in the purely scientific approach to management, Fayol emphasized common sense principles which were drawn from his own practical experience as a businessman and reflected many of the lessons learned in his long career as a manager. Fayol identified six principal managerial activities.[11]

1. *Technical activities:* production, manufacturing, adaptation
2. *Commercial activities:* buying, selling, exchange
3. *Financial activities:* search for an optimum use of capital
4. *Security activities:* protection of property and persons
5. *Accounting activities:* stocktaking, balance sheets, costs, statistics
6. *Managerial activities:* planning, organization, command, coordination, control

It was the last of these six activities that occupied most of Fayol's attention. These activities will be discussed at length later in this chapter.

Fayol also introduced into the literature basic principles of management. Among them are the division of labor, authority and responsibility, unity of command, scalar chain (chain of command), and centralization.[12] Many of these principles are in wide use today and have been discussed in Chapter 2.

Scientific principles of management have had a long-lasting and wide-ranging effect on the business world. They brought about great improvements in productivity through the elimination of waste and more efficient management techniques. Work simplification, time and motion studies, task specialization, analysis of work flow, and other improvements served to eliminate unnecessary motion and effort. The establishment of clear-cut goals and objectives, the implementation of improved lines of communication, and the development of better means of decision making and internal control have all contributed to improved organizational efficiency in the work setting. But the efforts of Taylor and Fayol and their disciples raised some nagging questions about the management of organizations that began to be answered with the advent of the Human Relations School of Management.

The Human Relations School

The human relations school of management theory followed the era of scientific management by only a few years. The behavioralists, as the followers of this school of thought were called, attempted to answer many of the questions that had been raised by Taylor, Fayol, and others in the scientific management school. The **behavioralists** believed that no amount of organizational restructuring would improve efficiency or productivity unless changes were made in the social relationships between the manager and the worker. In effect, the behavioralists recognized a basic defect in the scientific management approach—its over-reliance on artificial, mechanical means to improve production and its failure to acknowledge the importance of the human factor in organizational activities.

The behavioralists, as the name implies, were interested in discovering the meaning and nature of human behavior in an organizational setting and in developing theories that would maximize the potential of the individual worker. Followers of the human relations school do not belong to any one scholarly discipline, but rather incorporate the principles of sociology, anthropology, psychology, and related fields in their studies. The behavioralists did not attempt to develop concrete laws of management theory, but rather they attempted to develop and test hypotheses that would have practical utility for improving the organizational climate of the work setting. In the end, their efforts helped to improve organizational efficiency and increase worker satisfaction.

The Hawthorne Studies

The human relations school of management can be traced to the early works of Elton Mayo[13] and the studies conducted at the Western Electric Company's Hawthorne Plant in Chicago between 1927 and 1932.[14] The results of this research stimulated increased interest in the field of management and helped to clarify the role of the manager in the organization.

The Hawthorne studies brought into question many of the assumptions that had been routinely accepted by the students of the **scientific management school.** For example, the researchers discovered that the earlier belief of a simple and direct relationship between physical working conditions and rate of production did not always hold true. In some cases, in fact, it was found that productivity continued to increase while working conditions grew worse! This resulted in the formulation of the following hypothesis.[15]

> Increased production was the result of the changed social situation of the workers, modifications in their level of psychological satisfaction, and new patterns of social interaction. . . .

The Hawthorne studies significantly altered man's thinking about the interpersonal dynamics of organizational behavior and led to the development of many new theories of management. The major contributions of the Hawthorne studies to management theory were the following:[16]

1. The rate of productivity is determined by the social norms of the worker, rather than by his individual capacities.
2. Non-economic rewards are more important than economic incentives in influencing worker behavior.
3. Workers sometimes do not react as individuals but as members of a group in the occupational environment.
4. Informal group leaders can be more important than formal institutional leaders (i.e., foremen, supervisors, etc.) in setting and enforcing productivity standards.[17]
5. Employee participation in the decision-making process and democratic styles of leadership can significantly improve organizational efficiency and productivity.

Theory X and Theory Y   Following the Hawthorne studies, the human relations school of management attracted a number of followers. One was Douglas McGregor, a psychologist, who developed and expounded two contrasting sets of assumptions about the nature of human behavior in organizations. According to McGregor, these sets of assumptions could be related to two basically different types of management: Theory X (autocratic) and Theory Y (permissive).[18]

According to Theory X, the autocratic manager is presumed to make the following assumptions about employees.[19]

1. The average human being inherently dislikes work and will avoid it if he can.
2. Because of their characteristic dislike for work, most people must be coerced, directed, controlled, threatened with punishment, and otherwise forced to put forth effort to achieve organizational goals.
3. Most human beings prefer to be directed, do not like responsibility, have relatively little ambition, and desire security above all.

At the opposite extreme, McGregor's Theory Y postulated that the permissive leader holds these assumptions about workers.[20]

1. Physical and mental effort in a work situation is just as natural as play or rest.
2. Coercive measures are not necessarily required to motivate employees toward organizational goal achievement. Man can exercise self-direction and self-control if he is sufficiently committed to organizational objectives.
3. Commitment to objectives is related to rewards associated with their achievement.
4. Under proper conditions, the average human being learns not only to accept responsibility, but to seek it.
5. The capacity to exercise a relatively high degree of imagination, ingenuity, and creativity in the solution of organizational problems is widely, not narrowly, distributed in the population.
6. Under the usual conditions of modern industrial settings, the intellectual potential of the average worker is only partly realized.

McGregor's work led to a redefinition of the role and responsibilities of the manager. McGregor attempted to demonstrate, through his Theory Y, that human beings in an organizational setting can be motivated to work toward the objectives of the organization without the use of harsh or coercive measures. Moreover, McGregor believed that the organizational environment itself was not contrary to human nature and that the task of the manager should be to "harness" individual capacities and maximize the potential of employees in a way that achieves both individual and organizational interests.

Under the permissive style of management, as seen by
McGregor, the goals of the individual are closely aligned with
those of the organization. Individual commitment to the organization is solidified. Motivation is thereby increased as the
individual strives to achieve through a sense of self-fulfillment.
Permissive managers, unlike autocratic ones, rely heavily upon
personal involvement and less upon formal control methods.

McGregor's Theory Y was built around an implicit belief
in the dedication of the individual worker toward the goals of
the organization and the willingness of the worker to strive
toward the achievement of those goals. These beliefs closely
parallel several "assumptions" articulated by Haire to describe
the psychological orientation of the individual employee
toward the organization. The assumptions are that—[21]

- most people want more freedom in their work to decide
  for themselves, rather than wanting to be told what to do
  and how to do it in detail.
- most people have both the capacity and the desire to discipline themselves to a greater extent in their own work,
  rather than to have someone continually checking up to
  see if they are actually doing what they agreed to do.
- most people already have the competence to achieve significantly greater results than they are currently achieving;
  most people desire the chance to prove that they have this
  as yet untapped competence.
- most people work better and get more personal satisfaction
  from holding themselves to high standards in their work,
  rather than seeing how little they can do and still get paid.
- most people really want to learn how to do their own work
  better, to develop their abilities, and to reach for and attain higher standards, rather than to remain satisfied to
  coast through adult life on the momentum from their
  earlier education.
- most people feel that personal recognition and reward
  within the company should stem primarily from how much
  each contributes toward getting done what all have set out
  to achieve.
- most people want the door of opportunity to be open
  equally to all, with each individual's resulting success the
  direct result of his own unique combination of self-
  developed skill, competence, knowledge, and initiative,
  utilized within the needs of the business.

These assumptions, according to Haire, add up to a faith
in one's fellow man and the belief that "within each individual

employee there exists a potential for greater effort and contribution, greater than hitherto perceived or achieved; and that this can be realized with resulting greater recognition and reward."[22]

Haire is careful to point out, however, that these qualities are assumed to be, but are not, in all people, and that it must be left up to the individual manager to carefully assess his own organization to determine to what extent, if any, these qualifications exist among his subordinates. He should not be disappointed if all his subordinates do not exhibit these qualities, but he should operate under the assumption that some, if not most, will.

Contemporary Management Theories

A number of theories have been advanced in recent years that further define and clarify the role of the manager in the organization. Management theory has become a field of endeavor that has occupied the attention of an increasing number of social and behavioral scientists, and has been written about in thousands of professional journal articles and hundreds of texts. A few of the most noteworthy contributions to management theory are discussed below.

The Managerial Grid

Managers in the occupational environment have a dual responsibility. First, they must see to it that the work of the employee is directed toward the achievement of the goals of the organization. In this sense, they must be concerned with production. Second, they must concern themselves with meeting the needs of their subordinates. As we have seen already, individual needs and organizational efficiency are closely interrelated. In this second sense, the manager must be people oriented. How the manager strives to accommodate these sometimes conflicting demands will largely determine his management style. Blake and Mouton developed a typology of management styles based upon these two concerns (for production and for people) by arranging them on two intersecting continuums, forming what they describe as a managerial grid.[23]

The managerial grid (Figure 3-1) identifies five basic styles of management. In the 1,1 style, shown in the lower left corner of the grid, the manager is minimally concerned with either production or workers, and represents basically an attitude of indifference on the part of the manager. In the 1,9

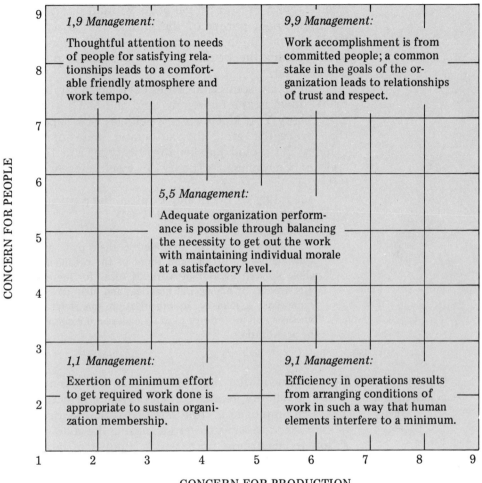

CONCERN FOR PEOPLE

CONCERN FOR PRODUCTION

1,9 Management:

Thoughtful attention to needs of people for satisfying relationships leads to a comfortable friendly atmosphere and work tempo.

9,9 Management:

Work accomplishment is from committed people; a common stake in the goals of the organization leads to relationships of trust and respect.

5,5 Management:

Adequate organization performance is possible through balancing the necessity to get out the work with maintaining individual morale at a satisfactory level.

1,1 Management:

Exertion of minimum effort to get required work done is appropriate to sustain organization membership.

9,1 Management:

Efficiency in operations results from arranging conditions of work in such a way that human elements interfere to a minimum.

Source: Robert R. Blake and Jane S. Mouton, "Managerial Facades," *Advanced Management Journal*, 31 (July, 1966), p. 31. Reprinted with permission.

Figure 3-1. Blake and Mouton's Managerial Grid.

style, shown in the upper left corner of the grid, the manager is almost wholly concerned with people and not at all concerned with production. Under the 9,1 style, shown in the lower right corner of the grid, there is little concern for people, but maximum concern for production. The 5,5 style of management, shown in the center of the grid, represents the middle-of-the-road approach that seeks to balance individual interests with organizational goals without upsetting either. In the upper right corner of the grid is the 9,9 style, which reflects the maximum concern for both people and production by integrating the worker into the productive purposes of the organization.

There are some similarities between the styles of management shown in the managerial grid and McGregor's Theory X and Theory Y. If McGregor's typologies were superimposed on the managerial grid, the autocratic style of management (Theory X) would parallel the 9,1 type, and the permissive style of management (Theory Y) would closely resemble the 9,9 type.

According to Blake and Mouton, the purpose of the managerial grid is to provide managers with

> ...a language system to describe their own managerial styles, those of others, and those of the organization as a whole as well as a framework of ideas for increasing the effectiveness of managerial practices and attitudes. With this framework, a man or an organization can strive to revise practices and procedures so as to achieve a 9,9 climate within the organization.[24]

Herzberg's Motivation-Hygiene Theory

We have previously discussed the fact that organizational efficiency is closely related to employee satisfaction, and that unless an employee is truly satisfied with his work, he will not be motivated to work toward achieving the goals of the organization to his utmost potential. A number of researchers have studied the phenomenon of employee satisfaction in the work setting. One such study was conducted by Frederick Herzberg and his associates.[25] Among other things, they found that those factors that produce job satisfaction among employees are separate and distinct from those factors that lead to job dissatisfaction. In other words, job dissatisfaction in the work setting is not merely the opposite of job satisfaction.[26]

Job dissatisfaction, according to Herzberg, occurs when certain factors associated with the job deteriorate to a level below that which the employee considers acceptable. These factors, which Herzberg refers to as "hygienic" because they "clean up" the work environment, include such things as physical work conditions, job benefits, administrative practices, and job security. While these factors can lead to job dissatisfaction, they are not associated with job satisfaction.

Herzberg suggests that job satisfaction is related to the ability of man to fulfill himself in the occupational environment. Those things which bring true job satisfaction to the employee Herzberg called "motivators," and are mainly psychological in nature. They include achievement, recognition, responsibility, and self-realization, and are intrinsic to the work being performed. Hygienic factors, on the other hand, are extrinsic to or beyond the actual job of the employee and apply to the work situation only.

Several researchers have amplified the findings of Herzberg and his colleagues and have contributed additional knowledge to our understanding of the needs of the individual in the organizational setting. In one study, it was shown that both job satisfaction (motivators), and job dissatisfaction (hygienics) are directly correlated with the level of the organizational hierarchy in which one is located. As one moves up the hierarchy, there is a tendency to be less motivated by hygienic factors and more motivated by job satisfiers. Thus, persons at the upper levels of the hierarchy in the organization will receive job satisfaction from factors different than those which produce job satisfaction for employees at lower levels.[27] These findings are important if we are to be able to create a working environment in which employees at all levels of the organizational hierarchy attain job satisfaction. Other studies have been conducted which tend to lend additional support to Herzberg's theory.[28]

Participative Management

Participative management incorporates many of the concepts and theories that have been previously discussed. Generally speaking, participative management attempts to absorb the individual employee in the decision-making process of the organization. It removes the "we-they" attitude that often exists between management and workers.

Participative management requires both a total commitment by top management to involvement of the worker in the management process and an entirely new way of thinking about the individual in the organization. It also requires a calculated risk—a gamble that the employee will respond in kind to the overtures of management. Accordingly, managers must not only dedicate themselves to more democratic methods of control and direction, but must re-educate their subordinates by instilling in them the notion that they are an

Metropolitan Police Dept., Washington, D.C.

Participative Management at Work

essential part of the organizational endeavor and are vital to
the success of the enterprise.

Participative management is the exact opposite of authoritative management. Whereas authoritative management requires the worker to involve himself merely in the physical
activities of his job, participative management attempts to
involve the employee both physically and psychologically in
the affairs of the organization. Authoritative management does
not receive the benefit of total commitment by the individual
to the organization, and often engenders resistance and half-
hearted effort by employees. Participative management strives
to convince the employee that his interests are closely aligned
with those of the organization, and thus stimulates a greater
sense of individual commitment.

One of the early attempts to implement a form of participative management in industry was the Scanlon Plan, so-called
because it was conceived by Joseph Scanlon and others in the
1930s and applied by a number of companies following World
War II.[29] Scanlon felt that employee interest in and contribution toward the organization could best be achieved by supply-
ing the employee with a maximum amount of information
concerning the goals, problems, and successes of the organization, and by soliciting his contribution as to how he felt the

problems might best be solved and the desired results best be achieved. The Scanlon Plan reflects a common sharing between management and the worker of information, ideas, problems, and goals.[30]

Participative management has become more popular in recent years, principally through the work of Rensis Likert, who has written extensively on the subject. Likert has suggested that, among other things, efficient management can be characterized as being—[31]

- employee-oriented, rather than production-oriented.
- more inclined toward general rather than close, supervision.
- non-punitive and helpful, rather than punitive and critical.
- communicative toward employees, rather than non-communicative.

Likert gives several reasons for the growing acceptance of the participative management approach in industry.[32] They are—

1. the increased pressures resulting from the highly competitive nature of business and industry, both domestically and internationally, resulting in a tremendous drive to discover new and better ways to increase individual productivity and organizational efficiency.
2. the general trend in our society to permit the individual greater freedom and initiative.
3. the higher level of education among workers today compared with former times.
4. the general dissatisfaction in business with traditional approaches to management.
5. the increasing technical complexity of American industry, in which the manager often knows less about the work he is supervising than those doing the work.

Like others in the field, Likert has developed a typology of management based upon a number of variables, such as communication, decision making, and control processes, all arranged on a continuum.[33] One end of the continuum he labeled the "exploitative authoritative" style of management, and the other he labeled the "participative" style. Between the two extremes were two intermediate management styles: "benevolent authoritative" (closest to exploitative authoritative), and "consultative" (closest to participative).

Each variable was described according to the four styles of management defined above. For example, under "communication—direction of information flow," an exploitative authoritative type of management is one in which all information flows downward through the organization. Under the benevolent authoritative style, information flows mostly downward. A consultative type of management is characterized as one in which information flows both up and down the organizational hierarchy. In the participative type of management, information flows down, up, and across the organization.

Similarly, under the variable "character of decision making process," the exploitative authoritative style of management is one in which most decisions are made at the top of the organizational hierarchy. In the benevolent authoritative type, policy decisions are made at the top of the organization, while some routine decisions are made at lower levels. Under the consultative style of management, even more decisions are made at the lower levels of the hierarchy. Finally, in the participative management style, decision making is widely decentralized through the organization.

According to Likert, organizational efficiency varies greatly among the different management styles. The level of production ranges from mediocre in the exploitative type to excellent in the participative style.

The style of management employed in any one organization will depend upon a number of factors, including the type of organization, the characteristics of its employees, the capabilities and skills of its managerial personnel, and the nature of the work performed by the organization. Participative management is rapidly gaining acceptance in a number of types of organizations, but has not really been employed with any degree of success in police organizations. However, as the level of professionalism among police increases, it is likely that participative styles of management will become a reality in a growing number of police organizations.

The Functions of Management

Organizations are created to tap the energies and resources of individuals and apply them collectively to common purposes. The task of the manager is to ensure that human as well as material resources are used to maximum potential. To this end, the manager performs a number of functions that apply equally to the management of a small department store and a metropolitan police department, although the characteristics of the two organizations vary considerably.

Planning   Planning is a fundamental responsibility of management. Moreover, it is the basis for all other management functions. Without adequate planning, the other functions of management cannot be sufficiently accomplished. Planning provides a blueprint for future activities. It is the platform from which future operations are launched. Planning involves a continuous process of review, evaluation, and adjustment.

> Only by committing himself to planning—by formulating and articulating policy, by implementing an adequate program, and by encouraging and supporting planning by personnel at all levels regardless of basic assignment—can the police chief executive assure himself that his agency will perform with increasing effectiveness in a changing environment.[34]

Planning plays an increasingly important role in the management of police organizations. Police executives can no longer expect to administer their departments effectively if they fail to look ahead to the future, developing sound and comprehensive plans of action. Fundamental to the process of planning is the establishment of goals and objectives. Too often, police organizations do not have clearly defined or well articulated goals and objectives by which the success or failure of their efforts can be measured. The following definitions may be helpful.

- Goal—A statement of broad direction, general purpose or intent. A goal is general and timeless and is not concerned with a particular achievement within a specified time period.

- Objective—A desired accomplishment which can be measured within a given time frame and under specifiable conditions. The attainment of the objective advances the system toward a corresponding goal.[35]

The planning process involves several logical steps, each of which is critical to the success of the planning process.

Identify the problem.   In any planning, it is first necessary to identify the problem that is to be solved. In a police department, for example, the problem under study may be an increasing number of traffic fatalities. The objective of the plan would be to devise a way to reverse the rise in fatal traffic accidents.

Research the problem.   Once the problem has been identified, all relevant facts associated with it must be collected and analyzed. Relevant information should include background data, which describes the development of the problem (e.g., how long have traffic fatalities been on the increase, what other factors might be associated with the increase, etc.), along with other pertinent information, such as approaches previously used by other agencies in solving the same or similar problems. A review of specific selective enforcement programs might be conducted to determine what control methods may have the most desirable effect.

Develop a plan.   Once the necessary information regarding the problem has been gathered and analyzed, it should be possible to develop a logical plan of action. It may be desirable to develop several alternative plans that allow for various approaches to the problem. Each approach should be tested and evaluated to determine its effectiveness.

A police department wishing to reduce the number of traffic fatalities in the city may experiment with various types of enforcement programs and techniques. These may include a concentration of enforcement efforts at particular locations within the city during specified periods of the day or the utilization of certain techniques, such as radar speed detection.

Review the plan.   Once a plan or set of plans has been developed, it must be evaluated to determine its effectiveness. The planner should try to determine which plan (if several are under consideration) is most likely to succeed. The probable cost of each plan must be established in order to ensure that the plan eventually selected can be implemented within existing budgetary limitations.

Implement the plan.   Once a decision has been made regarding which plan is most likely to succeed, it must be put into operation. At this point, it will be necessary to coordinate the implementation of the plan with all units in the organization that may be affected by it. Appropriate personnel must be committed to the plan and those directly involved in its operation must be thoroughly familiarized with its nature, scope, and objectives.

In the police organization, few plans affect only one unit or element. A plan to concentrate on certain types of traffic violations in order to reduce highway fatalities, for example, may involve both patrol officers as well as members of the traffic unit. To ensure the success of the plan, it should be thoroughly explained to all units of the organization that will be involved.

Adjust the plan. As the plan unfolds, it may be necessary to make modifications to the original design to allow for unforeseen developments. All good plans must be flexible in order to adapt to changing conditions and situations. Lack of flexibility in a plan may doom it to failure before it begins.

Evaluate the plan. Finally, the plan must be tested and evaluated to determine its strengths and weaknesses. How successful was the plan in achieving the desired effects? What unforeseen circumstances intervened to make modifications necessary? Is further modification needed? If more than one plan has been devised, the relative merits and defects of each plan should be compared. The plan that most effectively accomplishes the desired results should be retained and, if necessary, modified. If none of the plans developed prove successful, a new plan should be devised.

Planning is a continuous process that involves each of the steps outlined above. By omitting one or more of these steps, the planning process may be jeopardized. (Refer to Chapter 10 for additional information on planning.)

Organization

Organizing is a basic responsibility of management. Poor organization is reflected in loss of efficiency and wasted resources. A basic grasp of organizational principles is necessary if maximum efficiency of operations is to be achieved.

Police organizations are particularly in need of organizational strengthening and re-structuring. This fact was noted by the President's Commission on Law Enforcement and Administration of Justice in 1967 when it stated that:

... many police forces appear to have evolved over the years without conscious plan. These forces are characterized by diffusion of authority, confused responsibility, lack of strong lines of direction and control, and improper grouping of functions.[36]

Staffing

The third function of management is staffing. Staffing involves the recruitment, selection, training, and assignment of personnel within the organization. Since personnel are an organization's most valuable resource, staffing is critical to the success of the organization. Unqualified, incompetent, unmotivated, or untrained personnel will surely cripple an organization.

Staffing should be approached carefully and deliberately. Because a manager must attempt to match individual skills and capabilities with the needs of the organization, it is important to know exactly what kinds of personnel are required, what their qualifications should be, how to recruit them, and how they should be utilized once they are retained by the organization.

While many police departments complain of inadequate personnel, relatively few devote enough time to ensuring that existing personnel are being used properly. Some cannot even determine what are their exact manpower requirements. Instead, new programs are devised and additional personnel requested to staff them. As a result, police departments continue to grow in size, but do not experience a parallel growth in productivity or efficiency. The problem is often not a shortage of manpower, but a failure to utilize existing resources efficiently. This may be partially attributable to poor staffing.

Direction

Direction is the process of moving the operations of the organization along a predetermined path. Direction ensures that work progresses smoothly, on schedule, and according to plan. It is the process of leading and guiding subordinates and helping them to apply their individual skills and energies to organizational problems. Direction is a function of the relationship between a supervisor and his subordinates. At one time, direction was accomplished largely through the application of power and force. These tactics, however, are being replaced by other, more democratic forms of direction. "The successful direction of subordinates," according to Koontz and O'Donnell, "results in knowledgeable, well trained people who work efficiently toward the enterprise objectives."[37]

Control   Control is the process of ensuring that performance proceeds according to plan. Control can be exercised in a number of ways, including the use of periodic inspections, or audits. In the police organization, control over police operations is exercised through both external and internal devices. External control devices are those initiated by persons outside the police organization. Internal control devices are initiated within the department.

Internal Control   Internal control is that influence over organizational activities that is exercised by the chief executive and his designated representatives. Internal control consists of those activities within the organization which are designed to ensure compliance with established procedures. Internal control may be exercised through both formal and informal means. In smaller organizations, control is largely informal in nature, while in larger organizations, control becomes much more formalized.

The first means of control available to the police manager is the promulgation of policy statements, procedural manuals, written directives, and rules and regulations. These instruments provide guidelines by which organizational activity can be conducted and which assist the manager to better evaluate performance. Written policies and procedures are one example of a formal internal control device.

In a large organization, the chief executive may delegate all or part of the control function to a principal subordinate. In the police organization, this function is referred to as **inspection,** which is another example of a formal internal control device. Inspection attempts to ensure that all organizational activities are proceeding according to established plan and in accordance with accepted procedure. Inspection is accomplished by periodically examining all organizational activities. The principal elements of the inspection process are auditing, evaluating, adjusting, and correcting.

Auditing is the process whereby the functions of the organization and its subordinate elements are periodically reviewed. This review may be accomplished through the interview of personnel assigned to the unit, on-site observation of activities, or review of work records and other documents. Normally, auditing consists of a combination of these techniques.

An inspection team auditing the activities of a patrol force would probably first want to observe the procedures of the personnel assigned to that unit to detect any discrepancies in their performances. They would note whether or not established policies and procedures are being followed. They would probably also want to interview unit commanders and supervisors to discuss with them the operations of their respective commands. Finally, they would want to review the records of the unit to determine if the perfomance of the unit measures up to expected standards. If not, they would want to discover why.

Evaluating is the process of determining the effectiveness, or lack thereof, of an organization, activity, or program. Effectiveness may be expressed in both quantitative and qualitative terms. **Qualitative measures** refer to those aspects that cannot be directly counted, and are more subjective than quantitative measures. Qualitative measures are derived principally through observation of techniques and interviews with key personnel. **Quantitative measures,** on the other hand, can be directly assessed through written records and statistics. Crime rates, incidence of traffic violations, and arrest rates all provide quantitative measures of performance.

Evaluation attempts to determine whether or not a particular unit is performing as expected. Current levels of activity may be compared with previous activity periods, or with the activity levels of other units in the organization. If crime rates go up in one precinct and down in all others, questions may be raised about the efficiency of the one particular precinct.

Adjusting is the process of revising, amending, or correcting the activities of an organization or a unit so that they more closely correspond to established plans and procedures. Adjustments may be necessary if deviations from accepted policies are discovered in an operating unit.

Correcting is the means whereby deficiencies in existing operations may be eliminated or corrected. Correcting may be conducted simulataneously with adjusting, since both procedures involve changing the course or direction of existing activities. Adjusting is preventive in nature, while correcting is curative.

Inspection may be performed as either a line or a staff function.[38] As a line function, inspection is performed by the supervisor having immediate control over a particular activity or function. As a staff function, inspection becomes the duty of individuals who lack command authority over the operations being inspected but who are delegated authority to act on the behalf of the chief executive. Regardless of whether inspection is performed as a line function or as a staff function, the ultimate responsibility for ensuring internal control over organizational activities lies with the chief executive.

In large police organizations, staff inspection may be performed by one or more members of a designated unit within the department. Normally, the commander of the inspection unit will report directly to the chief of police. In the largest police agencies, the inspection unit will be staffed by many people, and individuals in the unit may specialize in their functions. Some personnel, for example, may be responsible for inspecting line operations while others may be responsible for staff functions. The commander of the inspection unit should devise a systematic process of review. Virtually all functions of the organization should be identified and an appropriate inspectional procedure developed. In the police organization, personnel, policies, procedures, facilities, and individual performance should be subject to periodic inspection and review.

Inspection should be a continuous process. Systematic procedures should be established to ensure that all activities of the organization are reviewed in a timely manner. Inspection schedules should be established and the commander of the inspection unit should ensure that such schedules are carefully followed.

Reports should be prepared by the individuals conducting the inspections. Such reports should be reviewed and approved by the commander of the inspection unit and should be channeled to the chief executive. Reports should indicate the scope of the inspection, deficiencies noted, and recommendations for improvement. Copies of inspection reports should be made available to the person in charge of the unit being inspected.

Since staff inspectors lack authority to take remedial action, they can only recommend that changes be made. The actual changes must be initiated by the commander of the unit in question. In cases of disagreement between the particular unit commander and the inspection staff, the chief executive must decide the proper course of action to be followed.

Staff inspectors should make every effort to ensure cooperation with members of the unit being inspected. Staff inspection personnel should not assume that they have the ultimate responsibility for controlling the affairs of a particular unit, but should regard themselves as an advisory body to the chief executive. They should attempt to convince members of the units being inspected that they are merely performing an administrative function that is intended to improve the overall efficiency of the organization. Inspection personnel should not set out to criticize or find fault with an operating unit, but should approach their tasks dispassionately and without bias.

In addition, members of the inspection staff have a responsibility to the chief executive to perform their duties thoroughly and completely. They must not allow their personal feelings to influence their judgement, nor should they permit themselves to overlook serious defects in operating policies because of a reluctance to discredit or embarrass fellow employees. The inspection function is vital to the success of the organization and must be carried out thoroughly, judiciously, and impartially.

Internal investigation is a unique form of internal control and is usually related to the investigation of incidents of police corruption or malpractice. Internal investigation, or internal affairs units, are concerned primarily with uncovering unlawful police practices and investigating allegations of police misconduct which may include any number of offenses including violations of departmental rules and regulations, laws, and ordinances. Allegations of police misconduct may derive from a variety of sources, including members of the department, other official and quasi-official bodies (e.g., better government associations, public prosecutors, the courts), or from the general public.

The police executive should ensure that there is a formal procedure set up for receiving, recording, and investigating allegations of police misconduct, and that all such allegations are carefully and honestly investigated. Failure to do so will result in a loss of public trust in the police and will ultimately have serious consequences on the morale and discipline of the department.[39]

External Control   External controls are those which are exercised by persons outside the formal structure of the organization. In private industry, external controls are employed by boards of directors, stockholders, consumers, and others who indirectly influence the operations of the organization. In public agencies, such as the police, external controls are exercised in a number of different ways by various groups and institutions.

Legislative controls over the police are the result of laws, statutes, and ordinances, which have the potential of limiting or constraining police activities. Laws tell the police what they cannot do and what they must do. Laws tell the police what types of behavior are permitted and which are prohibited. Laws may also dictate how much money a police department will have to conduct its activities, how many police officers may be employed, and how much they will be paid. Legislative controls are exercised by state legislatures, county boards of supervisors, and by village boards of trustees and city councils.

Judicial controls are exercised by members of the judiciary, including prosecutors, defense attorneys, and the courts. Prosecutors may refuse to try cases if there is insufficient evidence presented by the police, or if the means used to obtain the evidence appear questionable under the law. Defense attorneys may exercise a number of constitutional options designed to limit the authority of the police in criminal investigations. For example, they may advise their client not to answer any questions during a police interrogation. The courts, too, exercise great influence over police activities. Appellate court decisions concerning the admissibility of evidence and rights of the accused have a significant impact on police methods and procedures. Court decisions have had the effect of limiting the power of the police in many cases, and have in others interpreted police duties and responsibilities in greater detail than ever before.

Public controls. Members of the public can and do exercise control over the police, although not directly. The police have been accused in the past of being unresponsive to public needs and demands. For the most part, these allegations were true. But the fact remains that there are civil remedies for controlling misconduct on the part of the police. In addition, the police are subject to criminal prosecution for unlawful acts performed in the line of duty. In some cases, federal and state investigative agencies may be called upon by local authorities to investigate charges of police abuse. In other instances, special prosecutors, grand juries, and similar bodies may be called upon to investigate charges of police misconduct. But, the real responsibility for controlling and correcting unlawful or irregular police behavior must rest with the police executive. If he fails in this duty, public support of the police will be eroded and police effectiveness will be diminished.

In some cities, citizens groups have been formed to work with police executives in formulating policies and procedures regulating police conduct. While these efforts have met with resistance on the part of the police in some cases, they have been generally successful in the limited instances where they have been employed. There are a number of policy matters in which the community has a vested interest. These include use of deadly force by police officers and discretion in enforcing the law.

Police administrators should be encouraged to adopt a policy of making police actions subject to public review and criticism and to develop formal procedures whereby the public may have a more active role in determining police policies. The police *are* the servants of the public, and should never lose sight of that fact.

Public review and criticism of police policies and procedures will not be accomplished easily, and should be approached with care and thoughtful deliberation. Traditionally, the police regard criticism from outside the police agency as both uninformed and ill-advised. The police, however, are not unlike other groups of professionals in this respect. As Heydebrand points out:

> ... to the extent that professionals and professional organizations derive wealth, power, prestige, and symbolic rewards from their monopoly on specialized knowledge, they will resist attempts to have goals specified and operationalized, procedures prescribed and resources controlled by others.[40]

External controls can be an effective tool for placing limits on police authority. Unlimited police authority can have serious consequences, and the police executive should develop and encourage both internal and external controls that will serve to make the police more responsive to public expectations.

Coordination   As an organization grows and develops, and as its responsibilities become more varied and complex, it will recognize the need to divide its functions among specialized units. When this occurs, it becomes increasingly important that such units operate in harmony with each other. The efforts of separate units in an organization must be coordinated so that they will work in unison to achieve the goals of the organization in the most efficient manner possible. Coordination lends coherence of action and unity of purpose to organizational undertakings. Coordination is a basic principle of any organized activity. The successful coordination of organizational activities depends upon several factors.

Information

Information must be exchanged within the organization. Members of one unit must be fully informed about the activities of other units and individuals in the organization. This is particularly true of the police organization, in which a number of highly specialized operations are being performed simultaneously. All too often, inefficient and ineffective police work has been traced to a lack of coordination between various operating units within the police organization.

As an example, detectives must be aware of the activities and observations of patrolmen in order that they may know what is taking place in the field. Patrol officers, in a sense, are the eyes and ears of detectives. Without adequate information from patrol officers, detectives will be deprived of their "vital senses." On the other hand, patrol officers should know what detectives are doing. The informational process should involve a two-way exchange of information between the two units. A thorough exchange of information is essential if the two units are to perform their duties successfully and to work with a maximum degree of harmony.

Organization

A sound organizational structure is essential if members and units are to be properly coordinated. Proper organization implies coordination of efforts. A weak or improper organizational structure results in a lack of efficiency, inadequate control of operations, and difficulties in coordination.

Supervision

The key to maintaining effective coordination is the supervisor, whose job it is to ensure that the activities of those under his command are synchronized with the activities and operations of other individuals and units in the organization. Moreover, the supervisor must ensure that the activities of those under his control are directed toward the goals and objectives of the organization.

Personal Contact

In order to achieve effective coordination, it is essential that members of an organization have frequent contact with one another. If this is not possible through the normal work routine, it may be accomplished by periodic staff meetings, squad briefings, and by other similar means. In police organizations, personal contact is enhanced through a number of informal social activities and events that cut across the structural divisions of the organization. Personal contact also stimulates a greater exchange of information, and the two result in more effective coordination.

Policy Making

All organizations operate under some form of established policy, whether it be formal or informal. In larger police organizations, policy is highly formalized, while in smaller departments, policy may be largely verbal and informal, handed down from one generation of police officers to the next. Policy is an important tool for setting the tone of the organization and in directing the actions of its members. Without clearly defined policies, members of an organization will be unsure of what is expected of them.

Statements of policy are not normally specific in nature, but are rather broad in scope and general in content to permit flexibility. Policy statements may declare that certain things will be done, or may specify how certain activities will be accomplished. However, they will usually leave the matter of precisely "how" open to question, allowing room for individual judgement and discretion.

Why Have a Policy?

Policy offers the advantage of establishing, for the organization, a standard of operations upon which members may guide their actions. The absence of policy creates a vacuum in which persons may become uncertain as to exactly how to act in particular circumstances. Policy serves as a measuring stick by which individual behavior may be evaluated. Policies help to remove doubt and confusion that may be felt by members of the department if they are given no direction. Sound policy helps to establish and maintain continuity and consistency of actions throughout the organization.

In the absence of a policy, similar questions must be considered time after time. Lack of a policy means that the organization has established no continuing position. As a result, it is necessary to assess each situation on the basis of its own merits.[41]

In addition, the absence of established policy often results in duplication of effort, inefficiency, waste of manpower, money, and materials, and a generally poor and inconsistent level of performance by the organization.

The Policy-Making Process There are four basic steps involved in policy-making. These are: formulation, dissemination, application, and review and appraisal.[42] It should be kept in mind, however, that the policy-making process is a continuous one and operates in cyclical fashion—continuing from phase to phase.

Formulation. Policy formulation consists of assessing the present situation, projecting future trends, and determining needs. Facts must be gathered and analyzed. Questions must be asked and answered. What are the existing policies? Are they effective? If not, why? Tentative policy statements may be drafted and circulated for review among staff members. Staff meetings may be held to discuss impending policy development. After thorough research and evaluation, a statement of policy is issued.

Dissemination. Policies are normally issued in written form. This helps to prevent or minimize any misunderstanding of the exact intent of the policy. Policy statements should be written in language that is clear and concise. The exact intent of a policy statement should not be clouded by ambiguous generalities and convoluted phrases. Policy statements should provide sufficient detail to ensure the desired results, but should not be so specific as to limit the reasonable exercise of discretion.

An example of a clear policy statement is that of the Los Angeles Police Department regarding the use of force by police officers:

Use of Force. In a complex urban society, officers are daily confronted with situations where control must be exercised to effect arrests and to protect the public safety. Control may be achieved through advice, warnings, and persuasion, or by the use of physical force. While the use of reasonable physical force may be necessary in situations which cannot be otherwise controlled, force may not be resorted to unless other reasonable alternatives have been exhausted or would clearly be ineffective under the particular circumstances. Officers are permitted to use whatever force that is reasonable and necessary to protect others or themselves from bodily harm.[43]

Application.   New policies, particularly ones that deviate substantially from established policies, are sometimes difficult to implement. The chief executive of a police agency should recognize this fact and should allow for a reasonable period of adjustment. Policy directives should indicate the effective date of the policy and should allow for a period of adjustment, if possible.

Review and Appraisal.   The final step in policy making is that of review and appraisal. This phase is required in order that all existing policies be periodically reviewed in order to determine their relevancy. Since the conditions under which police organizations operate are changing constantly, and since new demands are frequently being imposed upon the police, it becomes necessary for policies to be periodically reviewed and, where necessary, updated. Operating conditions should be inspected to ensure that existing policies are being followed. Where deviations from policy are noted, remedial action should be taken. This is a function of the inspection process, as previously discussed.

Tradition alone cannot justify the existence of policy. Too many police agencies operate under archaic policy guidelines that have been handed down from generation to generation within the police establishment. The police operate in a dynamic environment, and the policies that guide police actions should be relevant to contemporary conditions. "Management cannot be satisfied with the status quo or accept a policy merely because it was enunciated by the founding fathers and made traditional by succeeding generations of managers."[44]

Decision Making   Decision making is the process of selecting from a number of alternatives, weighing the consequences of action, and choosing a suitable course of action for a given situation. Decision making is a complex and difficult process that cuts across other managerial functions. As Price has observed:

> Decision making involves, among other things, specification
> of a goal, formulation of alternative courses of action to
> achieve the goal, and selection of a course of action intended
> to optimize achievement of the goal.[45]

We all make decisions during the course of everyday
events. We decide what clothes to wear, what to have for
lunch, and how our paychecks will be spent. But the decisions
made by managers and chief executives are crucial to the well
being of the organization. Faulty decisions based upon insufficient information, or decisions made in poor judgement, can
seriously affect the effficiency and effectiveness of the organizations.

Decisions should be based on a logical and thoughtful
consideration of the possible choices of action, each weighed
for its logical consequences. Decision makers must objectively
evaluate the alternatives open to them and attempt to determine in advance the likely outcome of their decision. Thus,
decision making is a process of forecasting the probable results
of future events.

A successful decision maker must be fully informed. He
must have reliable, complete, and up-to-date information,
often relying upon subordinate staff members to provide such
information. In some cases, the chief executive may request
his immediate staff to join in the decision making process.
Other decisions he must make alone, for he alone is responsible for their consequences.

There are two general types of decisions which may confront the chief executive of a police agency: strategic and
tactical.[46] **Strategic decisions** are those which deal with long-
range plans and goals, operating procedures, and policy development. In the police organization, strategic decisions might
include, determining how best to utilize available manpower to
combat increases in crime, limitations on the use of lethal
force by police, or means of developing greater cooperation
between the police and the community. **Tactical decisions,** on
the other hand, involve short-term objectives, such as personnel assignments, allocation of work, employee grievances,
and so forth. In the police organization, many tactical decisions are made by first line supervisors and middle managers,
while strategic decisions are most often made by the chief
executive and his immediate staff.

Fiscal Management

Fiscal management is the process of planning and controlling the expenditure of funds. Police expenditures typically represent one of the largest single program areas in a municipal budget. As a result, the chief of police plays an important role, ensuring that public funds are administered wisely and effectively.

Budget Preparation

One of the most important tasks that will confront the police administrator each year is the preparation of the budget. The annual budget cycle begins several months before the final budget is ultimately approved. It begins with each department (police, fire, sanitation) assessing its own financial needs for the forthcoming fiscal year and translating those needs into dollar costs. New equipment may need to be purchased, or additional personnel hired. New programs may be called for as well. All these activities cost money and must be shown in the budget request.

A budget is simply a work plan with monetary values attached to it. In effect, a budget describes what the organization hopes to accomplish during the period the budget is in effect. The budget is also a planning guide which can be used by administrators to direct and control organizational activities.

Preparation of the budget is a long and complex process, involving a number of distinct functions, and occurring over an extended period of time. Although a police executive will not normally be involved in each phase of the budget process, it would be useful for him to know and understand the entire sequence of events that compromise the budget cycle. The elements of the budget cycle, which are described in detail in the International City Management Association publication, *Management Policies in Local Government Finance*, are policy setting, estimating expenditures, reviewing estimates, estimating revenues, forecasting, preparing the budget document, review and adoption, and execution.[47]

The police executive is responsible for preparing a budget request that is sufficient to meet the needs of his department and that is reasonable in view of anticipated programs and activities. Budgets have a habit of increasing year by year. This is inevitable, due to increased personnel costs and the overall effects of inflation. Nevertheless, a police executive must be prepared to have solid facts and figures to substantiate budget requests. Throughout the budget cycle, he may be called upon to justify the budget that he has submitted. At the same time, the police executive must be prepared to compromise. He must know what programs and costs in his budget are absolutely essential and which ones can be cut or trimmed down, if necessary.

The Budget Format   Budget formats vary from one jurisdiction to another. The most frequently used budget formats are the line-item type and the program budget (sometimes referred to as the Planning-Programming-Budgeting-System or PPBS). Under the line-item format, proposed expenditures are divided into specific categories, such as personal services (salaries and fringe benefits), operating expenses (supplies and materials), professional services, and capital outlays.

Under a program budget format, proposed expenditures are grouped according to function, or program area, such as department administration, patrol, traffic, criminal investigation, detention, training, and so on. The exact format of the budget will, of course, vary with the budgeting practices of the governmental jurisdiction. In many cases, however, the program budget format does offer a more realistic method of allocating resources according to planned programs and activities than the line-item format.[48]

Fiscal Control   A budget is a tool of management. It tells what programs and activities are planned, what resources are available to carry them out, and anticipated costs. However good the tool, though, the chief executive must exercise diligent control over expenditures to ensure that the purposes of the budget are achieved. The successful administrator is one who learns to plan expenditures wisely, operating within the means provided in the budget. Consistent budget deficits mean either that insufficient funds are being allocated to the department, or that they are not being controlled properly. In either event, the chief executive must assume at least partial responsibility.

Police executives must learn to detect emerging problems which may result in expenditures in excess of those provided for in the budget. Personnel shortages, for example, may result in more paid overtime than originally anticipated. Unusual occurrences, such as natural disasters, riots, or demonstrations may also require expenditure of funds beyond the sums originally budgeted. Such circumstances will require the police executive to carefully monitor the expenditure of funds.

The police executive should also maintain a close watch over expenditures for certain specialized operations, such as vice, narcotics, and intelligence, where "hidden accounts" may be used to the detriment of police credibility. The use of "buy" money, paid to informers, while often a legitimate police practice, should be closely supervised to prevent abuse.

Management Training

Popular belief once held that successful managers were born, not made. It was assumed that good managers just naturally had some unique or special qualities that enabled them to succed while others failed. However, a careful analysis of managerial functions has dispelled this notion, particularly in view of the increasingly complex nature of the duties and skills required of the manager today. While some managers are obviously more skilled than others, it is no longer assumed that managerial success is somehow related to an inherent trait or quality. Instead, managers must be created.[49]

Successful management requires wisdom, foresight, experience, and training. The art of management has advanced far beyond the point where it is possible for a person to advance through the ranks of an organization and eventually rise to command, even though this situation is still typical of many police organizations today. All too often, police executives are chosen because of their long service with the organization and in spite of the lack of a demonstrated ability to manage. Hopefully, this trend will be reversed in the future as it becomes more evident that seniority and tenure are no substitute for competency. While knowledge of police operations is admittedly a desirable prerequisite for a police executive, much more should be required. A successful police executive must not only be familiar with police operations, but should also be thoroughly trained in the fields of administrative theory, organizational behavior, and techniques and philosophy of management. The skills necessary for a manager to succeed are gained through a combination of experience, training, and personal development. A potential manager should be exposed to both informal and formal training if he is to develop those skills that will be required in the management of the police organization.

Informal Training   Informal training refers to the utilization of the resources available within the working environment of the organization to assist personnel in the development of management skills. Informal training is sometimes known as a career development program. A number of police agencies have initiated managerial development programs to ensure that individuals with the necessary interests and motivation may advance through the organization to eventually assume a managerial position. Management development programs are designed to acquaint supervisors and middle managers with the basic skills and techniques that will be needed as they advance to more responsible positions in police organizations.

Police executives, if they are concerned about the continued well being and effectiveness of the organization, have a responsibility to develop within their agencies the opportunity for subordinates to advance to management positions and to acquire the skills and abilities that will be required in those positions. Not all individuals, however, aspire to management positions. In the police field, some officers are quite content to remain in the lower ranks of the organization, and have no desire to accept the responsibility and authority that accompany higher positions. This is just as well, since promotional opportunities in police departments are usually sparse.

Police executives should carefully evaluate their subordinates in order to identify and evaluate candidates who express the desire and potential capability to assume managerial positions. As Koontz and O'Donnell have said:

> ... a prime qualification for manager selection is his keen desire to manage. Only a person with such motivation, provided he has the essential intelligence, will take full advantage of opportunities to acquire the wisdom of a mature executive. In other words, he must learn what he is taught; he must be able, and anxious, to absorb knowledge.[50]

Informal management training consists of exposing the potential manager to a wide variety of situations and conditions that are likely to confront him in his role as manager.

Among other things, he must become thoroughly familiar with all aspects of the organization, its functions, and its activities. This does not imply that he must necessarily have a detailed, working knowledge of all organizational functions, but rather that he should know how these functions fit together into the overall operation of the organization.

In police departments, career development programs expose potential managers to various phases of police activities by rotating them through a series of jobs and assignments within the organization.[51] **Job rotation** allows the managerial trainee the opportunity to apply skills and abilities to a variety of different situations in order to gain a better understanding of the problems of management. Job rotation also allows the individual to gain a better understanding of and appreciation for the various problems associated with coordinating and controlling specialized functions. In addition, it provides him with a broader perspective of the overall operations of the organization. In other words, it enables him to "get the big picture."

Job rotation is a common practice in many police organizations and has proven to be a successful technique for developing potential managers. But job rotation should not be conducted too frequently, lest it result in a loss of stability and continuity of operations. Nor should job rotation be conducted so sporadically or infrequently that it fails to serve the purpose intended, resulting in organizational and individual stagnation.

Another method by which potential managers may be prepared for the task of management is through delegation of authority. By delegating authority to subordinates, police executives may encourage potential managers to think and act like the managers they hope to become. Delegation of authority also encourages potential managers to assume the responsibility and authority that accompany the managerial role. Delegation of authority may be accomplished by transferring authority from the executive to the trainee. This transfer of authority is temporary, only intended to acquaint the trainee with the knowledge that comes with assumption of authority and responsibility. Authority so delegated may be withdrawn at any time.

Temporary appointments may also be used to familiarize the management trainee with the functions and responsibilities of management. Through temporary appointments, subordinates may be allowed to "get the feel" of the manager's role. Temporary appointments are doubly advantageous in the police organization. In addition to creating management potential in subordinates, they allow the chief of police to share some of the burdens of management. During the absence of the chief of police, one of his assistants may be designated as acting chief. During this time, the acting chief has the same authority and responsibility of the chief of police. There is no substitute for experience, and temporary appointments can provide the experience that is necessary to further the development and training of future managers.

Formal Training   Formal training should be required of all police executives. Unfortunately, in the past, this training has been lacking. During the past several years, however, an increasing number of schools, universities, and training institutes have turned their attention to the problem of providing quality training and education to police executives. In some cases, training programs are designed specifically to train police executives, while in other instances, police management training has been incorporated into a broader program of training for a variety of public institutions. One example is the School of Public Administration at the University of Southern California at Los Angeles, where a full range of courses have been developed to equip managers of a number of public institutions with the diverse skills and abilities that will enable them to manage their organizations successfully.

Many colleges and universities offer courses designed specifically to meet the needs of police organizations. In addition, most two- and four-year colleges and universities offer degree programs in police science, criminal justice, and related fields. Within these programs, there are usually a number of courses dealing with police organization, administration, and management. In addition to formal academic programs, there are several excellent training programs, institutes, and seminars on police management and career development offered by a variety of organizations, such as the International Association of Chiefs of Police, the Northwestern Traffic Institute,[52] the Federal Bureau of Investigation, the Southern Police Institute, and others. Funds to defray the cost of attending these courses are often available from state and regional criminal justice planning agencies. A partial list of these management training programs and pertinent information is included in the Appendix.

Summary

The management of men and organizations is a complex, difficult, and demanding task, for which few are prepared or qualified. This is no less true in police administration. Police executives must have a thorough understanding of sound management principles, organization theories, and administrative techniques, and they should be able to apply this knowledge to the practical, day-to-day realities of the police organization.

This chapter has attempted to provide a brief and general overview of the management function, and has drawn heavily from theories and principles that have been developed in the social sciences. Police organizations, like other organizations, must rely upon people, the most important resource, in fulfilling their responsibilities to the public. A knowledge of people, then, and the ability to maximize their potential, is a prime requisite for the manager of any organization.

Discussion Questions

1. *Explain the derivation and the meaning of the term "scientific management."*

2. *Explain why all managerial decisions have behavioral consequences.*

3. *Describe some of the contributions to management theory made by Frederick Taylor.*

4. *What are some objections to the scientific management approach?*

5. *What were the basic contributions of the Hawthorne studies to management theory?*

6. *Explain the differences between a goal and an objective.*

7. *What is the managerial grid? What is its purpose?*

8. *Discuss Herzberg's hygiene-motivation theory.*

9. *Describe the purpose and the process of inspection as it relates to the police organization.*

10. *Why is policy necessary? What are some of the consequences of a poorly defined or inappropriate policy?*

References

1. Harold Koontz and Cyril O'Donnell, *Principles of Management: An Analysis of Managerial Functions*, 4th ed. (New York: McGraw-Hill, 1968), p. 5.

2. Henri Fayol, *General and Industrial Management*, trans. Constance Storrs (London: Sir Isaac Pitman and Sons, 1949), pp. 5-6.

3. Douglas McGregor, *The Human Side of Enterprise* (New York: McGraw-Hill, 1960), p. 4.

4. Koontz and O'Donnell, *Principles of Management*, pp. 18-19; Justin G. Longenecker, *Principles of Management and Organizational Behavior*, 2d ed. (Columbus, Ohio: Charles E. Merrill, 1969), pp. 7-8.

5. Frederick W. Taylor, *The Principles of Scientific Management* (New York: Harper & Brothers, 1911).

6. An excellent discussion of the history and evolution of the scientific approach to management and the contributions of the early theorists can be found in L. Urwick and E. F. L. Brech, *The Making of Scientific Management, Vol. I: Thirteen Pioneers* (London: Management Publications Trust, 1949).

7. Taylor, *Scientific Management*, p. 7.

8. For a discussion of the concept of efficiency in public administration, see Emmette S. Redford, *Ideal and Practice in Public Administration* (Birmingham: University of Alabama Press, 1958), pp. 4-7.

9. Taylor, *Scientific Management*, p. 9.

10. Ibid, p. 10.

11. Fayol, *General and Industrial Management*, p. 3.

12. Ibid., pp. 19-20.

13. *The Human Problems of an Industrial Civilization* (New York: The Macmillan Co., 1933).

14. F. J. Roethlisberger and W. J. Dickson, *Management and the Worker* (Cambridge, Mass.: Harvard University Press, 1939).

15. Amitai Etzioni, *Modern Organizations* (Englewood Cliffs, N.J.: Prentice-Hall, 1964), p. 33.

16. Ibid., pp. 34-39.

17. See Chapter 2 for a discussion of informal organizations.

18. McGregor, *The Human Side of Enterprise.*

19. Koontz and O'Donnell, *Principles of Management*, p. 540.

20. Ibid.

21. Mason Haire, ed., *Organization Theory in Industrial Practice* (New York: John Wiley & Sons, 1962), p. 16.

22. Ibid.

23. Robert S. Blake and Jane S. Mouton, "Management Facades," *Advanced Management Journal*, 31 (July 1966), pp. 30-37.

24. Ibid, pp. 30-31.

25. Frederick Herzberg, Bernard Mausner and Barbara Bloch Snyderman, *The Motivation to Work*, 2d. ed. (New York: John Wiley & Sons, 1959).

26. Ibid., pp. 113-19.

27. Paul W. Cummings, "Does Herzberg's Theory Really Work?" *The Personnel Administrator*, 19 (October 1974), pp. 19-22.

28. Luis R. Gomez and Stephen J. Mussio, "An Application of Job Enrichment in a Civil Service Setting: A Demonstration Study," *Public Personnel Management*, 4 (January-February 1975), pp. 49-54; William J. Paul, Keith B. Robertson, and Frederick Herzberg, "Job Enrichment Pays Off," *Harvard Business Review*, 47 (March-April 1969), pp. 61-78.

29. Fred G. Lesieur, ed., *The Scanlon Plan: A Frontier in Labor-Management Cooperation* (Cambridge, Mass.: The MIT Press, 1958).

30. Fred G. Lesieur and Elbridge S. Puckett, "The Scanlon Plan has proved itself." *Harvard Business Review*, 47 (September-October 1969), pp. 109-18.

31. Rensis Likert, *New Patterns of Management* (New York: McGraw-Hill, 1961), pp. 1–25.

32. Ibid.

33. Rensis Likert, *The Human Organization: Its Management and Value* (New York: McGraw-Hill, 1967), pp. 14–24.

34. National Advisory Commission on Criminal Justice Standards and Goals, *Police* (Washington, D.C.: U.S. Government Printing Office, 1973), p. 119. (Hereinafter referred to as Goals Commission)

35. Ibid., p. 50.

36. President's Commission on Law Enforcement and Administration of Justice, *Task Force Report: The Police* (Washington, D.C.: U.S. Government Printing Office, 1967), p. 45.

37. Koontz and O'Donnell, *Principles of Management*, p. 50.

38. O. W. Wilson and Roy C. McLaren, *Police Administration*, 3d ed. (New York: McGraw-Hill, 1972), p. 199.

39. For an extended discussion of the subject of internal discipline in police organization, *see* Goals Commission, *Police*, Ch. 19.

40. Wolf V. Heydebrand and James J. Noell, "Task Structure and Innovation in Professional Organizations," in Wolf V. Heydebrand, ed., *Comparative Organizations* (Englewood Cliffs, N.J.: Prentice-Hall, 1973), pp. 300–301.

41. Justin G. Longenecker, *Principles of Management and Organizational Behavior*, 2d ed. (Columbus, Ohio: Charles E. Merrill, 1969), p. 104.

42. Ibid., pp. 106–11.

43. Goals Commission, *Police*, p. 599.

44. Longenecker, *Principles of Management*, p. 110.

45. James L. Price, *Organizational Effectiveness: An Inventory of Propositions* (Homewood, Ill.: Richard D. Irwin, 1968), p. 48.

46. Ibid., p. 61.

47. Richard W. Lindholm, David S. Arnold, and Richard R. Herbert, "The Budgetary Process," in J. Richard Aronson and Eli Schwartz, eds., *Management Policies in Local Government Finance* (Washington, D.C.: International City Management Association, in cooperation with Municipal Finance Officers Association, 1975), pp. 68–87.

48. For a brief overview of PPBS, see Lindholm, et al., *Management Policies*, pp. 88–92.

49. For a detailed discussion of the development and training of managers, see Koontz and O'Donnell, *Principles of Management*, pp. 506–533.

50. Ibid., p. 507.

51. Goals Commission, *Police*, p. 430.

52. The Traffic Police Administration Program at Northwestern University is described in R. Michael Buren, "A Police Management Training Program: Efficient Use of Man and Money?" *Journal of Police Science and Administration*, 1 (September 1973), pp. 294–302.

FOUR

Police
Patrol
Operations

General Observations . . .

The police organization is a complex and formidable structure, particularly in large metropolitan cities where police departments may number hundreds or even thousands of sworn and civilian personnel. As a police department grows and develops more responsibilities, it becomes increasingly specialized in its operations and procedures. In general, all police operations can be grouped into two rather broad but distinct categories: line services and support services.[1] Line services include the basic police functions of patrol, traffic enforcement, and criminal investigation. Support services include all other functions that support line operations, such as records, communications, personnel administration, and so forth. This chapter discusses the patrol operation and the administration, organization, and management of the patrol force.

The Purpose of Patrol

The word patrol is derived from the French word *patrouille* meaning, roughly, to paddle in the mud on foot. As one police authority suggests, the entymology of the word "clearly establishes the function as one which is arduous, tiring, difficult, and performed in conditions other than ideal."[2] In recent years, the job of the police patrol officer has gained increased attention from the public, particularly due to the romanticized versions of police exploits that have been portrayed in motion pictures, books, and television episodes. Nevertheless, the job of the police patrol officer is still largely misunderstood and thankless, even though it is the most important function of the police operation.

Basic police patrol is the primary vehicle by which the goals and objectives of the police organization are accomplished. Upon the patrol officer rests the major share of the burdens of the criminal justice system. It is the uniformed patrolman who must confront the enraged husband, the crazed drug addict, the frightened runaway, the grieving mother, the desperate criminal, and the uninformed, apathetic,

Courtesy of the Chicago Police Department

A patrol officer calls in.

and often hostile citizen. It is the patrol officer who must demonstrate that the system of criminal justice in America is still worthy of support. It is the patrol officer who is the target of public criticism and abuse (frequently), praise (seldom), and indifference (almost always). It is the patrol officer on the street who must set in motion the wheels of criminal justice; and, it is primarily he who determines the quality of justice that system produces.

Shoddy police practices, indiscriminate abuse of civil rights, vain, willful, corrupt and prejudicial police behavior all reflect unfavorably upon the police and the entire criminal justice system. Unethical, improper, and illegal behavior on the part of the police patrol officer, because it is more visible than other forms of governmental abuse, seriously erodes public confidence in and support for the police and other criminal justice agencies. Because the police patrol officer is in the vanguard of the struggle to achieve equal justice for all men, because he is sworn to protect the lives and property of those he serves, and because he has an obligation to preserve the fundamental principles of our democratic system, the burdens of criminal justice fall heavily (perhaps too heavily) upon him. The problems facing the men and women of the police patrol force are great and many. Continuously rising crime rates have seriously eroded public confidence in the police, despite the fact that the police alone cannot begin to solve the causes of crime—poverty, social injustice, and a deterioration of the moral fibre of our society. Increasing public concern regarding the integrity of governmental institutions and Federal and local government employees has hindered the police in their effort to perform their duties properly. The mission and role of the police, once clearly defined and accepted, has become vague and confused. The police themselves, unable to perform many of the duties expected of them, and unwilling to accept responsibility for others, have become uncertain of their proper role in society.

In the face of these mounting difficulties, police administrators have been sorely pressed to provide solutions and to demonstrate police effectiveness. While sound and dynamic police leadership will not solve all the problems confronting the police today, skillful and resourceful police managers can begin to create the climate in which solutions can be found. To do this, they must determine the most effective manner in which the resources of the police agency can be utilized.

Patrol Organization and Management

The police patrol force must be organized and managed in such a manner that will result in maximum available manpower in order to achieve the goals of the force to the greatest extent possible. In general, the goals of the police patrol force include the following: (1) enforcement of laws and apprehension of criminals; (2) preservation of the public peace and the maintenance of order; (3) regulating human conduct consistent with public needs and demands; (4) providing other public services as may be determined, consistent with the police role.

In order that these services may be provided in the most effective manner possible, police patrol forces are organized and deployed in such a way as to ensure their ready availability and immediate response in time of need. One of the basic weaknesses of police management today is that police administrators fail to utilize their personnel effectively, continuing to use custom and tradition, rather than actual need, as guidelines for allocating personnel resources.[3]

Patrol Force Allocation

A principal concern of all police administrators is the adequacy of manpower allocated to the patrol force. Since the primary burden of reducing crime and protecting life and property is placed on the patrol force, it is essential that an adequate number of personnel be assigned to this police function. The difficulty lies in the fact that no adequate formulas have been developed for determining acceptable manpower levels.

The number of personnel assigned to the patrol force depends, to a great extent, upon the total number of personnel available to the police administrator. Even though patrol is the backbone of the police operation, it is only one of several vital functions that are needed to make the organization effective. Depending on the size of the department, the proportion of personnel assigned to the patrol force may range from one-half to two-thirds of the entire department. Generally speaking, the larger the police organization, the smaller will be the percentage of total sworn personnel assigned to the patrol force. This is due primarily to the fact that as a police organization grows and develops additional responsibilities, it will become more specialized in its operations, and will allocate greater numbers of personnel to functions other than patrol.

In smaller departments, where there is little if any specialization, the patrol force will represent the bulk of the personnel assigned to the police organization.

The total number of police personnel in a given community is determined by a number of factors. These include the level of tolerance for criminal activities in the city, the willingness of the community to finance and support police services, and the ability of the police administrator to justify increased personnel allocations. It should be remembered, however, that the quality and efficiency of the police service in a given community cannot be measured by manpower figures alone. The types of persons recruited into the force, the nature and amount of training given them, the suitability of the equipment provided, and the efficiency of the department's operating procedures significantly affect the number of personnel needed to provide an acceptable level of police service. In addition, manpower utilization policies, such as management decisions about the use of one-man or two-man patrol units and foot patrol beats, also influence the quality and level of police service that can be provided.

There are no precise standards or formulas available for determining overall police personnel needs for cities of various sizes. While a particular staffing pattern might work well in one city, it might not in another. Variation of such factors as the degree of industrialization, ethnic composition, and social and economic characteristics all influence the need for police services. Official and citizen interest in the product of police services, the quality of the courts and prosecuting agencies, relationships with other law enforcement agencies, recruitment and training practices, and conditions of employment are other variables that must be considered. Moreover, whether or not the setting is urban or rural or whether it is part of a larger metropolitan complex, may also influence police needs and programs. To determine appropriate manning levels, the police administrator needs, first and foremost, sufficient information concerning police activities and demands for police service. Without such information, he can neither justify requested personnel increases nor effectively deploy the forces at his disposal.

Proper deployment of patrol personnel begins with the collection and analysis of data that reflects the community's need for various police services and the types of activities

performed by patrol officers. In some police agencies,
deployment data collection is nonexistent or inadequate.
In others the system lacks provisions for evaluating and
improving their deployment system or testing the efficiency
of new deployment techniques.[4]

Although deployment decisions should not be based
purely upon mathematical formulas and comparative standards,
such instruments are not without use.[5] Comparative standards
can certainly be helpful for formulating a perspective on the
manpower level in a given community. A better perspective
may be achieved if it is determined that the manpower allocations of a given department deviate significantly from established norms. While the factors mentioned earlier may account
for certain variations, it is considered useful to know how one
police agency's personnel strength varies from that of another,
particularly if the communities in which the two departments
are located are similar. An example of how manpower levels may
vary from community to community is shown in Figure 4-1.

The most useful method of determining adequate manpower requirements, particularly for the patrol force, is by
using data based on actual service demands. This requires that
an analysis be made of actual calls for service and other reportable police incidents, in order to compute minimum manning
levels. It is suggested that manpower requirements may be
determined by discovering how many patrol personnel are
required to handle a given number of calls for service and
other police activities.

It has been stated that approximately one-third of a
police patrolman's time is spent handling actual calls for
service.[6] The remainder of his time is spent performing administrative duties, such as report writing, on preventive patrol,
or performing other miscellaneous duties. Some studies, however, indicate that only about one-fourth of a patrolman's
time is spent handling actual calls for service and reportable
police incidents.[7] In addition, Kenney and his associates
determined that each case handled by the police patrolman
requires, on the average, about one half-hour to complete.[8]
With this information, it is relatively simple to compute the
actual number of patrolmen required to maintain an effective
manning level for patrol purposes.

Other factors that must be determined before attempting
to compute the strength of the patrol force are the anticipated

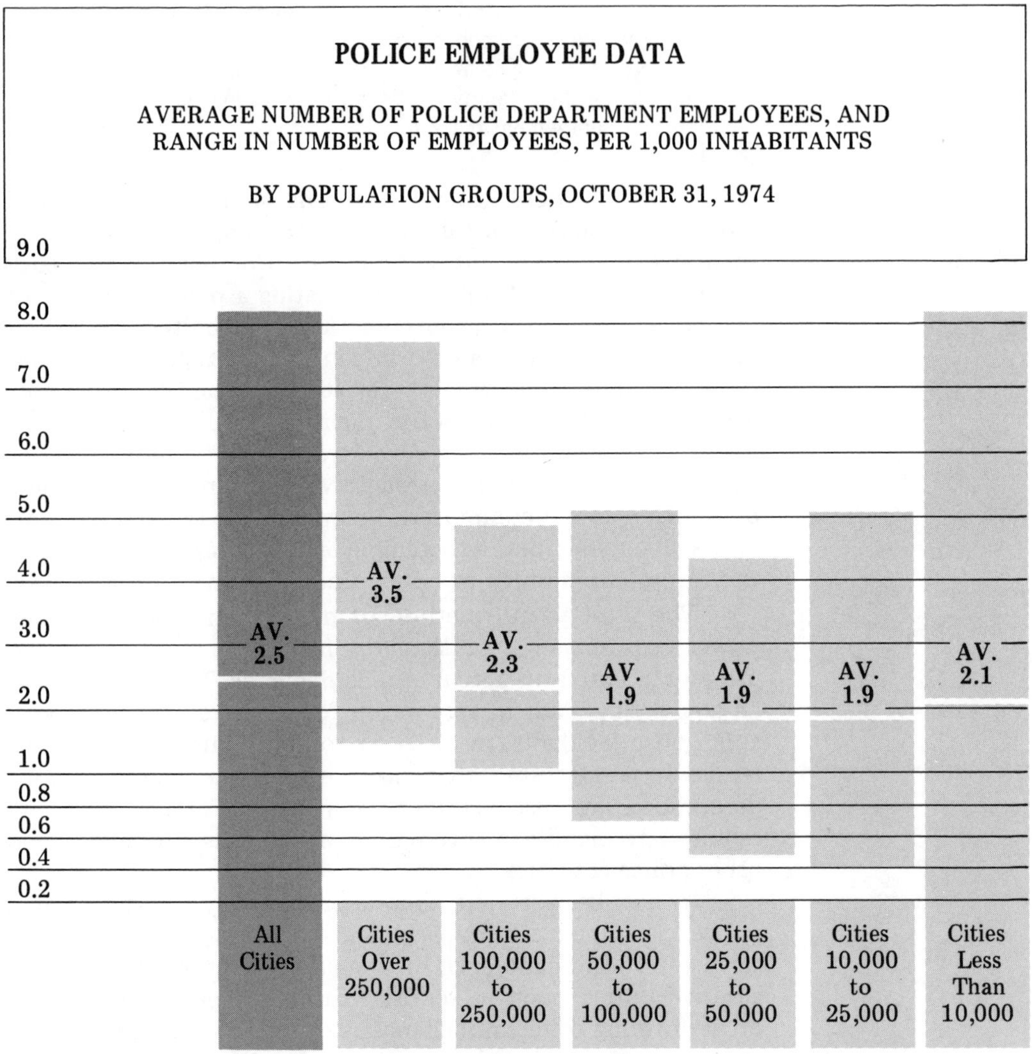

POLICE EMPLOYEE DATA

AVERAGE NUMBER OF POLICE DEPARTMENT EMPLOYEES, AND
RANGE IN NUMBER OF EMPLOYEES, PER 1,000 INHABITANTS

BY POPULATION GROUPS, OCTOBER 31, 1974

Source: Federal Bureau of Investigation, *Uniform Crime Reports — 1974* (Washington, D.C.:
U.S. Government Printing Office, 1975), p. 222.

Figure 4-1. Police Employee Data.

number of police incidents that the patrol force will be required
to handle and the **availability factor.**" The number of incidents
must be determined by examining past data and projecting
future trends. The availability factor is determined by sub-

tracting time from a patrolman's theoretical maximum number of working hours per year that will be devoted to holidays, sick leave, training, and so forth. The availability factor varies from department to department, depending upon the average number of hours each patrolman can be expected to be absent from his regular assignment, and may range from 1.5 to 2.0. An availability factor of 1.5 would mean that it would require 1.5 patrol officers to man one 8-hour beat 365 days per year.

The method of computing the availability factor is as follows:

Maximum manhours per year   (365 x 8)   =   2920.

Less:

Days off	832	
Vacation	80	
Sick Leave	48	
Holidays	80	
Training time	40	
Total Deductible		1080
Actual available hours		1840

The availability factor then becomes:

$$\frac{\text{Number of hours required to man one beat 365 days a year (365 x 8)} = 2920}{\text{Actual available hours} = 1840} = 1.6$$

According to the formula, the availability factor for the patrol force, or for any other unit in the police organization, can be computed easily. Availability factors will vary from organization to organization, depending upon sick time policies, holidays, and so forth. Once the availability factor has been determined, it is then possible to determine the actual number of patrol personnel required for the force:

$$\frac{\text{Number of Cases} \times \begin{array}{c}\text{Hours required to}\\\text{handle each case}\end{array}}{\begin{array}{c}\text{Percent of patrol-}\\\text{man's time devoted}\\\text{to handling calls}\end{array} \times \begin{array}{c}\text{Hours required}\\\text{to man one beat}\\\text{365 days a year}\end{array}} \times \begin{array}{c}\text{Avail-}\\\text{ability}\\\text{Factor}\end{array} = \begin{array}{c}\text{Number}\\\text{of Patrol}\\\text{Officers}\end{array}$$

Using the above formula, it would then be possible to determine the actual number of patrol personnel required to handle a given number of calls for service. If the anticipated number of calls for service were 15,000 for one year, the computation would read as follows:

$$\frac{15,000 \times .5}{.25 \qquad 2920} \times 1.6 = 16$$

According to the formula, it would require 16 patrolmen to handle the anticipated number of calls for service. The formula, of course, can provide only a rough estimate of the number of patrolmen actually required for a police department. Community characteristics, particular police problems, public expectations and demands, and other variables ought to be considered when determining the adequacy of the patrol force.[9]

Manpower Distribution

Once a sufficient number of patrol personnel have been assigned to the patrol force, they must be distributed according to actual need. Depending upon the size of the police jurisdiction, the patrol force may be divided up into beats or districts in a manner that will ensure that each geographic area of the city receives adequate coverage. In large cities, precincts or substations may be established, each representing a miniature police department. Within each precinct or substation, the deployment of patrol personnel is also arranged into beats, districts, or sectors of responsibility.

Another principal concern of the patrol force commander and the police administrator is the distribution of patrol personnel according to time of day. Police departments must remain in operation 365 days a year, 24 hours a day. At the same time, individual patrolmen do not normally work more than forty hours in any one work week, and are entitled to the same sick leave, holiday, and vacation privileges as other employees. The police administrator must therefore reconcile the need to provide adequate police coverage and his obligation to ensure that all personnel receive the benefits to which they are entitled.

In order to provide continuous, round-the-clock patrol coverage, the police patrol force is normally divided into three eight-hour shifts. In some cases, one or more overlap shifts may be used to provide additional coverage during peak activity hours.

Scheduling shifts is a problem, especially in small departments.[10] In too many cases, however, scheduling is taken for granted, with little thought given to allocating personnel according to actual demands for services. Too often, an equal number of officers are assigned to each shift, despite the variation in workload from shift to shift. Such variation creates an imbalance with the result that some officers are required to handle proportionately more cases than others. This is not an efficient use of manpower and should be avoided.

Each police agency should initiate its own manpower-workload analysis in order to schedule and deploy patrol officers according to actual need. The smaller the department, the less problem such studies pose. In larger police agencies, where computers are available, weekly or monthly data printouts may be obtained to simplify the task of manpower allocation.

When conducting manpower workload studies, it is important to differentiate between different types of calls for service. Some types of police activities require more time than others. A minor traffic accident, for example, may require less time than an arrest for a felony. For this reason, different types of police incidents should be grouped into separate categories, and their average time computed. Then, each type can be assigned a weighting factor when computing total time required to deal with all calls. For example, the following average times and assigned weights might be used.

Type of Activity	Average Time Required	Assigned Weight
Criminal	60 minutes	1.0
Traffic	45 minutes	.75
Services	30 minutes	.50

More sophisticated analyses might include greater detail,

separating arrests from investigations, and criminal offenses by type or degree.

By applying weighted scores to actual police activities, it is possible to obtain a much clearer picture of workloads on a shift-by-shift basis. The data shown in Figure 4-2 clearly shows a significant variation of activity levels between the three patrol shifts.

The purpose of such analysis is to allocate police patrol personnel as nearly as possible according to actual need on a shift-by-shift basis. The weighting factors shown in the examples, of course, are merely illustrative of the *method* of determining patrol shift manpower distribution, and are not meant to be taken as exact formulas to be used in a given police jurisdiction. Police administrators should initiate similar studies to determine the proper manning levels for the patrol stifts in their own departments. In addition, police administrators should be alert to the fact that manpower needs as well as police activities are subject to fluctuation. Certain types of police incidents may rise sharply in summer months in some jurisdictions and dip slightly in others. Therefore, seasonal characteristics should be taken into consideration when making long-range plans concerning patrol assignments. Moreover, the activities of the patrol force should be periodically audited to determine whether or not current manpower levels are commensurate with actual needs. Activity trends may change for one reason or another, and the police administrator should be alert to spot such changes and adjust personnel assignments accordingly. Too many or two few patrol personnel can be detrimental to the overall efficiency of the police organization.

One final factor should be considered regarding shift assignments in the patrol force—the assignment of days off to patrol personnel. Obviously, not all officers will be lucky enough to have free weekends. In fact, most of the patrol force must content themselves with days off during the middle of the week. Levels of police activity fluctuate according to the day of the week, the hour of the day and by season. As a result, some days represent low levels of police activity and others account for considerably more police incidents. The typical police department might encounter higher activity levels on Fridays and Saturdays, and lower levels during the middle of the week. Because of unique local conditions, police jurisdictions may find that their peak activity levels occur on Wednesdays and Thursdays rather than on weekends.

Type of Incident	First Shift 12:00 midnight – 8:00 AM				Second Shift 8:00 AM – 4:00 PM				Third Shift 4:00 PM – 12:00 midnight			
	Number	Weight	Score	% of Total	Number	Weight	Score	% of Total	Number	Weight	Score	% of Total
Criminal[a]	356	1.0	356	26.8	464	1.0	464	34.9	508	1.0	508	38.3
Traffic[b]	168	0.75	126	17.1	360	0.75	270	36.7	452	0.75	339	46.1
Service[c]	1644	0.50	822	33.1	1332	0.50	666	26.9	1984	0.50	992	40.0
Total[d]	2168			29.8	2156			29.7	2944			40.5

NOTES: [a] Criminal incidents include all reports, investigations, and arrests involving criminal offenses
[b] Traffic incidents include traffic accident investigations, pedestrian and vehicular control, and traffic enforcement
[c] Service incidents include all other police activities not included in either of the first two categories
[d] Totals for percents are read across the columns

Figure 4-2. Hypothetical Example Showing How Different Types of Police Incidents can be Weighted to Determine Proportionate Levels of Police Activity on a Shift-by-Shift Basis.

Overlapping Shifts   Frequently, peak activity periods may cross shifts. For example, a peak activity period in many cities is between the hours of 10:00 PM and 2:00 AM. Since this activity period would normally extend across both the end of the third shift and the beginning of the first shift, it might be advisable to assign an additional shift to buttress the patrol force during this period. An overlap shift assigned from 8:00 PM to 4:00 AM would provide the necessary additional personnel to handle increased activity that may exceed the normal manpower capabilities on either of the two shifts. In addition, it would provide additional patrol coverage during the critical time when the first shift is relieving the third shift. An overlapping shift, arranged in this manner, will provide for continuous patrol coverage in the event of incidents requiring immediate response. The overlapping shift, or fourth shift, as it is sometimes called, may consist of only a few patrol officers, or may constitute a regular patrol shift, equal in strength to the other patrol shifts.

The Platoon System   The platoon system enjoys great popularity among police personnel in general and is widely used among police departments in the United States, despite its general unsuitability for effective patrol force distribution and the detrimental effect it has upon the responsibility to match manning levels with actual need. Under the platoon system, an equal number of patrol officers are assigned to each of three or more patrol shifts. These shifts, or platoons, operate as units and rotate shifts on a regular basis. As an example, in a given department, each platoon might rotate from one shift to another every thirty, sixty, or ninety days. In some departments, platoons rotate as often as once each week.

The primary disadvantage of the rotating platoon system is that it does not provide for the assignment of patrol personnel to shifts according to actual need as determined by activity levels. Instead, the same number of patrol officers are assigned to the day, evening, and morning shifts. The platoon system is inefficient in that it does not achieve maximum utilization of manpower, resulting in an excess of personnel during low activity periods and a shortage of personnel during high activity periods.

The basic rationale behind the platoon system seems to involve the concept of maintaining each shift, or platoon, as an integral unit in order that the officers can function together more effectively. While this idea is not without merit, its effectiveness is compromised when the platoons are periodically shifted without regard to activity levels. Police administrators should carefully assess the needs of their patrol forces, in terms of activity levels, before adopting the platoon rotation system.

The 4-10 Plan A relatively new development in deployment of police personnel has emerged in recent years. Called the 4-10 Plan, the concept departs from the traditional practice of scheduling patrol personnel to an eight-hour day, five-day work week. Instead, patrol officers are scheduled to a ten-hour day, four days a week.[11] The principle objectives of the 4-10 plan are to increase effectiveness of police patrol personnel allocation procedures and to improve individual job satisfaction among employees. The 4-10 plan was first developed in private industry and was adopted in California on an experimental basis by the Huntington Beach Police Department in February 1970. Subsequently, it has been adopted by several other police departments in Southern California and elsewhere in the United States.

An important feature of the 4-10 plan is that it provides the same number of total hours (40) to be worked by patrol personnel, but distributed in a different manner. The result is a reduction in the number of personnel assigned to the early morning (first) shift during periods of light activity, an increase in the number of personnel assigned to the evening (third) shift during peak activity periods, and a basic restructuring of the traditional working hours of the day shift. See Figure 4-3. It also provides for an overlapping of shifts and allows for a greater number of personnel to be on duty during periods when activity levels are highest without requiring the assignment of a fourth shift. The potential advantages of the 4-10 plan include the following:

1. An increase in patrol strength during periods of peak activity.
2. Increased operational efficiency of the patrol force.
3. Increased morale among members of the patrol force, due to the fact that they gain one additional day off each week.
4. Improved economy of the patrol operation.

The 4-10 plan, however, is not without adverse limitations. Among the disadvantages inherent in the 4-10 plan are

Figure 4-3. Typical patrol schedule for the 4-10 plan, comparing average number of personnel on duty on 10-hour and 8-hour shifts.

Source: Paul M. Whisenand, George M. Medak, and Bradley L. Gates, "The Four-Day — Forty-Hour Workweek," in *Criminal Justice Monograph: Innovation in Law Enforcement* (Washington, D.C.: U.S. Department of Justice, Law Enforcement Assistance Administration, National Institute of Law Enforcement and Criminal Justice, 1973), p. 146.

	a.m.						p.m.							a.m.							
Time	7	8	9	10	11	12	1	2	3	4	5	6	7	8	9	10	11	12	1	2	3	4	5	6	7

Watch I: 20 patrolmen; 3 sergeants
Watch II: 23 patrolmen; 3 sergeants
Watch III: 13 patrolmen; 3 sergeants

Average on 10-hour shift

56 patrolmen	11.40	13.10	20.50	7.40
9 sergeants	1.71	1.71	3.42	1.71
3 lieutenants	0.71	1.71	1.00	0.00

Current average on 8-hour shift

Patrolmen	11.40	14.30	12.90
Sergeants	2.14	2.14	2.14
Lieutenants	0.71	0.71	0.71

the following:

1. The need for additional personnel to bolster auxiliary staff functions.
2. Increased utilization of patrol vehicles during peak manning periods.
3. Problems associated with adjusting individual work schedules.

In general, however, the 4-10 has proven successful in those police agencies where it has been adopted. It remains a useful alternative to traditional manpower deployment systems. Police administrators faced with the problem of allocating patrol manpower to meet unusual activity needs should carefully examine the 4-10 plan to determine its applicability to their own situation.[12]

Shift Rotation   Rotating shifts, a common feature of the patrol force deployment system of many American police departments, provides for the transfer of personnel from one patrol shift to another on a regular basis. Either individual officers or whole groups of officers may be rotated simultaneously. Shift rotation offers a number of advantages to the police administrator. These include—

1. Shift rotation is an equitable solution to the problem of determining which personnel will be assigned to what shifts. Since some shifts are more desirable than others, it is sometimes necessary to assign personnel to shifts they do not like. As a result, morale may be lowered and internal conflict may develop.
2. Shift rotation permits officers to become more thoroughly familiar with all aspects of the patrol operation, which may vary greatly at different times of the day. Officers who remain on one shift for extended periods of time are likely to lose touch with routine occurrences on other shifts. Shift rotations helps to make the patrol officer proficient in his duties both during the day and evening hours.
3. Shift rotation forces the individual officer to be constantly alert during his tour of duty. Officers who remain on the same shift for extended periods may have a tendency to become complacent and neglectful in their duties, overlooking critical events. Complacency is one of the worst enemies of the patrol officer.

Rotating shifts may be achieved in a number of ways. One common practice is to rotate the whole shift, or platoon, as described earlier. The platoon system, however, is not considered to be an efficient method of deploying patrol forces. Another method of rotating shifts is on an individual basis, whereby each officer automatically rotates from one shift to the next in such a manner that the composition of each shift is continually changing. One disadvantage of this method is that it makes the scheduling of officers difficult. Another disadvantage is that because the members of the shift are continually changing, it is difficult for the supervisor to get to know his men and to establish a standard supervisory technique. Officers who have worked together for an extended period of time pose less of a challenge to the field supervisor, who knows what to expect from subordinates.

A third method of accomplishing shift rotation is by periodically requiring all officers to rotate shifts, but allowing them to choose the shift they wish to work by a system of bidding. Bidding for shifts may be done by seniority, or by reverse seniority, thus ensuring that all members of the patrol force are given an equal opportunity to obtain the shift of their choice. Under the bidding system, a roster is posted once every thirty, sixty, or ninety days with the names of all members on the patrol force listed by seniority. Each officer then indicates the shift he wishes to work for the following period, along with the days off he wants. In some departments, it is customary to require officers to choose a shift different from the one which they have been working, ensuring some turnover in personnel each bidding period.

Despite its popularity in many police departments, and the benefits it offers, the rotation system has some distinct disadvantages which should be considered when the police administrator contemplates initiating a system of shift rotation.[13]

First, the frequent rotation of personnel from one shift to the next creates difficulties for the domestic affairs of the individual officer. It makes the planning of family and social events more difficult. Officers whose working assignments and days off are continually changing have difficulty becoming involved in activities outside their job. Officers who wish to attend school are often unable to do so. In addition, shift rotation discriminates against patrol officers, since other members of the police organization usually are assigned to fixed shifts. Finally, periodic rotation of shifts is a physical hardship on the patrol officer. Some people are less able to change living, eating, and sleeping habits frequently; a periodic rotation of their work assignments may constitute a serious threat to their health and welfare, jeopardizing their proficiency on the job. For such reasons, the police administrator should carefully weigh the advantages and disadvantages before implementing a policy of shift rotation. However, officers who wish to rotate their shifts by changing with other officers should be permitted to do so, as long as it can be done without disrupting the work schedule.

Patrol Procedures

Effective police patrol can only be accomplished if the personnel assigned to the patrol force are logically and thoughtfully deployed and if they utilize proper techniques and procedures in the performance of their duties. Police patrol is not, or should not be, a random or haphazard exercise. It should be carefully planned and performed. Officers should patrol their assigned areas with great diligence, giving careful attention to the persons, places, and things around them. They must be ready to respond quickly to calls for service, especially if they are emergency calls. Patrol officers must be alert to detect and investigate unusual occurrences and suspicious activities. They must remain vigilant in the enforcement of the law and the apprehension of violators. Moreover, they must be alert to the fact that they are always in the public eye. What they do and how they do it will make a lasting impression on the members of the community in which they work.

Foot Patrol   Foot patrol is the oldest patrol method known to the police. Although it has diminished greatly since the advent of the automobile, foot patrol still plays an important role in the patrol operations of many American police departments.

Foot patrol is particularly effective in downtown areas, where the frequent sight of a uniformed police officer is likely to inspire public confidence and deter criminal activity. Because he has the opportunity to make many personal contacts stopping to talk with people on an informal basis, the patrolman has the advantage of becoming acquainted with many of the people on his beat. As a result, he can become more familiar with the public he serves and can respond more effectively to their needs.

The foot patrol officer can also develop sources of information often denied to other officers. This information may lead to the apprehension of offenders and the solution of crimes. In addition, the foot patrol officer can become more familiar about the characteristics of his beat. He can more readily spot suspicious circumstances and persons whose presence might warrant investigation. He is closer to the daily routine of his beat and is in a better position to detect criminal activity and to apprehend persons committing or about to commit crimes. The foot patrol officer becomes an authority on his beat and the persons and places in it.

The foot patrol officer, however, operates under definite limitations. He is unable to respond as quickly as motorized units to emergency situations where his presence may be required. The use of foot patrol officers is also less economical than a motorized patrol unit, because foot patrol officers can only cover a limited geographic area. In addition, foot patrol officers are also limited by weather conditions. Most are ineffective in heavy snow or in rainstorms, for instance.

Nevertheless, the foot patrol officer can be a real asset to the patrol operation, and the police administrator should endeavor to use them to their utmost advantage. One city in New York credited its high rate of crime clearances to its foot patrol officers, who represented a substantial part of the patrol force. One veteran police officer remarked that, in his opinion, ". . . there is no better way to control crime and to prevent it before it even starts than by having some of our men walking beats at all times."[14]

Motorized Patrol   With the advent of the automobile, police forces developed a new patrol technique—motorized patrol. Using automobiles, police patrol officers were able to cover more areas and respond more quickly when called. Today, the automobile has become a standard item of police equipment, and motorized units are the basic form of police patrols. The automobile offers the patrol officer many advantages: he can move about in inclement weather easier than the foot patrol officer; he can carry necessary items of equipment, such as firearms, ammunition, first aid and investigation kits; he can pursue and apprehend criminals who are also equipped with automobiles; and he can respond to calls from citizens more promptly. Nevertheless, the police patrol car has some rather serious disadvantages.

First, the officer in the patrol car is physically, and perhaps psychologically, isolated from the people in the community. He does not have the advantage of being able to stop to talk with people and does not have the opportunity to get to know the people on his beat. The patrol car officer is always on the move, trying as best he can to cover the area in his beat as completely and thoroughly as possible. The patrol car acts as a mechanical cocoon that separates him from the community and weakens the bond that should exist between the patrol officer and the citizen.

Second, the officer in the patrol car is not able to perceive his surroundings as well as the foot patrolman. Driving down city streets at 25 or 30 miles an hour, a patrol officer cannot carefully study his surroundings to detect suspicious circumstances or persons. As a result, much criminal activity may go unnoticed by the patrol car officer, no matter how keen may be his powers of observation or how diligent he may be in patrolling his assigned area. Moreover, many patrol officers in cars often fail to stop at various times and places during their tour of duty to make physical inspections. Automobile patrol officers somehow seem anchored to the seats of their cars, unable or unwilling to remove themselves and venture about on foot. As a result, they are not able to patrol their assigned areas thoroughly.

Finally, patrol cars are expensive to operate and maintain. They are often in use almost continuously throughout the day and night, and frequently they do not receive the preventive maintenance they deserve. As a result, they wear out quickly, and must be repaired or replaced. In addition, police officers sometimes abuse the automobiles assigned to them, thus causing even more wear and damage. Frequent breakdown of police patrol cars due to misuse or overuse is a constant source of worry to the police administrator.

One-Man vs Two-Man Patrol Units

For several years a controversy has raged among law enforcement authorities concerning the question of one-man versus two-man patrol units.[15] For every argument developed in favor of one-man units, a contrary argument can be advanced. To date, there is no general consensus on the subject, even though the trend in recent years has been away from two-man patrol units toward one-man units.[16]

The police administrator is in a difficult position. He has a responsibility to provide to the public the best police service possible and to do so economically. Obviously, two-man patrol units are not economical, because two officers are being used to do the job of one. On the other hand, he is under pressure from policemen's groups to ensure the safety of the officers under his command. One of the arguments favoring two-man units is that they are safer, in terms of the welfare of the individual officer. The police administrator is often forced to reconcile these points of view and to make an intelligent decision on the issue.

On the whole, one-man patrol units are used much more extensively than two-man units, although there is considerable variation according to size of police agency and type of shift assignment. One-man patrol units are found most frequently in smaller cities and on the day and afternoon shifts, while two-man patrols are normally found more often in larger cities, usually restricted to the night shifts.

One-man patrol units offer several advantages. First, they are more economical. Obviously, fewer officers can cover much more area in one-man patrol units. Second, since it is possible to deploy more one-man units than two-man units, the patrol force can be distributed over a larger area. As a result, response time can be reduced, and the likelihood of apprehending a suspect in the act of committing a crime is enhanced. In addition, one-man patrol units are generally considered to be more effective than two-man units, although there is considerable disagreement on this point. Proponents of one-man patrol units argue that a single officer can concentrate his entire attention to the circumstances around him, while a pair of officers may tend to become engaged in idle conversation that may detract from their abilities of observation. Finally, many police authorities believe that one-man patrol units offer more protection for the officer, since an individual officer is not lulled into a false sense of security by relying too heavily upon his fellow officer to protect him in a difficult situation. This is another issue that generates heated argument among police.

Statistics gathered by the Federal Bureau of Investigation do not shed much light on the issue. In 1974, for example, 18.7 percent of all reported assaults on law enforcement officers were perpetrated upon one-man, unassisted patrol units, compared to 22.8 percent upon one-man assisted patrol units, and with 37.4 percent two-man patrol units.[17] Since there are relatively fewer two-man patrol units in use, it would appear that the officers assigned to such units become victims of assault disproportionately higher than would normally be expected.

In a more comprehensive study involving an analysis of several hundred reported assaults on police officers in five southwestern states (Texas, Oklahoma, New Mexico, Arkansas, and Louisiana), it was discovered that while 63.1 percent of all officers assaulted were assigned to one-man patrol units, only 12.4 were unassisted at the time of the assault.[18] This suggests two things. First, officers assigned to one-man patrol units were not without assistance from back-up units during the assault; and second, the presence of one or more additional officers at the scene did not prevent the assault. The researchers also found no significant relationship between the number of officers present and the extent of injuries received by the victim officer concluding that, "the data do not support the premise that officer safety is enhanced through the use of two-man motor patrol assignments."[19]

Team Policing   One of the greatest problems affecting the police today is their relationship with the communities they serve. We know by now that the police will not be successful in their attempts to prevent crime and maintain social order unless they are able to develop and maintain a substantial degree of public confidence in and support for their programs and activities. Team policing is one method that has been tried in order to gain that confidence and support.

Team policing first developed in Aberdeen, Scotland, shortly after World War II. It was initiated originally to improve morale and reduce boredom among police officers patrolling quiet neighborhoods. A variation of the team policing concept, known as "**unit beat policing**," was developed in the town of Accrington, in the County of Coventry, England, in 1966. The purpose of unit beat policing, however, was not to reduce boredom, but to make more effective use of limited personnel by organizing them into teams assigned to specific areas.[20]

Team policing, under a variety of forms and under several different names, has been adopted in many cities in the United States in recent years. In each case, the purpose of the team policing plan seems somewhat different. In Syracuse, New York, the team policing model was used in the development of **crime control teams**, which were assigned to permanent districts, largely as an effort to reduce crime. In Los Angeles, the TEAM (Team Experiment in Area Mobilization) plan was somewhat more ambitious, but also directed at crime reduction. In other cities, team policing has been used in an effort to lessen the gap between the police and the community. The central purpose of the team policing models developed in Dayton, Ohio, and Holyoke, Massachusetts was better police-community relations. Still other versions, with slightly different purposes, have been developed in New York City, Richmond, California, and Cincinnati, Ohio.

Generally, team policing is viewed as a *method* of policing which exhibits the following attributes—

1. geographic stability of patrol through the permanent assignment of police teams to small areas or neighborhoods.
2. maximum communication, interaction, coordination, and cooperation among team members, fostered through the practice of working together to solve common problems.
3. Better communications between team members and residents of the neighborhoods to which they are assigned.[21]

In addition, team policing is viewed as an alternative to traditional police organization models and management philosophies. Team policing, for example, usually employs the following methods of organization and management.[22]

1. **Unity of supervision.** Team members have the advantage of working for the same supervisor for long periods of time. As a result, the level of supervision is more consistent than might otherwise be expected.
2. **Decentralized decision-making.** Team members are encouraged to make decisions for themselves which ordinarily would be made by upper and mid-level management. This encourages team members to assume greater responsibility for their actions.
3. **Emphasis upon generalist approach.** Each member of the police team is a generalist, even though some members may have specialist skills. To the extent possible, problems developing within the team's sector of responsibility are handled by team members without outside specialist assistance.

In a sense, team policing employs the technique of participative management, because it encourages each member to share in decision making, giving them an equal share in goal achievement. As Kenney points out, team policing "presupposes that all personnel have a contribution to make to the operation of the department, are capable and motivated to make that contribution and that there will be acceptance, if worthy, of the contribution."[23]

Because of its radical departure from traditional police organization models, team policing has encountered stiff resistance from some quarters. In particular, it has been resisted by police middle managers, who see it as an encroachment upon their spheres of influence and authority.[24] As a result, the record of team policing in the United States has been scored with failures as well as successes. Until more research is undertaken to assess the strengths and weaknesses of team policing, its future is not clear.[25]

Other Patrol Methods   Police patrol, if it is to be effective, must be flexible and adaptable to changing conditions and circumstances. Police jurisdictions vary greatly in the nature of the conditions in which the police officer must operate. The problems confronting the patrol officer vary from city to city and from state to state. Methods that produce desired results in one locale may not work well in another; procedures that are effective in one location may not be as effective in another. One of the greatest challenges facing the police administrator is the effective utilization of the forces at his disposal. Innovation, imagination, and adaptability are essential if the police administrator is to be able to meet his responsibilities to the public. A number of alternative patrol methods are available to the police administrator to increase the effectiveness of his patrol force. While the utility of these methods may be more limited than traditional techniques, nevertheless, they offer definite advantages in terms of meeting particular needs and unique situations.

Horse patrol is used almost exclusively in large metropolitan areas and for specific purposes, such as patrolling parks, forest preserves, and other locations which are generally inaccessible to motorized patrol units. In addition, horse patrols are used by the National Park Service (to patrol national parks), and by police and sheriff's departments in rural and mountainous areas for search and rescue operations and to track down wanted persons.

Bicycle patrols are an extremely effective means to deploy personnel for special tactical purposes. Many police agencies have used bicycle patrols, manned by both uniformed and plain clothes officers, for patrolling residential areas and business districts. Bicycles are quiet to operate and can be

Courtesy of the United States Park Police

The U.S. Park Police are among many law enforcement agencies that utilize horse patrols.

used in areas where conventional patrol units cannot operate efficiently, such as shopping centers, playgrounds, and parks. On the other hand, bicycle patrols are not as fast as motorized units and cannot operate under severe weather conditions.[26]

Motorcycle patrols are used by municipal police agencies almost exclusively for traffic control purposes. Motorcycles have enjoyed great popularity since they were introduced into police work several decades ago, primarily due to the fact that they are relatively less expensive to operate than automobiles, and can be easily maneuvered in traffic. In recent years, however, the use of motorcycles in law enforcement has been seriously questioned. It has been demonstrated, for example, that motorcycles are generally more hazardous to operate than automobiles and are ineffective in inclement weather, and thus cannot be operated year round in many police jurisdictions.

Some major cities have reduced their motorcycle squads, while others have abandoned use of motorcycles altogether. In Washington, D.C., the Metropolitan Police Department's motorcycle fleet was officially disbanded in March, 1974, after an extensive study revealed that the motorcycle was not cost effective.

Police administrators should carefully examine the needs of their departments and their communities before making a determination as to the practicality of implementing motorcycle patrols. If such patrols are currently being used, their effectiveness should be carefully and systematically evaluated. ". . . [P]olice executives should assess, very carefully, the need for solo motorcycle use and be certain that such conveyances can do the job well enough to offset the factors of increased cost, hazard, and lack of all around utility."[27]

Aircraft patrols.   Both fixed-wing aircraft and helicopters have been used effectively by law enforcement agencies in the

Courtesy of the Delaware State Police

Helicopter and fixed-wing aircraft provide support for regular patrol units.

United States for a number of specialized purposes. In addition to using aircraft for routine patrol functions, they have been employed for surveillance, traffic control, search and rescue missions, and the pursuit and apprehension of criminals. Although the costs to local governments to purchase and operate aircraft patrols is considerable, they have gained popularity in recent years and use by law enforcement agencies is expected to increase.[28]

Marine patrols. Police agencies that have law enforcement and police responsibilities along waterways—lakes, rivers, and oceans—must have some means of patrolling the areas. Marine patrols have been used in several large cities, including Chicago, New York, and Cleveland, along with a number of smaller cities. Using a variety of craft and equipment, marine agencies provide a number of police services, including rescue operations, preventive patrol, security patrol, and enforcement of water safety regulations and maritime laws. In many instances,

Courtesy of the San Joaquin Sheriff's Dept., Stockton, California

Marine patrols are used by police departments to supplement their patrol operations.

marine agencies work closely with Coast Guard units, enforcing statutory provisions relating to waterways and performing rescue operations.

Canine patrols. Police dogs have been used for centuries by law enforcement agencies to assist them in providing public protection and in patrol operations. Dogs were first introduced to American law enforcement shortly after World War I, by the New York City Police Department. Dogs continue to be valuable aids to law enforcement agencies and can be used for a variety of purposes—

- search and rescue operations;
- pursuit and apprehension of criminals;
- security and preventive patrol around commercial and industrial facilities;
- detection of contraband, such as explosives and hard drugs.[29]

In addition, police dogs have been used for crowd and riot control; although the negative public reaction to such use should be considered carefully before using dogs for such purposes. When dogs are to be used for crowd control purposes, guidelines should be issued detailing the manner in which the dogs may be used and the proper restraints that should be imposed on such use.

Preventive Patrol

This chapter has explored the purpose and nature of the police patrol function, and has briefly described particular types of patrol strategy. It has been noted that routine patrol is a basic tool of the police used to prevent crime and detect unlawful behavior. This discussion has rested on the assumption (shared by most police administrators) that preventive patrol is a fundamental role of the police. Indeed, preventive patrol has historically been regarded as the *principal* function of the police. All other police activities—records, communications, investigation—are, in a sense, ancillary. Most, if not all, police forces are built around the patrol operation, and the greatest share of most police budgets is devoted to maintaining and supporting the patrol force. Preventive police patrol is considered by many to be the essence of the police function. In fact, many veteran police officers have been known to refuse promotions and assignments to specialized functions because they prefer to remain in the patrol force, where the "real" police work is accomplished.

However, the effectiveness of preventive patrol has been questioned recently. After years, even centuries, of relying upon preventive patrol as the principal means of thwarting criminal acts and apprehending offenders, some authorities have begun to doubt that traditional preventive patrol really serves any useful purpose. Slowly but surely, nagging doubts about the value of preventive patrol have begun to surface. Though most police forces in the United States continue to place their faith in preventive patrol, a few researchers and police practitioners have begun to examine this subject in greater detail. To date, the most noteworthy attempt to explore the usefulness and effectiveness of preventive police patrol was undertaken in the Kansas City (Missouri) Police Department, under the auspices of the Police Foundation, which provided a grant for the study. The study, lasting twelve months, was concluded in 1973, and produced some significant and surprising results.[30]

The Kansas City study involved variations in the level of routine preventive patrol within fifteen police beats in the city. The beats were randomly divided into three groups, or districts. In one ("reactive") district, routine preventive patrol was eliminated entirely, and police officers only responded to actual calls for service. In the control district, routine preventive patrol was maintained at its usual level of one car per beat. In the remaining ("proactive") district, preventive patrol was intensified by two or three times its usual level through the assignment of additional patrol cars in the district. Based upon citizen interviews, victimization surveys, and detailed police service and crime statistics, it was discovered that the variations in the three levels of patrol "appeared not to affect crime, service delivery and citizen feelings of security in the way the public and the police often assume they do."[31] Among other findings, the study revealed the following:[32]

1. The experimental conditions had no significant effect on residence and non-residence burglaries, auto thefts, larcenies involving auto accessories, robberies, or vandalism—

crimes usually thought to be deterable through preventive patrol.

2. Few significant differences and no consistent pattern of differences occurred across experimental conditions in terms of citizen attitudes toward police services.

3. . . . [C]itizen fear of crime was not affected by the experimental conditions.

4. Experimental conditions had no significant effect on either police response time or citizen satisfaction with police response time.

Undoubtedly, many police administrators will choose to ignore the findings of the Kansas City experiment and will continue to rely upon preventive patrol as the basic technique for deterring and detecting crime. Certainly, the results of the study cannot themselves, unsupported by further research and analysis, justify a general revision of police patrol methods and procedures. The value of the Kansas City study is not that it resolves the question of the value of preventive patrol. It does not. Rather, the findings reinforce beliefs held by many police practitioners and researchers that police agencies can no longer continue to rely solely on traditional approaches to the problem of crime control and detection, and that innovation and experimentation must be undertaken if the police are to be able to respond effectively to the new and evolving problems that confront them. As the authors of the report suggest, many of the findings "point to what those in the field have long suspected—an extensive disparity between what we want the police to do, what we often believe they do, and what they can and should do."[33]

Summary

The patrol function remains the backbone of police operations; it will probably remain so. That alternative methods of police patrol techniques will be forthcoming is questionable. For the present, police forces will continue to rely upon a variety of patrol tactics and techniques to safeguard the lives and property of citizens, to deter unlawful conduct, and to apprehend offenders.

Police administrators should be encouraged to give thoughtful attention to the particular needs of their communities when allocating resources to the patrol force and when determining effective patrol strategies. Imagination and wisdom, rather than custom and tradition, should guide the police executive in making the most effective use of resources. Innovation and experimentation are necessary if maximum efficiency of limited resources is to be realized.

Discussion Questions

1. *Explain the difference between line and staff police operations.*

2. *What are the four basic goals of police patrol?*

3. *Explain why there can be no precise methods for determining police personnel needs in all cities?*

4. *What is the availability factor? How is it computed?*

5. *Under what conditions is it advisable to employ overlapping shifts?*

6. *Briefly describe the advantages and disadvantages of the following:*

   a. the platoon system
   b. shift rotation
   c. the 4-10 plan
   d. foot patrol

7. *What are the basic limitations of motorized patrol units?*

8. *What are the goals of team policing?*

9. *Under what conditions are bicycle patrols particularly effective?*

10. *Why have some cities abandoned use of motorcycle units?*

References

1. Some texts divide "support services" into staff services, which include such functions as personnel administration, training, and planning, and auxiliary services, which include communications, records, and detention. In this text, the term *support services* is used to describe all non-line functions.

2. Samuel G. Chapman, *Police Patrol Readings*, 2d ed. (Springfield, Illinois: Charles C. Thomas, 1970), p. ix.

3. John P. Kenney, George T. Felkenes, Carl Bloom, and Michael O'Neil, "Field Patrolmen Work Load in California: Cities with 25,000 to 100,000 population," *Journal of California Law Enforcement*, 4 (January, 1970), pp. 124-31.

4. National Advisory Commission on Criminal Justice Standards and Goals, *Police* (Washington, D.C.: U.S. Government Printing Office, 1973), p. 200.

5. See Calvin Clawson, "A Theoretical Approach to the Allocation of Police Preventive Patrol," *The Police Chief*, 40 (July, 1973), pp. 53-59.

6. O.W. Wilson and Roy C. McLaren, *Police Administration*, 2d ed. (New York: McGraw-Hill, 1972), p. 365.

7. John P. Kenney, *Police Administration* (Springfield, Illinois: Charles C. Thomas, 1972), p. 157.

8. Ibid.

9. Another method of determining manpower requirements and allocating police patrol forces is described in James D. Caldwell and James M. Nehe, "Implementing Unit Beat Policing: Patrol Distribution in Arlington County," *The Police Chief*, 41 (September, 1974), pp. 47-49.

10. One method of scheduling police manpower in the small department is discussed in William H. McGinnis, "Small Department Duty Schedule," *The Police Chief*, 41 (July,

1974), pp. 61-62; more sophisticated methods of patrol force distribution are described in Thomas J. Sweeney and William Ellingsworth, *Issues in Police Patrol: A Book of Readings* (Kansas City, Mo.: Kansas City Police Department, 1973), pp. 241-261; see also, James P. Damos, Peter Richman, and Eldon Miller, "P·R·E·W·A·R·N·S· . . . A Police Response Early Warning System, *The Police Chief*, 40 (August, 1973), pp. 24-27.

11. See Paul M. Whisenand, George M. Medak, and Bradley L. Gates, "The Four-Day—Forty-Hour Workweek," in *Criminal Justice Monograph: Innovation in Law Envorcement* (Washington, D.C.: U.S. Department of Justice, Law Enforcement Assistance Administration, National Institute of Law Enforcement and Criminal Justice, 1973), pp. 143-63.

12. For additional information regarding the application of the 4-10 plan to law enforcement, see William Cann, "Our 4/40 Basic Team Concept," *The Police Chief*, 39 (December, 1972), pp. 56-64; William A. Allen, "Four-Day Work Week: Another Approach," *The Police Chief*, 40 (January, 1973), pp. 48-49.

13. Wilson & McLaren, *Police Administration*, 3rd ed., pp. 328-329.

14. Robert Dyment, "A Case for the Foot Patrolman," in Chapman, *Police Patrol Readings*, p. 186.

15. For a more lengthy discussion of the one-man versus two-man controversy, see Chapman, *Police Patrol Readings*, pp. 212-244.

16. The increased presence of female police officers in patrol units has not escaped the author's attention. However, for the purposes of simplicity, the terms *one-man* and *two-man* will be used to describe both male and female patrol officers.

17. Federal Bureau of Investigation, *Crime in the United States 1974* (Washington, D.C.: U.S. Government Printing Office, 1975), p. 246.

18. Samuel G. Chapman, et al., *Perspectives of Assaults in the South Central United States*, Vol. I (Norman, Oklahoma: The University of Oklahoma, 1974), p. 141.

19. Ibid., p. 145.

20. Lawrence W. Sherman, Catherine H. Milton, and Thomas V. Kelly, *Team Policing: Seven Case Studies* (Washington, D.C.: Police Foundation, 1973), pp. xiii, ff.

21. Ibid., pp. 4-5.

22. Ibid., pp. 5-6.

23. John P. Kenney, *Police Administration*, rev. 3d ed. (Springfield, Ill.: Charles C. Thomas, 1975), p. 94.

24. A few of the typical problems encountered in implementing a team policing plan are discussed in Sherman, et al., *Team Policing*, pp. 91-96.

25. The Cincinnati Community Sector Team Policing Program (COMSEC) is the single team policing program to be extensively evaluated to date. See Sumner N. Clarren and Alfred I. Schwartz, *An Evaluation of Cincinnati's Team Policing Program*, Working Paper: 3006-11 (Washington, D.C.: The Urban Institute, October 8, 1974); Alfred I. Schwartz and Sumner N. Clarren, *Evaluation of Cincinnati's Community Sector Team Policing Program, A Progress Report: The First Six Months, Summary of Major Findings*, working paper: 3006-4 (Washington, D.C.: The Urban Institute, July 30, 1974).

26. George D. Eastman and Esther M. Eastman, eds., *Municipal Police Administration*, 6th ed. (Washington, D.C.: International City Management Association, 1969), p. 82; Chapman, *Police Patrol Readings*, pp. 200-203.

27. Ibid., p. 82.

28. C. Robert Guthrie and Paul M. Whisenand, "The Use of Helicopters in Routine Police Patrol Operations: A Summary of Research Findings," in S.I. Cohn, ed., *Law Enforcement Science and Technology II* (Chicago: IIT Research Institute, 1968), pp. 151-55.

29. Chapman, *Police Patrol Readings*, pp. 656-658.

30. George E. Kelling, Tony Pate, Duane Dieckman, and Charles E. Brown, *The Kansas City Preventive Patrol Experiment: A Summary Report* (Washington, D.C.: Police Foundation, 1974).

31. Ibid., p. 3.

32. Ibid., pp. 3-4.

33. Ibid., p. 4.

FIVE

Specialized
Police
Operations

General
Observations . . .

As a police agency grows in size, assuming new and more complex responsibilities, it must acquire new capabilities. Since each member of the department cannot be thoroughly trained in all the specialist areas needed in modern law enforcement, special units must be developed. The extent of specialization within any police agency is usually proportionate to the size of the organization. In small police departments, there can be little formal specialization, although individual officers may acquire specialist skills to be exercised as the need for them arises. In larger departments, specialization is widespread.

Although specialized police operations have become essential to modern law enforcement agencies, they sometimes grow disproportionate to their need. For example, it is common, even in medium-size police departments, to create a specialized traffic unit to be wholly responsible for the investigation of traffic accidents, and the enforcement of traffic laws and parking ordinances. In some cases, however, traffic enforcement could be more effective if it were the responsibility of the patrol force. Specialized police operations are important and usually necessary, but the current trend seems to be away from highly specialized units back to the concept of police generalists.

An example of the trend away from specialization is the emphasis placed upon a generalist orientation that has emerged from the team policing concept discussed in the previous chapter. Even in traditional police organizations, it is generally agreed that over-emphasis on specialization can have adverse effects upon the efficiency of police operations.[1] For instance, some police departments have discontinued the practice of requiring detectives to respond to all criminal complaints and have allowed uniformed patrol officers greater leeway in the conduct of routine criminal investigations. In this way, trained investigators are used to supplement, not replace, the skills of patrol officers.

When determining the extent to which specialized police operations should be undertaken, several factors should be considered. Two principal considerations are—[2]

1. Personnel assigned to specialized operations almost always are drawn from the ranks of the patrol force. As a result, the patrol force is weakened and the overall effectiveness of the line operation may be impeded.
2. The circumstances that require the application of specialized police operations may cease to be a problem after a period of time has elapsed. In other words, such problems may be only temporary. More often than not, however, specialized units created to meet temporary problems continue to outlive their usefulness, devoting their energies to finding the means to justify their existence.

Selection for Specialized Assignment

The selection of personnel for specialized operations poses a difficult problem for the police administrator.[3] Specialized assignments are often a point of contention within the police agency; they are viewed by many police officers as a reward for past exemplary performance. If some officers fail to receive specialized assignments, they may feel that their efforts are not being sufficiently recognized or rewarded.

Assignment to a specialized unit within the police agency often gives an officer a sense of superiority over former colleagues. He may feel that he now "has it made," and has been elevated to a loftier position in the organization. Such attitudes contribute to internal conflicts and bad feelings among the members of the organization. Therefore, the police administrator should take steps to ensure that the selection and assignment of persons to specialized operations is undertaken with great fairness and deliberation. Following are a number of considerations to be kept in mind when assigning personnel to specialized operations.[4]

Personnel records system. Every police agency should maintain an adequate personnel records system which details the skills, aptitudes, experiences, and interests of all persons within the agency. This information should be compiled when the individual enters the police agency. Such records should be periodically reviewed and updated. This information should be used by the police administrator to determine which members of the organization have the requisite skills and training necessary for them to successfully perform specialized functions.

Vacancy announcements. Vacancies in specialized positions should be announced throughout the police organization and all qualified persons should be encouraged to apply. Announcements should describe the position to be filled, the nature of the work to be performed, and the minimum requirements for the position. Requirements for the position should be established, and should be based on education, the amount and extent of specialized training necessary, and related experiences.

Personal interview. All candidates for specialized assignments should be interviewed to determine their suitability, aptitude, and mental attitude toward the position. Interviews should be conducted by the chief executive or a member of his command staff, together with the commander of the unit in which the specialized operations will be performed. The purpose of the personal interview is merely to evaluate a number of candidates and choose those who are best qualified for the assignment.

Background investigation. In some cases, an investigation into the applicants' recent backgrounds and activities may be necessary to determine suitability for a specialized assignment. For instance, a background investigation may reveal that an applicant has developed financial difficulties. This fact alone might not affect the officer's performance in his regular assignment, but it could become a serious liability if he were assigned to an operation such as vice, gambling, or narcotics, where the temptation to gain personal profit through official action can be great.

Specialized training. In most cases, persons assigned to specialized operations will require additional training to prepare them for the new assignment. This may be accomplished through formal training courses designed specifically for such purposes, or it may consist only of a brief period of in-service or on-the-job training conducted by members of the unit.

Temporary assignments. Persons assigned to specialized police operations should be required to complete a suitable probationary period during which competence for the new position can be evaluated. Permanent assignment to specialized positions should be made only after the individual has demonstrated his aptitude for the new position.

Periodic rotation. Persons in specialized assignments should be periodically rotated to other positions or assignments within the police organization, for several reasons. First, if left too long in one position, operational specialists may lose sight of the overall duties of the agency. They tend to place too much emphasis on their own operations at the expense of the rest of the department. Due to their own technical expertise, operational specialists may lose their objectivity and perspective. An officer assigned to vice operations, for example, may tolerate criminal violations by his informants simply to gain information. Such a policy can undermine police effectiveness and should not be encouraged.

A second reason for rotating persons in specialized assignments is that they often become exposed to corrupting influences that may compromise their effectiveness. Because of the nature of the work in which they become involved, particularly in the areas of vice and narcotics, officers assigned to specialized operations are in a unique position to realize personal gain from their official status. In recent years, many scandals have involved officers assigned to such specialized operations.

Finally, periodic rotation of those in specialized assignments helps to ensure a fresh and objective approach to problems. New ideas and procedures may result by having new personalities drawn into the operation. Persons who remain too long in one position have a tendency to become "stale" and remain content to apply traditional techniques and procedures rather than being creative and innovative in their problem-solving efforts.

There are a number of specialized operations in police organizations, particularly the larger ones. In the following section, attention will be focused on juvenile operations, criminal investigation, traffic enforcement, vice investigation, narcotics enforcement, and intelligence operations.

Juvenile Operations

In 1973, one out of every four persons arrested for a criminal offense was under the age of eighteen. According to arrest records, nearly one-half of all thefts were committed by juveniles. In addition, over 50 percent of all auto thefts and burglaries, and one-third of all robberies were committed by juvenile offenders.[5] Clearly, offenses committed by the young constitute a serious police problem. Due to the sensitive nature of the problem of handling youthful offenders, and the specialized training and techniques that are required, specialized juvenile operations are usually mandatory in most police agencies.

Juvenile offenders represent a unique challenge to the law enforcement agency for several reasons. First, most states require that persons classified as juveniles be treated differently than adult offenders.[6] Second, the enforcement policies and preventive strategies used for adult offenders are not appropriate for juveniles. A young person's behavior is often susceptible to modification through methods and techniques that would not be appropriate for adults.

Finally, the successful treatment and rehabilitation of the juvenile offender may have a significant impact upon his or her adult career. The manner in which a juvenile is treated today may affect conduct in future years. Thus, the successful treatment of the juvenile offender may have a substantial impact upon the criminal justice system in the future. Conversely, the failure of the police and other criminal justice and community service agencies to deal effectively with juveniles represents a failure of those institutions to fulfill their responsibilities to the community.

> Clearly it is with young people that preventive efforts are most needed and hold the greatest promise. It is simply more critical that young people be kept from crime, for they are the Nation's future, and their conduct will affect society for a long time to come. They are not set in their ways; they are still developing, still subject to the influences of the socializing institutions that structure—however skeletally—their environment: Family, school, gang, recreation program, job market. But that influence, to do the most good, must come before the youth has become involved in the formal criminal justice system.[7]

Unfortunately, the influences that shape the behavior of the young people in our society have not yet reached the ultimate goal of deterring criminal conduct by young persons. As a result, the police are still left to intercede where society has failed.

Under the strain of other responsibilities, the police officer is often unable to devote the necessary time required to

Courtesy of the Dallas Police Department

Dealing with young people is an important part of the police officer's job.

apply many of the techniques that are used in dealing with juvenile offenders. Specialized knowledge and training are required to deal successfully with youth-oriented problems. Special skills, techniques, and aptitudes are also necessary because of the singular nature of juvenile problems. As a result, it is neither practical nor economical for a police agency to attempt to train all police officers in juvenile policies and procedures. Thus, many police agencies carefully select a few qualified officers, give them proper training, and assign them the responsibility of dealing exclusively with offenses committed by juveniles.

No specific criteria can be developed to determine the proper scope and structure of juvenile operations for all police agencies. Instead, the particular requirements of the individual police jurisdiction must be considered when a decision is to be made concerning the development, implementation, and operation of a specialized juvenile unit. Factors that should be considered include: past trends and future projections of juvenile-related incidents and offenses; the number or proportion of young people in the community; the existence of athletic fields, recreation centers, and other attractions in the community that might contribute to an increased volume of juvenile activity; and the values and expectations of the community regarding treatment and disposition of juveniles.

The number of personnel assigned to the juvenile unit depends upon the number of cases involving juveniles. The National Commission on Criminal Justice Standards and Goals recommended that, depending upon the nature and extent of juvenile problems within a given community, a police department with more than fifteen employees should have some sort of juvenile investigation capability in addition to its other functions. This capability may consist of one or more full- and part-time positions.[8] In smaller departments, one member of the department may be designated as the juvenile officer in addition to a regular assignment. In larger departments, the juvenile operation is usually performed by a number of specialists, employing a wide range of skills and techniques.

Personnel Selection

The selection of personnel assigned to the juvenile units is extremely important.[9] The effectiveness of a specialized juvenile operation will depend, to a great extent, upon the quality and dedication of the personnel assigned to the unit. Therefore, it is important that careful consideration be given to establishing standards for selection which ensure that only qualified and properly motivated personnel are assigned to specialized juvenile operations.

One issue confronting the police administrator is that of determining whether or not the juvenile specialist should be a sworn officer or a civilian employee. There are advantages and disadvantages to both options. On the one hand, a sworn police officer will undoubtedly be more familiar with the overall police operation, and will be able to mobilize the resources of the agency to the best advantage. In addition, a sworn officer will probably enjoy more mobility within the police organization and will possibly receive greater cooperation and support from his fellow officers than would a civilian. On the other hand, a civilian juvenile specialist may be more sensitive to the unique problems posed by juvenile offenders, be better educated and trained in juvenile procedures and policies, and be more objective and less conventional in his approach to youth-oriented problems than a sworn officer might be.

Whether a civilian or a sworn officer is appointed to the juvenile specialist position depends upon the particular circumstances of the individual police agency. If qualified sworn personnel are available within the ranks of the police department, there is little advantage to be gained by appointing a civilian to the position. On the other hand, requirements for the position of juvenile specialist should not be lowered merely because there is no one in the organization with the necessary qualifications. If no one in the organization has the required training, education, and experience, it might be quite appropriate to appoint a well-qualified civilian to the position. A number of desirable characteristics should be apparent in the juvenile specialist including

1. a positive attitude toward the goals of juvenile work, particularly as they relate to the rehabilitation of juvenile offenders and their diversion from the formal system of criminal justice.
2. an aptitude for and an interest in the field of juvenile behavior. Persons assigned to the juvenile unit should be highly motivated and should be capable of working with young people in a variety of situations.
3. a personality that will allow the juvenile specialist to establish and maintain meaningful relationships with young persons of all backgrounds and temperaments.
4. the ability to work effectively under minimum supervision and to use initiative and imagination in the solution of problems.
5. a working knowledge of law enforcement, police operations, and the juvenile justice system; and the ability to establish and maintain an effective working relationship with other criminal justice and public service agencies.
6. a level of education and training that clearly establishes

that the individual has an awareness of and an appreciation for the principles of sociology, psychology, counseling, and rehabilitative techniques.

Promotion and Compensation

Persons should not be assigned to juvenile specialist positions in lieu of promotion through the regular rank structure of the department. Normally, specialist positions should not be considered as having a higher rank status than positions in the patrol force. Specialist positions should be created due to a need for a specific type of skill and expertise, not because of a desire to increase promotional opportunities in the agency. Similarly, persons assigned to specialist positions should be so assigned because of their ability and desire to fill the positions, not because of promotional incentive.

Rank within the juvenile unit should be limited to those positions that are supervisory in nature. In large departments, for example, it may be necessary to create a supervisory position because of the number of personnel assigned to the juvenile unit. However, since the juvenile specialist should be able to work with a greater deal of independence than other persons in the police organization, the need for supervisory positions should be minimal.

It is customary in some police departments to reward persons assigned to juvenile specialist positions with an increase in salary. The necessity and practicality of this practice is subject to question. In general, the assignment of an individual to a specialist position should not be accompanied by an increase in salary unless the nature of the work required in that position, in terms of its complexity and sophistication, is substantially different than other non-specialized positions in the organization.

While juvenile work may be no more (and no less) important than the work performed by patrol officers, it may be more demanding and may require the application of greater skills and energies. Therefore, it is the nature of the work to be performed that should determine whether or not a person assigned to a specialized unit should receive an increase in pay.

Organizational Considerations

Another issue facing the police administrator is the organizational relationship of the juvenile unit to other units in the police department. In the past, juvenile units have evolved as a specialized function of the investigation unit due to the fact that, at one time, juvenile specialists were concerned mainly with investigating crimes involving juveniles and were not particularly involved in prevention and rehabilitation of delinquents. Due to the evolving nature of the juvenile justice process and the increased emphasis being placed on delinquency prevention, diversion, counselling, and rehabilitation, there is little reason to believe that the juvenile operation should continue to be a subcomponent of the investigative unit.

There are a number of reasons why the juvenile unit should be separated from the investigative unit. First, the nature of the functions performed by the two units are distinctly different. While criminal investigative units are concerned almost exclusively with the investigation of crimes and the apprehension and prosecution of criminal offenders, juvenile specialists are more concerned with the prevention and control of juvenile delinquency and the diversion of the juvenile offender from the formal criminal justice system.

A second disadvantage of locating the juvenile unit under the operational control of the investigative unit is that juvenile specialists may sometimes be required to assist regular investigators in criminal cases instead of devoting their entire energies to juvenile matters. As a result, the effectiveness of the juvenile operation may be seriously weakened. It is preferable, therefore, to place the juvenile unit under the operational control of someone other than the commander of the criminal investigation unit. The exact placement of the juvenile unit depends largely upon the size of the police agency and its existing organizational structure. If possible, the juvenile unit should be located in close organizational proximity to other units whose functions are similar in nature, such as crime prevention and community services. In addition, the juvenile unit should closely coordinate its activities with those of the criminal investigation unit.

Policies and Procedures

The proper operation and management of a specialized juvenile unit requires that definite guidelines be established to prescribe the duties of unit members and their operating procedures. Policies and procedures should be periodically reviewed and revised to reflect changing conditions.[10] Policies and procedures established to guide the operation of the juvenile unit should include the following:

1. goals and objectives of the juvenile unit;
2. functions and responsibilities of juvenile specialists;

3. policies regarding the interview, interrogation, detention, and incarceration of juvenile offenders;[11]
4. policies regarding the maintenance of juvenile records and their disclosure to other parties;[12]
5. internal relationships with other organizational units;
6. policies regarding the disposition of juvenile offenders.

Duties and Responsibilities

The duties and responsibilities of the juvenile specialist should be clearly delineated in policy statements and procedural guidelines. The typical duties of the juvenile specialist include—

- the investigation of crimes in which juveniles are involved, either as victims or suspects;
- counselling juveniles who have been involved in crimes, or who are suspected of having committed crimes, or who are believed likely to become delinquent;
- the detection and prevention of crimes by juveniles;
- the mobilization of other resources in the criminal justice system and available through other community services agencies which have a capability to provide youth services.

Development of Community Resources

The police are hard-pressed to perform many of the duties expected of them. They often lack the necessary technical skills and resources needed to deal with many of the problems that confront them. This is particularly true in the case of juvenile problems. Due to the evolving nature of the juvenile justice system, with its increased reliance on counselling, referral, rehabilitation, and diversion, many police agencies are ill prepared to handle effectively many of the complex problems associated with youth prone to delinquency.

To compensate for the lack of capability, police administrators should strive to develop additional resources that serve youth within the community and to place greater reliance on existing community service agencies that are better prepared to handle juvenile problems. Youth service bureaus, diversion projects, and educational programs are among the many types of programs in which the police may become involved, along with other community agencies.[13] An effective youth-services program, expanding the role of the juvenile specialist, can help to identify, develop, and utilize resources available within the community and to strengthen its entire juvenile operation.[14]

Investigative Operations

A primary responsibility of the police is the investigation of crimes and the apprehension of criminal offenders. Since most persons who commit crimes are not apprehended at the time of the offense, it becomes necessary to conduct an investigation to determine the identity of the perpetrator(s) and to collect sufficient evidence to present against defendants in court. Criminal investigation requires specialized training, skills, and techniques that are not normally available to the patrol force. In addition, criminal investigations may require long hours of painstaking work that patrol officers could not afford to take from their regular patrol duties. Thus, it becomes necessary in all but the very small police departments to form a specialized investigative unit to handle this important function.

Investigative Responsibilities

The investigation of crime is a highly complex process, involving a number of distinct processes, including—

1. an examination of the crime scene and the surrounding area;
2. interviews with the victims of crimes and all witnesses, if any;
3. the identification, collection, and preservation of all items of physical evidence;
4. an analysis of items of evidence by trained specialists;
5. a review of all offense reports and related documents;
6. collaboration with other law enforcement and investigative agencies to determine possible suspects;
7. a check of investigative files, criminal offense histories, fingerprint files, and vehicle registration files;
8. the identification, location, apprehension, and prosecution of offenders;
9. preparation of written investigative reports and summaries;
10. presentation of physical evidence and oral testimony in court.

While all of these duties may not be required in every criminal case investigated, they are generally inclusive of the general nature of an investigator's responsibilities.

Over-specialization   The need for specialized criminal investigators in all but the smallest police jurisdictions is evident. However, one concern with which the police administrator must cope is the tendency to overspecialize within the investigative unit itself. Although particular investigators may have particular skills and interests over-specialization can greatly limit the effectiveness of the investigative unit and should be kept to a minimum. This point was emphasized by the National Advisory Commission on Criminal Justice Standards and Goals.

> As a result of the mobility and sophistication of modern criminal techniques, police agencies have tended to over-specialize, particularly in criminal investigation. In at least one agency, criminal investigators are assigned on the basis of geographic division, specific crime activity, type of business involved, and weapon involved: investigators may be referred to as the North Division liquor store armed robbery team. Such specializations often increase effectiveness in a limited area, but it usually results in less manpower for general investigative activities.[15]

In the small- and medium-size police departments, therefore, emphasis should be placed on making criminal investigators generalists rather than specialists, in order that the work load may be more evenly distributed. This does not mean, of course, that individual investigators should not be encouraged to develop particular investigative skills and be allowed to apply them when needed. For example, one investigator may be very proficient in handling crimes of violence (rape, robbery, homicide), but he should not be used exclusively for this purpose if his skills are needed in other areas, such as burglary or auto theft.

Investigative Phases   The investigation process is usually conducted in two distinct and separate phases: the **preliminary investigation** and the **follow-up investigation**. The preliminary investigation is normally conducted by the patrol officer after the crime has been reported to the police, while the follow-up investigation may be conducted at some later time by the investigator assigned to the case. Some police departments rely too heavily on their limited investigative resources and fail to take advantage of the capabilities of their patrol forces in the investigation of criminal offenses. For example, it is the practice in some police agencies to have detectives handle both the preliminary and the follow-up investigations, while the patrol officer may be used only to contact the victim at the crime scene and await the arrival of the investigators assigned to the case. This practice is not cost-effective and fails to recognize the fact that the actions of the patrol officer at the crime scene may very well determine whether or not the case is solved and the perpetrator apprehended.[16] Indeed, in too many police departments today the myth of the detective as the supreme crime fighter, with investigative skills and intuitive powers second to none, still prevails. Too often, police administrators fail to recognize the capabilities of their patrol officers and choose instead to turn routine cases over to detectives for follow-up.

In most cases, the follow-up investigation will be conducted by a member of the investigative unit. Follow-up investigations are almost always conducted when the perpetrators of crimes are unknown, but they may also be conducted in those cases where suspects have been arrested by the patrol force. Detectives, for example, may wish to question persons in custody in order to gain additional information about the offense for which they have been arrested, or about other offenses about which they may have information. In narcotics cases, for instance, detectives will usually want to question persons arrested for possession of dangerous drugs to determine what information they can about sources, methods of distribution, principal dealers, and so forth.

In those cases where a suspect has not been taken into custody, the follow-up investigation should begin where the preliminary investigation ends. The offense report prepared by the patrol officer should be reviewed, evidence examined, and witnesses and victims contacted again, if necessary. Similar crimes committed in the immediate or surrounding area should be reviewed to determine if there is a possible pattern. Other law enforcement and investigative agencies should be contacted to determine if they have information that may be vital to the investigation, such as the names of possible suspects who have been arrested for similar crimes in their jurisdictions.

Criminal history files, wanted-persons bulletins, and vehicle registration files should be checked to obtain possible clues to the identity of responsible persons. Items of evidentiary value, such as blood stains, fingerprints, and hair samples, may need to be examined by a laboratory technician to aid in the solution of the case. If the investigation is successful, the person(s) responsible will be identified, located, arrested, and prosecuted. Arrest and search warrants may be needed and additional items of evidence may be seized and analyzed. The investigator must then prepare his case for court. Consultation with the district attorney or prosecuting attorney may be necessary to determine what charges are to be filed, or to decide whether or not the evidence against the defendant is sufficient to sustain a criminal charge. Ultimately, the investigator will be called upon to testify in court as to the methods and results of his investigation.

Courtesy of the Metropolitan Police Dept., Washington, D.C.

Scientific investigation leads to the solution of many crimes.

Organization and Staffing

The investigative unit is a line operation. As such, it should be placed in close organizational proximity to other line operations, such as traffic and patrol. The three functions of traffic control, criminal investigation, and patrol are typically grouped under the command of one individual in many police agencies to ensure greater control and coordination of services.

The rank structure in the investigative unit should depend upon the number of personnel assigned to the unit and the need for supervisory positions. As in the case of the juvenile unit, assignment to the investigative unit should not be considered an advancement in rank, nor should it carry with it an increase in salary unless the duties performed by the investigators are clearly superior to those performed by patrol officers.

The number of personnel assigned to the investigative unit must be determined by the number of cases for which the unit is responsible. Work loads and activity levels provide the basis for determining the number of personnel needed to staff the investigative unit. Several things must be known before a police administrator can make an intelligent and rational decision regarding the appropriate manning level for the investigative unit. These include—

1. the expected number of cases referred to the investigative unit;
2. the approximate time required for each investigation;
3. the expected number of man-hours available to the investigative unit.

Studies have shown that, on the average, one hour is required to complete each case referred to the investigative unit.[17] In addition, it has been estimated that detectives spend approximately one-third of their time performing duties directly related to the investigative process, and two-thirds of their time performing activities relating to administration, coordination, and related functions.[18] The exact times allotted to these functions and the length of time spent investigating individual cases, of course, will vary with each police jurisdiction.

The anticipated number of cases referred to the investigative unit can only be established by using data derived from past experiences and projecting future trends. For example, if a police department has experienced an average 5 percent annual increase in the number of criminal investigations conducted each year, this figure can be applied to current figures to determine future caseloads.[19]

Notwithstanding unforeseeable and unpredictable events which may significantly affect a department's investigative caseload, it is possible to project future activity levels with a reasonable degree of accuracy. In addition, it is possible to predict the actual number of man-hours that will be available to the investigative unit, based upon past experiences. An example of how information derived from personnel files and past work schedules may be used to determine availability of manpower is shown in Table 5–1.

Table 5-1   **Average Number of Investigative Man-Hours Available per Year**

Potential Man-Hours (52 × 40)	2080
Deductible Man-Hours[a]	
Vacation	90
Sick Leave	40
Holidays	72
Training (In-service)	40
Court Time (On duty)	400
Compensatory Time	48
Total Deductible Man-Hours	690
Available Man-Hours (Potential less deductible)	1390

[a]Deductible Man-Hours are based on the average for each investigator from information derived from personnel files

Table 5–1 shows that 1,390 man-hours per individual investigator would be available to the investigative unit annually. This information, along with the information described earlier, can be used to determine the actual number of personnel that will be required to handle the number of cases assigned to the investigative unit. If, for example, it could be predicted that a police agency can expect to handle approximately 5,400 cases requiring investigation in a given year, the following computation could be made.

$$5,400 \text{ cases} \times 3 \text{ hours per case} = \frac{16,200}{1,390} = 11.7$$

Based upon the above computation, it can be estimated that 11.7 (or approximately 12) investigators would be sufficient to handle the number of cases in the unit. Of course, for such calculations to be possible, it is imperative that detailed records be prepared and maintained. The figures given are merely for purposes of illustration, and cannot be applied universally. The police administrator should see to it that adequate records are maintained so that information necessary for such computations can be compiled and extracted when needed.

Case Priorities Few police agencies have sufficient numbers of qualified investigators to thoroughly investigate all cases reported to them. Some cases are considered more important than others and are given immediate attention, while others may never be investigated. To ensure that cases requiring more attention are treated adequately, it is necessary to develop a system of priorities. Investigative priorities should be established as a matter of police policy rather than being left to the discretion of the individual investigator. Policies establishing investigative priorities will ensure that cases deserving immediate attention are not neglected, and that cases not deemed important are not investigated to the exclusion of others.

Investigative priorities will also ensure that all cases are handled uniformly within the investigative unit, and that none are given preferential treatment because of the personal prejudices, biases, or interests of individual investigators. For example, one investigator may have a tendency to devote most of his time to certain cases to the exclusion of all others, because of personal interests. As a result, those cases which deserve a higher priority may be unnecessarily neglected. The lack of a system of priorities may result in a failure of investigators to treat all cases uniformly and consistently.

The exact system of priorities established for the investigative unit depends upon the particular circumstances of the police agency, including the nature of criminal acts which pose the most serious threat to the community, the characteristics of the community itself, and the systems of values of those responsible for making policy decisions. The following list might be a typical priority system.

Priority Rank	Type of Case
1	Serious crimes against persons (homicide, rape, robbery)
2	Serious crimes against property (burglary, theft, auto theft)

Priority Rank	Type of Case
3	Lesser felony crimes, with suspects
4	Serious misdemeanors, with suspects
5	Other felonies and misdemeanors, with no known suspects

Case Clearances   Police investigators, unlike their counterparts in the patrol force, are concerned almost exclusively with criminal matters. Their entire function revolves around the investigation of crimes and the apprehension of offenders. While patrol officers may be concerned with providing a wide range of services and performing a number of different duties, the task of the police investigator is more narrowly defined.

Once of the problems facing many police administrators is that of evaluating the effectiveness of the police operation. One useful and generally accepted method of evaluating the effectiveness of the investigative function is through the use of clearance rates.[20]

Clearance rates indicate the number of crimes cleared or "solved" by the police jurisdiction. A crime is generally considered cleared when the police agency identifies the perpetrator, has sufficient evidence to present a case in court against the guilty party, and takes someone into custody. In addition, crimes may be considered cleared under exceptional circumstances when something beyond the control of the police agency precludes placing formal charges against the offender. An example of an exceptional clearance would be a case in which the offender is known but the victim refuses to prosecute (as in many marital disputes). Another type of exceptional clearance is that in which prosecution is denied because the suspect has been prosecuted elsewhere for a crime committed in another jurisdiction. A third type of exceptional clearance would be in the case of the police agency being unable to prosecute due to the incapacity of the offender, as in a murder-suicide.[21]

Clearance rates may vary from jurisdiction to jurisdiction and for different types of crimes. On the average, one out of every five serious crimes[22] in the United States was cleared by arrest in 1973.[23] The clearance rates for the United States for the Index Offenses in 1974 are shown in Figure 5-1.

One of the dangers involved in using clearance rates as a measure of police effectiveness is that it places too much emphasis on reaching a statistical plateau that may be unreasonable or unrealistic for a particular police agency. Just as there are

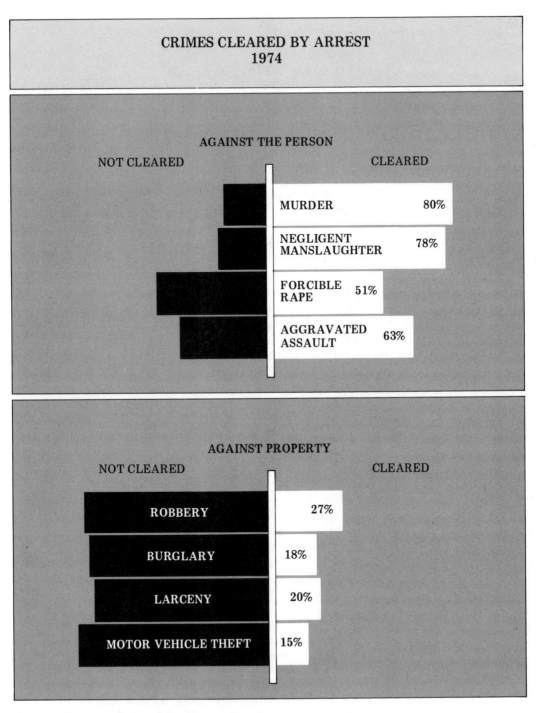

CRIMES CLEARED BY ARREST
1974

AGAINST THE PERSON

NOT CLEARED   CLEARED

MURDER   80%

NEGLIGENT
MANSLAUGHTER   78%

FORCIBLE   51%
RAPE

AGGRAVATED   63%
ASSAULT

AGAINST PROPERTY

NOT CLEARED   CLEARED

ROBBERY   27%

BURGLARY   18%

LARCENY   20%

MOTOR VEHICLE THEFT   15%

Source: Federal Bureau of Investigation, *Uniform Crime Reports — 1974* (Washington, D.C.: U.S. Government Printing Office, 1975), p. 43.

Figure 5-1. Crimes Cleared by Arrest, 1974.

a number of factors beyond the control of the police which, nevertheless, influence the level of criminal activity in a police jurisdiction, there are many things that affect an agency's rate of case clearances. These include the availability of victims and witnesses and their willingness to assist in prosecution, the quality and capacity of the prosecutorial and judicial agencies to process criminal matters, and the character of the community.

Placing too much emphasis on clearance rates also has the effect of compromising the integrity of the persons responsible for reporting and investigating crimes. Patrol officers may be pressured into not reporting crimes, or "unfounding" them in order to reduce the crime rate and thereby increase the rate of clearances.[24] Detectives may attempt to "downgrade" offenses by classifying burglaries as thefts or criminal trespass in order to improve their clearance rates.

That it is often difficult to determine whether or not a high (or low) clearance rate is due to the quality of the preliminary investigation (normally a function of the patrol force) or the quality of the follow-up investigation (a function of the investigative unit) is another reason for not using clearance rates as an indicator of investigative effectiveness. One possible solution to this problem is to record separately those crimes cleared by the patrol force (such as in the case of on-site arrests), and those cleared by the investigative unit. In any case, the clearance rate should be used with caution when used as a measure of investigative efficiency. Other measures that may be used to evaluate the effectiveness of the investigative effort include the percent of all stolen property recovered, the percent of all arrests resulting in conviction, and the level of citizen satisfaction with the efforts of the investigator.

The National Advisory Commission on Criminal Justice Standards and Goals suggested the development of quality control procedures to measure investigative effectiveness.

> Quality control procedures should be applied to criminal investigation operations to insure that each reported crime receives the investigation that it warrants. Procedures include constant review of reported crimes, preliminary investigation reports, and followup reports. In smaller agencies this review may be conducted by a unit administrator or supervisor. In large agencies certain personnel may be assigned as case supervisors. The review of reports should determine the comprehensiveness of the investigation, and the report should aid in coordinating investigative activities, particularly in developing pattern analysis and method of operation.[25]

Traffic Enforcement

Basic Principles Managing the orderly flow of traffic and preventing accidents is a basic and principal responsibility of the police. It is commonly accepted that traffic can best be controlled and accidents most effectively prevented through the application of the three Es: engineering, education, and enforcement. While the police have primary responsibility for enforcement efforts, the police administrator shares the obligation of engineering and education with other public officials. The police agency of a city must—

1. provide the traffic engineer with the necessary data for sound traffic engineering and correction of deficiencies, and support him by securing compliance with control efforts;
2. provide the local traffic safety agency and other concerned citizens groups with the data on which educational programs can be based, and actively participate in such programs;[26]
3. provide the level and kind of traffic enforcement necessary to minimize losses to the community incurred through traffic congestion and accidents.

Basic to all successful programs in engineering, education, and enforcement efforts are accurate and complete data on traffic accidents. These data constitute the statistical base necessary for the analysis of traffic problems and the development of appropriate remedies.

The Traffic Enforcement Index The principal quantitative measure of the level of traffic enforcement in the community is the Traffic Enforcement Index (TEI). The index is merely a statistical representation of the relationship of the number of traffic citations for hazardous moving violations that result in conviction to the number of motor vehicle accidents in which persons were either injured or killed.

A generally accepted norm for enforcement efforts is a TEI of 20. This figure does not represent an absolute, but it is the point at which many agencies dealing with traffic enforcement have found that enforcement efforts result in some measure of control over the incidence of traffic accidents. In effect, this guideline says that to stop or reverse a rising frequency of traffic accidents, the conviction of about 20 drivers and pedestrians for hazardous violations is required for each fatal or non-fatal personal injury accident occurring in the city. It should be pointed out that there are limitations to the TEI as an indicator of enforcement efficiency. Traffic fatalities and personal injury accidents can occur in spite of good enforcement. Police efforts, for instance, can have little influence over such factors as the failure of persons to use appropriate safety equipment, equipment failures, and inclement weather, all of which can have an impact on traffic accidents.

Figure 5–2 shows the Traffic Enforcement Index for a hypothetical city and compares it with the number of traffic accidents reported to the police jurisdiction in that city. It is readily apparent that over a period of several years a definite inverse relationship between the TEI and the pattern of accidents can be established. That is, as the TEI goes down, the number of traffic accidents increases. Theoretically, at least, to reverse or stop this trend—to decrease the number of traffic accidents—the TEI should be increased. Briefly stated, the enforcement effort should be accelerated.

While there is no guarantee that a higher TEI will ensure a lower rate of traffic accident frequencies, the principle is generally accepted in modern police agencies and the police administrator should strive to monitor the effect of the traffic enforcement efforts of his department on the incidence of traffic accidents and make adjustments in enforcement programs where necessary.

The need for accurate and timely traffic accident and enforcement data cannot be emphasized two strongly. Many police agencies do not maintain up-to-date traffic information with which to evaluate the needs of the department or to identify problem areas. In addition, reliable information regarding conviction rates on traffic offenses is also lacking in some jurisdictions. In agencies large enough to have a specialized traffic enforcement unit, one person should be responsible for collecting and analyzing all traffic information so that an effective traffic enforcement program can be developed and that the effectiveness of that program can be monitored. Information should be collected on all traffic accidents occurring in the city, by time, location, and cause, along with information on the extent and nature of property damage and personal injuries. Enforcement data should also be maintained and measured against accident figures to determine what effect, if any, the enforcement activities have on accidents. On the basis of this information, the traffic enforcement program of the agency should be continually reviewed and updated.

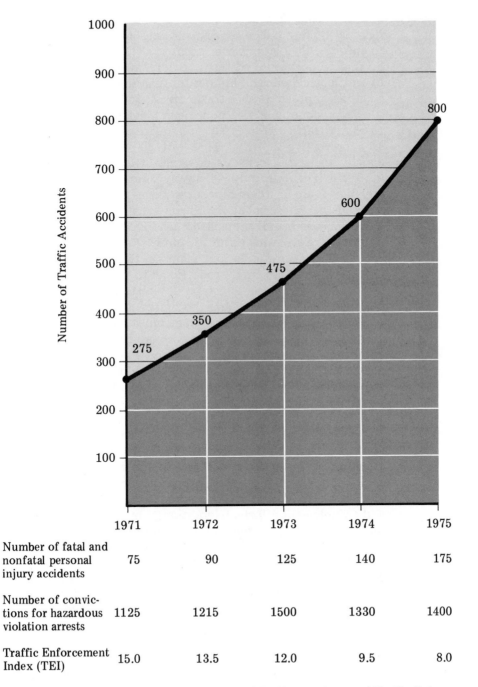

	1971	1972	1973	1974	1975
Number of fatal and nonfatal personal injury accidents	75	90	125	140	175
Number of convictions for hazardous violation arrests	1125	1215	1500	1330	1400
Traffic Enforcement Index (TEI)	15.0	13.5	12.0	9.5	8.0

Figure 5-2. Comparison of Annual Number of Traffic Accidents and Traffic Enforcement Index

Selective Enforcement

Selective enforcement of traffic laws is desirable for several reasons. First, a police department does not have the resources to enforce all violations that occur at all times and at all places. Second, the purpose of traffic enforcement is the prevention of traffic accidents and injuries through the deterrent effect of penalties imposed through traffic arrests and convictions. Unfortunately, some chiefs of police and elected officials continue to regard traffic enforcement as a source of revenue rather than as a preventive activity. Since not all violations contribute equally to traffic accidents, it serves little purpose to enforce all traffic laws uniformly. Obviously, some types of infractions are more serious than others, requiring different levels and methods of enforcement. Third, selective enforcement, if properly managed and controlled, can be a positive means of improving relationships with the public.

Selective traffic enforcement is the practice whereby enforcement efforts are "proportional to traffic accidents with respect to time, place, and type of violation."[27] In order for a selective traffic enforcement program to be effective, the officer in charge of the program must have access to comprehensive, up-to-date information on traffic problems and conditions. In larger departments where police information is automated, this data can usually be produced weekly, and in some cases, daily. In smaller departments, it may be necessary to tabulate such information manually and less frequently.

Once collected, the information may be transferred to pin maps and charts showing the distribution of traffic accidents by time of day, day of week, location, and type of violation. These maps and charts should be updated as often as possible, so that current information can be readily available, permitting a constant reevaluation of traffic problems and enforcement efforts. In addition, it may be useful to maintain such charts and maps on both monthly and annual bases in order to detect and compare trends that may emerge.

After traffic problems have been identified, it is then possible to plan and execute meaningful enforcement strategies. The enforcement tactics to be put into effect depend, of course, upon available manpower. Whether a department has a specialized traffic unit, or whether traffic enforcement is the responsibility of the patrol force, will make a difference in the enforcement strategies adopted.

If the department has no specialized traffic unit, then it will be up to the commander of the patrol force or individual patrol shift commanders to plan and oversee the department's selective enforcement program. The absence of a specialized traffic unit, however, should be no reason not to employ a selective enforcement program. Indeed, all patrol officers should be impressed with the importance of selective enforcement as a regular part of their patrol assignments.

The Need for Uniformity

Traffic ordinances vary from state to state and from community to community. Uniform policies and procedures concerning the enforcement of traffic laws are all but nonexistent. In addition, the enforcement of traffic laws rests exclusively with the individual police officer, who determines what laws will be enforced and what types of enforcement practices will be applied.[28] Some officers may rely heavily on written warnings as an enforcement technique, while others may prefer to enforce all violations with citations and arrests. Some officers may place a greater emphasis on violations of the speed limit, while other officers may concentrate their attention on other infractions.

The impact of these discrepancies in uniformity on the individual citizen is, at best, disconcerting. Unlimited discretion in the enforcement of traffic laws may provoke charges of police abuse, partiality, and prejudicial treatment from various sections in the community. While limited discretion must be exercised by the individual officer, it must be accompanied by reason and guided by administrative policy. Each police agency should develop appropriate guidelines that will assist traffic officers in their enforcement functions.

> Written guidelines, understood and adhered to by each officer, provides [sic] a means whereby the individual officer can exercise proper discretion, use good judgment, make acceptable decisions, establish reasonable priorities, and at the same time, promote uniformity of enforcement action throughout the jurisdiction.[29]

Other Specialized Functions

Narcotics Investigation

The control and suppression of the illicit distribution and use of dangerous drugs is an important responsibility of the police. Drug control operations usually require specialized training and techniques not normally available to the patrol force. While all police officers must have a basic knowledge of drug enforcement policies and procedures, the actual investigation of drug-related cases in most police agencies having specialized investigative units is usually delegated to a narcotics section or detail. There are a number of reasons why a specialized drug investigation unit is necessary.

1. Drug offenses are more difficult to investigate than other types of offenses because the victim is often the offender. As a result, information concerning illegal drug activities is extremely hard to obtain. As a rule, persons involved in drug activities are not willing to assist the police in obtaining information. Consequently, the police must use extraordinary means of obtaining information, including: (a) paid informants; (b) undercover investigators; (c) surveillance techniques. All of these methods require special training and expertise.
2. Drug offenses frequently overlap with other forms of criminal activity. A drug user must often rely upon other types of illegal activity, such as burglary or robbery, to support his habit. As a result, drug investigators often must deal with other types of crimes and other offenders, frequently coordinating their efforts with other investigative units.
3. Drug abuse problems are ubiquitous, respecting no jurisdictional boundaries. Drug investigators must be free to move about in the community and beyond to investigate drug offenses and to apprehend persons suspected of being involved in drug activities. In addition, they must develop and maintain a close working relationship with federal, state, and local drug enforcement agencies.
4. Drug investigations require many man-hours and often extensive and exhaustive investigative efforts. A team of narcotics investigators may work for several weeks or even months to conclude a major case.

The investigation of drug offenses is particularly difficult and is a phase of police operations that requires careful planning and the development of systematic guidelines that will assist narcotics investigators in performing their duties efficiently. Several factors complicate the task of drug enforcement.

1. The ambivalence of attitudes toward drug use neutralizes public support of the police in their enforcement and

apprehension efforts. Particularly when that enforcement effort involves the lesser drugs, such as marijuana, there is a considerable divergence of opinion regarding the legitimacy of current laws and police procedures. As a result, some states have taken steps toward decriminalization of the simple use and possession of marijuana, while other states have laws that retain harsh penalties for the same offenses. Adequate research has not yet been conducted to determine what harmful effects, if any, the use of certain drugs may incur. Until greater consensus is reached regarding the psychological and physiological efforts of such drugs, and until acceptable laws are passed by the legislatures, this ambivalence will continue to handicap the police in their enforcement efforts.

2. The secretive nature of drug use, its clandestine operations, and the ease with which drugs may be imported and distributed, also limit the enforcement efforts of the police. As a result, the police themselves have had to rely on irregular and sometimes questionable tactics to develop information necessary to apprehend and prosecute offenders.[30] Many of these tactics are offensive and have gained the police the enmity of segments of the public.

3. The impact of constitutional guarantees regarding searches and seizures, and the interpretations of these guarantees by the courts, have limited police practices and have seriously impeded law enforcement agencies in their attempts to control drug abuse.

4. The reluctance of the courts to impose harsh penalities on persons convicted of drug offenses—particularly the youthful and first offenders—have resulted in the dismissal of many drug charges, despite evidence of considerable investigative efforts by the police.

These factors should be carefully considered by the police administrator when developing policies and procedures to guide the operation of the drug investigation unit.

Investigation of Vice   Vice is a broad term that is variously applied to a number of offenses, such as pornography, lewd conduct, gambling, and sex crimes—crimes that have been referred to as victimless crimes. It is the duty of the police to enforce the laws enacted by federal, state, and local legislative bodies. It is not the duty of the police to judge or place values on the rightfulness or wrongfulness of those laws, nor is it their prerogative to determine which laws should be enforced more vigorously than others. Nevertheless, the police often become the scapegoat of those who would criticize the "overreach" of the criminal law.

For years, scholars, academicians, and other interested parties have debated the propriety of legislating against the so-called victimless crimes.[31] A number of authorities have taken the position that laws regulating conduct which is otherwise harmless to others are improper violations of individual choice and should not be enforced.

Morris and Hawkins, for instance, have severely criticized laws that attempt to regulate morals. "The function, as we see it, of the criminal law is to protect the citizen's person and property. . . .We think it improper, impolitic, and usually socially harmful for the law to intervene or attempt to regulate the private moral conduct of the citizen."[32]

The enforcement of legislation against gambling, drunkenness, narcotics, and sexual behavior continues to be a police responsibility, despite growing arguments for the abolishment of such laws. It would appear that, in the years to come, many of these laws will be "erased" from the statute books, and the police will be relieved of many of the responsibilities of unpopular enforcement. In the meantime, however, the police must attempt to strike a balance between the need to enforce existing laws and the desire of the individual citizen to engage in conduct that is considered illegal.

The problem of the police administrator is to establish a system of realistic priorities by which a reasonable enforcement effort may be formulated and applied. A police administrator has limited resources at his disposal, and he should try to make the most effective use of them. If his investigative unit is unable to handle the criminal cases assigned to it, then it would appear unreasonable to allocate a substantial share of the investigative resources of the agency to offenses that have a minimal impact on the peace and welfare of the community. If, on the other hand, a particular form of vice activity appears to be growing out of proportion to other crimes, or if there is a growing public concern about certain types of vice offenses and a demand for the police to act, there may be justification for increased enforcement efforts. The primary goal of the police administrator, with respect to vice operations, should be to provide reasonable and necessary enforcement measures in line with existing resources. What constitutes reasonable and necessary enforcement, of course, depends on the values and expectations of the public to whom the police are responsible. The police administrator should endeavor to assess public sentiments regarding such issues and to incorporate them, whenever possible, into statements of policy and operational procedures.

Intelligence Operations   Intelligence operations[33] are a unique form of the investigative function and may or may not be performed by members of the general investigative unit. The intelligence function consists largely of gathering, analyzing, and disseminating information about particular individuals and groups and their activities; it differs from general criminal investigation due to the nature of the information gathered and the manner in which it is used. The information gathered by intelligence specialists differs from information generated through regular criminal investigations in the following respects.

1. The information contained in intelligence files is highly confidential and sensitive. Access to it is severely restricted.
2. The information contained in intelligence files is usually catalogued by the names of individuals and groups and consists of chronological records of their activities and other pertinent information.
3. Much of the information contained in intelligence files may be non-criminal in nature. For example, newspaper clippings are usually a valuable source of intelligence information.
4. Intelligence information is not normally used for prosecution purposes, but is rather used to develop a greater body of knowledge about individuals and their organizations and activities (i.e., associates, daily routines, telephone numbers, addresses, car registrations, and so forth).

Intelligence units probably originated as a response by law enforcement agencies to the urgent need to develop more complete and reliable data about organized crime figures and their operations. The earliest forerunners of modern intelligence units were the Central Information Bureau (CIB) of the New York City Police Department and the Chicago Intelligence Division (CID) of the Chicago Police Department. Both of these organizations were formed near the turn of the twentieth century and were established to deal with particular types of criminal activities. In recent years, these units have been reorganized and presently exist almost exclusively to develop, analyze, and process information concerning the activities of high-level crime syndicates.[34] In addition, the function of modern intelligence units has been expanded in most police agencies to compile information about other types of illicit activity, such as narcotics rings, terrorist groups, and suspected espionage activities.

While properly maintained and controlled intelligence files and operations are essential to the discovery and eradication of sophisticated forms of organized crime, the misuse of intelligence files and the misdeeds of members of intelligence units can prove to be a serious liability to the police administrator. Many police departments maintain some sort of intelligence files, and although they may not have a formal intelligence unit, there is often a lack of awareness of the true purpose of intelligence operations. In some cases, there is a lack of adequate policy guidelines or established procedures to guide members of intelligence units in their activities. In other instances, no direct control is exercised over the types of information placed in intelligence files or the manner in which that information is gathered and disseminated.

Another basic weakness of many police intelligence gathering operations is the failure to substantiate or document "raw" data. Unverified reports concerning the activities of individuals and organizations can be a source of professional embarrassment to a police organization and its chief administrator. James Ahern, the former Chief of Police in New Haven, Connecticut, has related in great detail the risks involved in relying upon unverified and unsubstantiated intelligence information concerning suspected terrorist activities.[35]

The preparation and maintenance of intelligence files, or dossiers, on law-abiding citizens without reasonable evidence of criminal culpability, is a serious encroachment on fundamental individual freedoms, constituting an invasion of privacy. Such activities should not be condoned. Moreover, reckless and irresponsible actions by members of intelligence units who have no firm policies to guide them in their operations pose serious consequences for the police administrator.

Policies and procedures governing the operations of intelligence units and the maintenance of intelligence files should be reviewed and evaluated to ensure that adequate controls over such activities exist and are being enforced. If no firm policies exist, they should be established. Strict guidelines should be established that will cover, among other things, the following:

1. the proper use of, access to, and dissemination of intelligence information;

2. the nature and types of information to be collected and maintained;
3. acceptable practices, procedures, and techniques for the collection of intelligence information;
4. minimum and maximum retention periods for intelligence data;
5. operational relationships with and responsibilities to other intelligence-gathering organizations;
6. relationships between members of the intelligence unit and other units in the police organization.

Summary

Specialized police operations are found in most police agencies, although they vary in scope and complexity with the size of the agency. In small departments, specialization is rather informal, and exists on an as-needed basis. In larger departments, specialization is more institutionalized.

There is a growing tendency to deemphasize specialization in law enforcement, and to return some of the duties formerly performed by specialists, such as detectives, to patrol officers. Police specialists should be utilized to supplement the skills of patrol officers, not replace them. In a sense, the police specialist is an extension of the patrol function.

The danger of emphasis upon specialization should be recognized and avoided. Police specialists should not be allowed to forget that their primary purpose is to provide assistance to the patrol officer. Too often, police specialists are allowed to carve out for themselves a small fiefdom into which they can retreat from the everyday rigors and stresses that confront the patrol officer. This frequently leads to internal strife and jealousy which is not conducive to effective police operations. A blend of specialist and generalist skills is needed in any police organization.

Discussion Questions

1. *Why are specialized functions necessary in the police organization?*

2. *Describe several requirements that are essential for the proper selection and appointment of personnel to specialized assignments.*

3. *Discuss several reasons why persons in specialized positions should be rotated periodically.*

4. *Why do juvenile offenders pose a unique challenge to police agencies?*

5. *What factors should be considered when developing and implementing a specialized juvenile unit?*

6. *Give several reasons for using patrolmen as preliminary investigators.*

7. *List and describe the information needed to determine adequate manning levels of investigative units.*

8. *Give several reasons why clearance rates are not the best means of evaluating investigative efficiency?*

9. *Describe several factors that necessitate the assignment of persons to specialized drug enforcement activities.*

10. *How can misuse of intelligence information be harmful to the police agency?*

References

1. National Advisory Commission on Criminal Justice Standards and Goals, *Police* (Washington, D.C.: U.S. Government Printing Office, 1973), p. 207. (Subsequently referred to as National Goals Commission.)

2. V.A. Leonard, *The Police Detective Function* (Springfield, Ill.: Charles C. Thomas, 1970), pp. 4-5.

3. National Goals Commission, *Police*, pp. 213-16.

4. Ibid., pp. 214-16.

5. Federal Bureau of Investigation, *Crime in the United States 1974* (Washington, D.C.: U.S. Government Printing Office, 1975), p. 194.

6. States vary in the age at which a person is considered to be an adult; in general, persons below the age of 18 are defined as juveniles.

7. President's Commission on Law Enforcement and Administration of Justice, *The Challenge of Crime in a Free Society* (Washington, D.C.: U.S. Government Printing Office, 1967), p. 58.

8. National Goals Commission, *Police*, p. 223.

9. Portions of the following section are drawn from material contained in Steven M. Ward, "Individual Technical Assistance Report in Response to a Request for Technical Assistance by the Augusta, Georgia, Police Department," (Chicago: Public Administration Service, 1974).

10. National Goals Commission, *Police*, p. 222.

11. Such policies are usually the subject of state laws.

12. National Goals Commission, *Police*, p. 222.

13. Charles D. Hale, *Police-Community Relations* (Albany, New York: Delmar Publishers, 1974), pp. 133-44).

14. George H. Shepard, "Youth Services Systems: An Innovative Concept in Prevention," *The Police Chief*, 40 (February, 1973), pp. 48-53.

15. National Goals Commission, *Police*, p. 235.

16. Peter W. Greenwood and Joan Petersilia, *The Criminal Investigation Process, Volume I: Summary and Policy Implications* (Santa Monica, Ca.: The Rand Corp., 1975), p. vii; John P. Kenney, *Police Administration* (Springfield, Ill.: Charles C. Thomas, 1972), p. 164.

17. Kenney, *Police Administration*, pp. 160-172.

18. Ibid.

19. Other factors which may contribute to fluctuations in case loads include: (a) changes in policies and procedures which may have an impact on overall activity levels (i.e., more patrol personnel which may result in increased arrest rates); (b) changes in state and local laws which may substantially change the pattern of a police department's enforcement operations (i.e., the "decriminalization" of offenses relating to marijuana usage, gambling, and prostitution); and (c) changes in the socio-economic structure and characteristics of the community (i.e., fluctuations in unemployment rates or changes in migration patterns).

20. The subject of evaluating police effectiveness is described in greater detail in Chapter 10.

21. Federal Bureau of Investigation, *Crime in the United States 1974*, p. 42; see also Federal Bureau of Investigation, *Uniform Crime Reporting Handbook* (Washington, D.C.: U.S. Government Printing Office, 1965), p. 48.

22. Serious crimes, or Index Offenses, are those identified by the FBI as being the most serious types of offenses and those which represent the greatest concern to local police agencies. They are murder, forcible rape, aggravated assault, robbery, burglary, theft, and auto theft.

23. Federal Bureau of Investigation, *Crime in the United States 1974* (Washington, D.C.: U.S. Government Printing Office, 1975), p. 42.

24. Jerome H. Skolnick, *Justice Without Trial: Law Enforcement in Democratic Society* (New York: John Wiley & Sons, 1966), p. 170.

25. National Goals Commission, *Police*, pp. 235-36.

26. For example, most police agencies routinely report traffic accident data to local and state jurisdictions, as well as to the National Safety Council, for the purpose of compiling local, state, regional, and national traffic statistical summaries.

27. Gordon H. Sheehe, Police Traffic Supervision, in George D. Eastman and Esther M. Eastman, eds., *Municipal Police Administration*, 6th ed. (Washington, D.C.: Interna-

tional City Management Association, 1969), p. 115.

28. John A. Gardiner, *Traffic and the Police: Variations in Law Enforcement Policy* (Cambridge, Mass.: Harvard University Press, 1969), pp. 150-65.

29. The Traffic Institute, "Position Statement: Uniform Traffic Law Enforcement," (Evanston, Ill.: Northwestern University, p. 4.

30. Skolnick, *Justice Without Trial*, pp. 112-63.

31. Edwin M. Schur, *Crimes Without Victimes: Deviant Behavior and Public Policy* (Englewood Cliffs, N.J.: Prentice-Hall, 1965).

32. Norval Morris and Gorden Hawkins, *The Honest Politician's Guide to Crime Control* (Chicago: The University of Chicago Press, 1970), pp. 4-5.

33. For a comprehensive treatment of the police intelligence function, see E. Drexel Godfrey, Jr. and Don R. Harris, *Basic Elements of Intelligence* (Washington, D.C.: Technical Assistance Division, Office of Criminal Justice Assistance, Law Enforcement Assistance Administration, U.S. Department of Justice, 1971).

34. President's Commission on Law Enforcement and Administration of Justice, *Task Force Report: Organized Crime* (Washington, D.C.: U.S. Government Printing Office, 1967), p. 13.

35. James F. Ahern, *Police in Trouble: Our Frightening Crisis in Law Enforcement* (New York: Hawthorne Books, 1972), pp. 51-56.

SIX

Personnel Recruitment, Selection, and Training

General
Observations . . .

Personnel recruitment, selection, and training are related problems that demand the devoted attention of the progressive police administrator. Over 2500 years ago, Confucius wrote: "The successful administration of government depends entirely upon the selection of the proper men." This aphorism is still applicable. The day is gone when the police administrator can afford to depend upon chance to recruit and induct qualified and dedicated personnel into the police service. No longer can tradition and custom serve to guide police training programs.

Personnel are a police agency's most valuable resource. It is by the individual and collective actions of the men and women recruited into the police service that police performance will be judged by the community. The quality of the personnel recruited, selected, and trained by the police department will eventually determine public attitudes toward the police. As Wilson and McLaren have observed:

> Incompetent, untrained, and undisciplined policemen invariably provide unsatisfactory service; they damage the reputation of their own departments and promote unfavorable public opinion throughout the country. There is no place in a modern, progressive department for stupid, inept, uncouth, lazy, dishonest, or insolent officers; and their presence on a force is evidence of the failure of their administrative head to give careful attention to his personnel management duty.[1]

There are presently about a half-million full-time and part-time police employees in the United States. To recruit and retain qualified personnel, police departments must enter a highly competitive labor market. Though many police agen-

174

cies have an abundance of applicants, relatively few who apply for police positions are selected. This is due largely to the high standards and rigid selection procedures necessary to ensure that only the most qualified are admitted into the police profession. As a result, many police departments find themselves continually understaffed and face severe recruitment problems.

Shortages of personnel place a wearisome burden on the police administrator who must maintain operational effectiveness and deliver an acceptable level of police services to the community. There are no easy solutions to this perplexing problem. It would be simpler to lower the entrance requirements for the police service, and thereby increase the number of persons who successfully apply for police positions. Lowering standards, however, would have an adverse impact upon the level of professionalism that the police seek to maintain.

A second alternative, obviously preferable to the first, might be to increase the effectiveness of the selection process. This could be achieved by (1) enhancing the desirability of the police service through increased salaries and improved conditions of employment, and (2) employing better selection standards and procedures.

Recruitment

Recruitment is the first step in the selection process. Recruitment is a procedure involving several tasks, including: (1) identifying personnel requirements; (2) securing necessary permission to fill personnel vacancies; (3) determining personnel qualifications; and (4) attracting a sufficient number of applicants to fill the vacant positions. The number of applicants should always exceed the number of positions to be filled to ensure that only the most qualified are selected.

The recruitment process varies with the size of the police department. In small rural communities, police recruitment may be a simple and informal process. In large urban communities, however, police recruitment can be a very expensive and time-consuming operation.[2] In all cases, the recruitment process should have as its ultimate goal the selection of the most qualified persons that can be found.

Selection

Selecting the suitable candidate for the police service is an imperfect science. No one has yet defined, with any degree of certainty, those qualifications needed to ensure a successful police career. As a result, the selection standards and procedures used by police agencies today are more often than not the product of custom and tradition rather than empirical evidence. Without a doubt, many persons who would make exceptional police officers are disqualified for questionable reasons, while a few of those who are selected later prove to be poor choices.

> A task as important as the selection of police personnel should be approached positively; police agencies should seek to identify and employ the best candidates available rather than being content with disqualifying the unfit. The policy of merely eliminating the least qualified results in mediocrity because it allows marginal applicants to be employed along with the most qualified.[3]

Ensuring Equity in the Selection Process

Police administrators are obliged to ensure that only the most qualified candidates are admitted into the police service. At the same time, they must employ selection standards and procedures that are fair and equitable. In the past, police selection standards and procedures have, intentionally or unintentionally, discriminated against certain classes of people in our society, namely minority groups and women. As a result, regulatory agencies, such as the Equal Employment Opportunity Commission, have initiated guidelines that prohibit discriminatory hiring practices for all public employers, including police departments. In addition, a number of court decisions have been handed down to ensure fairness in police hiring practices. As a result, most public agencies have been forced to modify their hiring practices and to implement acceptable affirmative action plans to ensure that no person will be denied employment simply on the basis of age, sex, ethnic background, or religion.

One obstacle to ensuring equity in the selection process is the lack of valid, job-related selection criteria. Major studies have been initiated to develop entrance requirements and selection criteria that do not discriminate against any class of persons and that effectively assess an applicant's aptitude for a particular position. While no definitive results have been published yet, efforts in these areas are continuing.[4]

Affirmative Action Plans

Most local public administrators are familiar with the term "affirmative action." Affirmative action may be defined as any plan, procedure, or program designed to eliminate discriminatory employment practices. The purpose of affirmative action is to ensure that all *qualified* persons seeking employment in the public service are judged solely upon their individual merit. Under affirmative action, public employers may not, intentionally or otherwise, discriminate against applicants based upon reason of sex, age, race, religion, or national origin.

Over the years, it has become apparent that some public employers did in fact discriminate against certain classes of persons seeking employment. Such discrimination, however, was not always intentional. Intentional or not, discriminatory hiring practices are no longer permitted. In a landmark court decision (*Griggs vs. Duke Power Company*)[5], the U.S. Supreme Court held that unintentional discrimination is equally as wrong as conscious bias, and could not be tolerated. As a result, public employers were required to reexamine their hiring practices and selection standards and to eliminate those elements that could be construed to be discriminatory in effect as well as in purpose.[6]

Several steps must be undertaken in the implementation of a successful affirmative action plan.[7]

1. Make strong organizational commitment to the philosophy of affirmative action, institutionalized through formal policy.
2. Assign authority and responsibility for implementing the program to a top official in the organization.
3. Analyze the job force to determine positions, units, and departments where minorities are underemployed.
4. Set specific, attainable goals for the selection and/or promotion of minorities in each case where they are underrepresented in the work force, and make supervisors and managers responsible for meeting these goals.
5. Examine selection standards to ensure that they reflect actual job needs.
6. Locate minority group representatives who possess the qualifications necessary to fill vacant positions.

7. Review and, if necessary, revise employment procedures to ensure that they are free from discriminating effects.
8. Initiate training and career development programs designed to fill the needs of minorities who have not had access to such programs in the past.
9. Develop systems to monitor the process of the program on a regular basis. Adjust the system, as desired, to ensure that program goals are met.

Although the police executive may not be directly involved in the development or implementation of an affirmative action program (a task usually reserved for a personnel specialist within the municipal government), it is likely that he will be involved in the administration of the plan indirectly, and must be concerned with its impact upon the recruitment and selection procedures of the police department. Therefore, a police administrator should fully understand the purposes of the affirmative action program, what it is intended to accomplish, and the manner in which it will be administered.[8]

Minority Recruitment

Members of ethnic minority groups have traditionally been underrepresented in police departments in the United States. A number of national commissions have attributed many of the problems the police experience in dealing with minority populations to their failure to actively recruit minorities into the police service. The President's Commission on Law Enforcement and Administration of Justice, for example, severely criticized police departments for their poor showing in recruiting members of minority groups and emphasized the advantages to be gained from a higher proportion of minorities in police agencies:

> In order to gain the general confidence and acceptance of the community, personnel within a police department should be representative of the community as a whole. . . . The frequent contact of white officers with officers from minority groups on an equal basis can help to reduce stereotyping and prejudice of white officers. Minority officers can provide a department an understanding of minority groups, their languages, and subcultures, that it often does not have today. . . . Personal knowledge of minority groups . . . can lead to information not otherwise available, to earlier anticipation of trouble, and to increased solution of crime.[9]

Courtesy of the Dallas Police Department

Recruiting a sufficient number of minority applicants is a pressing problem for many police executives.

There are a number of causes to which the underrepresentation of minority group members in police departments can be attributed. First, they have frequently been systematically discriminated against in their efforts to gain police employment.[10] Second, the high standards employed by most police agencies often tend to eliminate minority group members for social, cultural, and physical reasons.[11] Aptitude tests, for example, are often biased in favor of whites, who have benefited from higher educational opportunities. In many cases, blacks growing up in slum neighborhoods are more likely to have minor arrest records than whites from suburbia. Finally, it has become increasingly difficult to attract minority group members into the police service due to the negative image of the police that has developed in minority neighborhoods.

Nevertheless, police executives must redouble their efforts to open the doors of police departments to blacks, Mexican Americans, and other ethnic minorities.[12] Minority recruitment efforts are particularly essential in the large cities and urban centers where there are sizeable minority populations. In some cases where the police have failed to enact aggressive minority recruitment programs, the courts have intervened, often with disastrous results. A number of cities have been ordered by the courts to eliminate discriminatory hiring practices and taken positive measures to make their police departments more representative of the community as a whole. Firm efforts on the part of the police administrator to recruit minorities may forestall court intervention and the concomitant adverse consequences to the police department.

Women in Policing

Throughout its history, law enforcement has been considered a male profession. Women employed by police agencies, with few exceptions, have been traditionally assigned to such limited duties as typing, dispatching, and juvenile work. Women have been discriminated against in the law enforcement profession to a greater extent than minorities. However, the 1970's have witnessed a major revolution in law enforcement; women are being recruited into the law enforcement profession in greater numbers today than ever before. They are being assigned to duties that were once considered the exclusive province of the male officer. In many cities in the United States, women investigate traffic accidents, perform regular patrol duties, make arrests, and supervise other police officers (male and female) in field duties. As a result, women are subjected to the same police hazards as their male counterparts. In 1974, the first death of a policewoman was recorded in the Metropolitan Police Department in Washington, D.C. The officer was killed in an attempt to apprehend an armed suspect.

Clearly, women have found a new role in police work. More and more police agencies are abandoning (either voluntarily or through coercion) their exclusionary policies and are actively recruiting, selecting, and promoting women. In 1973, the Los Angeles Police Department adopted a "unisex" policy, whereby the classification "policeman" and "policewoman" were consolidated into a single classification of "police officer," with the same opportunities for employment, assignment, and promotion for both sexes. The Chicago Police Department adopted a similar policy in 1974, and the St. Petersburg, Florida, Police Department has had such a policy since 1972.

Women still have a long way to go in their struggle to gain equal rights in employment, assignment, and promotion

Courtesy of the Metropolitan Police Dept., Washington, D.C.

The role of women in policing has changed dramatically in recent years.

in police agencies. According to a survey conducted in 1972 by the Urban Data Service Center of the International City Management Association, women comprised only about 1.0 percent of the total uniformed force in 300 of the largest police agencies in the United States.[13] The same survey revealed that only one out of five cities assign women to patrol duties. Larger cities (more than 500,000 inhabitants) were more likely to assign women to patrol duties than were smaller cities.

In the next several years, it can be expected that sex will no longer be a consideration for employment in the police service. Indeed, the Civil Rights Act of 1964 (Title VII) requires that all jobs must be open to both men and women alike unless it can be demonstrated that sex is a "bonafide occupational qualification necessary to the normal operation" of the duty or position.[14] At least one major study, undertaken to assess the potential of women in law enforcement, has found no significant differences between the performance of men and women in similar police duties.[15]

Selection Standards

If the police are ever to become recognized as professionals, it would appear essential that they develop a uniform standard of selection. To date, selection standards for the police vary widely from state to state and from city to city. While it probably would not be useful to impose rigid selection standards on local units of government, it seems highly desirable that all states adopt uniform minimum standards to ensure a higher level of professionalism within the law enforcement service.

This effort has been underway for several years, and a majority of states now have adopted legislation establishing peace officer standards and training comissions. The first such commissions were established in New York and California in 1959. The California Peace Officer and Standards Commission (POST) was initiated largely through the efforts of the state's police officers.[16] The basic purpose of such commissions is to establish and maintain a high professional standard of law enforcement throughout the United States. This purpose is achieved—

1. by setting realistic and attainable standards for police selection and training;
2. by providing technical assistance to law enforcement agencies in their attempts to adopt and implement such standards.
3. by making necessary financial assistance available to law enforcement agencies in order to permit them to adopt and implement the standards.

Statewide standards of selection and training are a commendable effort to ensure uniformity in the quality of law enforcement personnel. In agencies that are financially unable to meet higher standards, resources can be made available to assist them. Local prerogatives, however, should be maintained. The function of state peace officer standards and training commissions should be to assist local jurisdictions to adopt minimum standards, not to impose arbitrary requirements that are unreasonable in view of the particular needs or circumstances of the agency. In addition, local authorities should be encouraged, wherever possible, to exceed minimum standards.

On the other hand, appropriate measures should be taken to ensure compliance with minimum standards wherever possible. The National Advisory Commission on Criminal Justice Standards and Goals has recommended that:

> States should employ the [peace officer standards and training] commissions to inspect for compliance with the standards and certify only the police officers who meet them. Failure of an individual to meet state standards should deny him employment as a police officer.[17]

State commissions notwithstanding, determining selection standards for the police department remains largely a local problem, one that requires careful deliberation and sound judgement. There are normally two opposing forces at work in determining appropriate selection standards. If standards are set too low, there is a probability that the quality of personnel recruited into the police agency may fall below that considered necessary to provide professional police services. On the other hand, if standards are too high, the police agency may find itself faced with a problem of too few qualified applicants to fill vacant positions.

Of critical importance in the development of appropriate selection standards is the need to match entrance requirements with the skills and knowledge required to adequately perform the job. There is little justification for setting standards of selection higher than those that are necessary. Selection standards for the police service, particularly those concerning physical requirements, are in a state of flux, and continue to vary among police agencies. A few of the more common selection standards are discussed in the following sections.

Citizenship

Almost without exception, an applicant for police employment in the United States must be a citizen of this country. This is no doubt due to the recognized need for a strict sense of loyalty to the laws of the nation and the dedication to community values that a police officer must possess. Moreover, the citizenship requirement no doubt reflects the rather parochial custom of granting public jobs only to citizens.

Education

During the last two decades, law enforcement has witnessed the advent of the college educated police officer. Though a majority of police officers in the United States still do not have college degrees, an increasing number of them are attending college, and the overall educational level of the police officer is inching upward.

A number of police agencies have taken measures to upgrade the educational level of their police officers. About one out of five cities having between 250,000—500,000 inhabitants now requires some college education for entry into the police service.[18]

The first non-federal police agency in the United States to require a four-year college degree was the Multnomah County Sheriff's Department in Portland, Oregon.[19] By 1967, only about two dozen police departments in the country required any college education, and most of these were in California.[20] The President's Commission on Law Enforcement and Administration of Justice recommended, in 1967, that all police agencies should strive toward a goal requiring all police officers to have baccalaureate degrees. In 1973, the National Advisory Commission on Criminal Justice Standards and Goals recommended the following standards for police agencies:[21]

1. a one-year college requirement for all police officers immediately;

2. a two-year college requirement for police officers by 1975;
3. a three-year college requirement for police officers by 1978;
4. a four-year college requirement for police officers by 1982.

While it is doubtful that these standards can or will be accepted universally by police agencies in the United States, they do provide standards toward which police agencies should strive. Raising the educational level of the police has been facilitated by the tremendous increase in college degree programs in law enforcement, police administration, and police sciences. In addition, federal programs to support law enforcement education programs and local education incentive plans have served to spur interest in college education for police officers.[22]

The concept of increasing the educational level of police officers is certainly meritorious, yet it poses definite problems for the police administrator. Studies have demonstrated that college educated police officers generally are less satisfied with the often dull and routine aspects of the police function and soon lose interest. As a result, attrition rates among college educated police officers are usually higher than those for police officers with more limited educational backgrounds.[23] A study of police performance and background characteristics in the New York City Police Department revealed that one-third of all college educated police officers recruited in 1957 had left the force by 1968, compared to less than one out of five officers who had not graduated from college.[24] In addition, few police departments give proper recognition for college education in assignments and promotions. Officers with college education are given no special consideration when assignments or promotions are made, and thus, become easily frustrated when they discover that time in grade and seniority count more than educational achievement.

If educational standards for police officers are to continue to rise, then it is important that police agencies adapt their organizational structures, personnel procedures, and operations to recognize the true worth of college education. Officers with college degrees, if they are to be retained in the police service, must feel that their educational achievements are properly rewarded. This can be achieved through: (1) creating positions that challenge the advanced knowledge of college educated officers, such as planning and research, community relations, youth services, etc.; (2) providing salary incentives to police officers with college education; and (3) giving credit for college education in the promotional process.

At the same time, it must be recognized that a substantial portion of the police officer's work is not sufficiently challenging or intrinsically rewarding to attract and retain the interest of college educated men and women. Moreover, it is not likely that small cities will, in the foreseeable future, be able to pay the high salaries necessary to attract college graduates. Finally, there is yet no hard evidence to support the belief that a college education is necessarily a condition of successful police performance.[25] Consequently, while a higher level of education for all police personnel remains a desirable goal, it is unlikely that it will be easily achieved. In fact, there is some doubt as to whether it is even a practical one.

Physical Requirements

Police work is an occupation of physical and emotional extremes. At times, it is dull, boring, and emotionally fatiguing; at other times, it is exciting, challenging, and physically demanding. Accordingly, physical requirements have traditionally played an important role in the process of selecting personnel for the police service. Unfortunately, in the past, many police agencies have relied too heavily upon physical standards that have little or no bearing upon the ability of a police officer to satisfactorily perform the duties that will be expected. As a result, many otherwise qualified candidates have been excluded from positions in law enforcement. Such factors as age, height, weight, hearing, and eyesight obviously have a great deal to do with the ability of a person to perform effectively as a police officer, but they should be weighed against other qualifications, such as intelligence, emotional stability, and maturity, which are equally as important in the police role. In addition, inflexible physical requirements (i.e., weight and height) sometimes discriminate against certain ethnic minorities and women, violating equal employment opportunity provisions. Moreover, rigid physical requirements may unnecessarily exclude candidates whose mental attitude, bearing, and emotional stability might make them ideally suitable to the police service.

Today, the tendency is generally toward the relaxation of physical requirements for police officers. This is due primarily to (1) the general realization among police authorities that physical qualifications alone do not necessarily determine the professional competence of a police officer, and (2) court decisions that have prohibited entrance qualifications that cannot be proven to be job-related and essential for the successful performance of the police function.

Age Requirements   Most police departments restrict entrance into the police profession to persons between 21 and 35 years of age, although minimum and maximum age requirements vary considerably among individual agencies. In recent years, there has been a tendency to lower the minimum age for police officers below 21 years. This is due in part to changing state laws that have lowered the age requirements for voting, consumption of alcohol, and other matters relating to adulthood.

There are dangers inherent in lower age limits for police officers, however. In many cases, men and women are not mature enough to accept the awesome responsibility of police service while still in their teens. Accordingly, age alone should not be a determining factor, but should be considered along with judgement, bearing, and mental attitude.

One method of overcoming the problems associated with age requirements in police departments is through the use of police cadet or community service officer (CSO) programs. Under police cadet programs, young men and women who aspire to a career in law enforcement, but who do not meet the minimum age requirements (assuming they are qualified in all other respects), are assigned to various police tasks that do not require the attention of a regular sworn officer.

Police cadet programs offer several advantages. First, they relieve sworn officers of many of the routine duties that occupy much of their time. For example, police cadets may be used to handle parking problems, work the complaint desk, take minor police reports, and so on. These are duties that needlessly consume many precious hours of a patrol officer's time.

Second, police cadet programs are excellent in-service training programs. Generally, by the time a young man or women has completed the cadet program, he or she will have gained much valuable experience that will serve them well later in their police career. Indeed, police cadets often learn more about the workings of a police department, through their exposure to many different tasks and assignments, than do police officers in a similar period of time.

Third, the police cadet program serves as a more thorough screening device than anything else available to the police administrator. During the cadet program, a cadet may be continually evaluated to determine his or her suitability. At the completion of the cadet program, the police administrator will be able to make a very realistic assessment of the individual's aptitude for a career in law enforcement.

Courtesy of the Columbia, South Carolina Police Department

Police cadets can be a valuable resource to a police agency.

Finally, the cadet program allows the police administrator to attract individuals with a college education. In
most cases, police cadets are required to attend regular college
classes in some field relating to law enforcement and to maintain a passing grade average. By the time an individual has
completed the cadet program, it is likely that he or she will

have attained at least a two-year college degree and will be inclined to continue with his or her college education.

Residency Requirements

Police departments frequently require applicants to be a resident of the community either prior to or soon after being appointed to the police department. In 1961, the International Association of Chiefs of Police reported that three out of four police departments surveyed reported residency requirements ranging from six months to five years prior to appointment.[26] A more recent survey by the International City Management Association revealed that about half of the largest police agencies in the country required the applicant to be a resident prior to initial appointment.[27]

The history of residency requirements dates back several decades to an era when public employment jobs were considered appropriate rewards to bestow on persons who were politically loyal to the existing power structure. Obviously, some cities also feel that someone appointed to the police department from outside the city would not understand nor appreciate the unique problems of the community as well as a resident.

In major metropolitan areas, however, there is little, if anything, to be gained from requiring police officers to live in the city in which they work. In is not unusual for other workers to commute 100 miles each day to their jobs. To require police officers or other public employees to live in the city in which they work poses an unnecessary hardship and is clearly discriminatory. Both the 1967 President's Commission on Law Enforcement and Administration of Justice and the American Bar Association recommended the abolition of preservice residency requirements for police officers.[28]

In many cases, residency requirements for public employees have been ruled unconstitutional. In Youngstown, Ohio, for example, a civil service regulation providing that police employees must reside within the city limits was ruled unconstitutional [Fraternal Order of Police Youngstown Lodge, *et al. v.* Hunter *et al.*, 303 N.E. 2d. 103, Ct. Com. Pls. (1973)]. In a more recent decision, however, the courts have ruled residency requirements to be a constitutionally valid employment qualification (*McCarthy* v. *Philadelphia Civil Service Commission*, Pa. Commonwealth Ct., 339 A2d 634). Thus, it would appear that a city may, if it chooses, impose residency as a legitimate qualification for employment. Whether or not such a requirement is necessary would depend upon the circumstances of the individual jurisdiction.

Selection Procedures

Selecting police personnel is a time-consuming and often complex process that may take several months. For this reason, many larger departments have full-time staff who do nothing but administer the recruitment and selection program, thus ensuring a continual flow of applicants and sufficient candidates to fill vacancies without undue delay. In other departments, where only a few vacancies may occur each year, the selection process is more sporadic and is conducted only as needed.

Selection procedures vary significantly from one police department to the next. In smaller departments, the selection process is rather simple and informal. In larger departments, it becomes more complicated and time-consuming. The following selection procedures are typical of those found in a majority of police departments in the United States.

The Formal Application

The first step in the selection process is customarily a screening of employment applications by those who have expressed an interest in the police service. In some police departments, employment applications may be submitted at any time; in others, they will only be accepted when there are vacancies to be filled. Whenever possible, persons desiring to apply for a police position should be interviewed briefly at the time they submit their application. This is done to ensure that the application form has been filled out completely and accurately, and to answer any questions the applicant may have. It is also done to screen out immediately any persons who have physical defects or other undesirable characteristics (i.e., age, bad eyesight, not a citizen, etc.) that may automatically disqualify them from employment.

In some cases, a department may receive a request for an employment application from someone who lives some distance away. In such instances, it is advisable to mail the applicant an instruction sheet and a position description, describing the duties, pay, and benefits of the position, along with the application form.

The application form should be as brief and simple to complete as possible. At the same time, it should provide sufficient information for evaluating the background and the qualifications of the applicant.[29] Since the application form will provide the basis for subsequent investigation into the prior work history, character, and family background, information should be as complete and accurate as possible. Applicants should be advised that intentional falsification of the application form may be cause for automatic disqualification from the police service.

The Written Examination

Written examinations are used by most police departments to determine whether or not applicants possess the intelligence necessary to perform the difficult tasks required of a police officer. Written tests are generally a combination of IQ tests and aptitude examinations. Although most police authorities continue to uphold the utility of IQ tests to measure an applicant's general suitability for police work,[30] the exact relationship, if any, between IQ score and satisfactory police performance has not yet been ascertained. In one study, researchers found no important relationship between IQ scores and police performance.[31]

Recent court decisions and guidelines published by state and federal regulatory agencies (e.g., U.S. Civil Service Commission, Equal Employment Opportunity Commission) have forced many municipalities to reexamine their entry-level testing procedures to ensure that they are non-discriminatory and that they are truly predictive of acceptable job performance. As a result, a number of studies are currently underway to test the validity of traditional testing procedures and to develop new ones.

Physical Agility Tests

A police officer is often required to perform unusual physical feats in the performance of his duties, such as pursuing a criminal on foot, climbing fences, and so forth. For this reason, most police departments require applicants for the police service to successfully complete some sort of physical agility tests. These tests are (and should be) usually simple, and only persons with obvious physical defects fail them.

TESTING ROOM

Courtesy of the Dallas Police Department

Police applicants taking the written examination.

Physical agility tests should be conducted in such a manner that they test only job-related physical attributes. There should be a proven correlation between the trait being measured and the duties that will be required of the police officer. Agility tests may be graded either on a pass-fail basis (the candidate must successfully pass each phase of the test), or on a cumulative basis (each activity is scored separately and the total points determine the applicant's final score).

Once appointed to the police department, officers should endeavor to remain in good physical shape. Periodic physical examinations should be conducted to detect physical ailments that may have developed subsequent to the officer's appointment. In addition, police administrators should attempt to provide suitable physical fitness programs and facilities, such as exercise areas, that will encourage officers to remain in good physical condition.[32]

The Medical Examination

Routine medical examinations are required of police applicants to determine any physical defects that may, if undetected, subsequently lead to substandard performance, early retirement, or an incapacitating injury. Time lost due to injuries can be expensive to the police agency. Pre-employment and post-employment physical examinations can help to ensure that members of the force are in top physical condition.

The leading causes of nonaccidental retirement for physical disability among police officers, in order of occurrence, are: (1) heart and circulatory diseases; (2) back disorders; and (3) peptic ulceration.[33] Many of these problems can be averted if a thorough physical examination is required prior to a candidate's appointment to the force.

The physical examination is usually a pass–fail proposition—either a person is physically qualified or he is not. The decision rests with the physician conducting the examination. The normal physical examination will usually consist of chest and back X-rays, blood pressure readings, urinalysis, blood count, electrocardiogram (EKG), and vision and hearing tests. In some cases, more thorough examinations may be required.

The Polygraph Examination

The polygraph, or "lie detector," as it is commonly called, has been used by law enforcement agencies for years in the investigation of criminal offenses. The polygraph is used primarily to determine whether persons suspected of crimes respond truthfully when questioned about their involvement in illegal activities. While the results of polygraph examinations are generally not admissable in a court of law, they can be useful in determining a person's innocence, thereby narrowing the focus of an investigation.

Polygraph examinations are frequently used by law enforcement agencies when screening applicants. They can be a valuable aid in verifying the information provided by the individual on his application form, and they may also be used to clarify questions that may have developed during other phases of the screening process. For example, the polygraph may be used to verify an applicant's honesty in answering questions about prior criminal involvement and work history.

The types of questions asked during the polygraph examination and the manner in which the applicant's responses are evaluated are crucial issues. Indications of criminal misconduct early in an individual's life, particularly if those offenses were minor and not indicative of a general pattern of dishonesty or criminal behavior, should not be the sole basis for disqualifying a person from the police service. In addition, vague, general questions about a person's sexual experiences should be avoided unless they are intended to substantiate or clarify information uncovered during other phases of the screening process.[34]

Polygraph examinations should only be conducted by trained and qualified polygraph operators. These may be members of the police agency, a nearby police department, or a licensed polygraph operator.

The character of the polygraph operator is extremely important. He must not only be competent, he also must be dedicated to a professional code of ethics that will ensure that the information gathered during the examination will be kept confidential and will be divulged only to authorized persons. Unscrupulous and unethical polygraph examiners may do a great disservice to the agency and to the individual if they fail to observe professional standards. Polygraph operators should not allow their personal feelings to color their professional judgement of an applicant's suitability for police service. No questions should be asked during the polygraph examination that are not directly related to an individual's suitability for police service. Questions designed to embarrass or discredit the applicant should not be asked unless they are directly related to qualifications necessary to become a police officer.

The Background Investigation

The background investigation is one of the most important elements of the screening process. The background investigation, if conducted thoroughly, provides important information about the applicant that may not be obtainable through other means. The background investigation may be conducted by (1) personal interview; (2) telephone; (3) teletype; and (4) mail. Usually, the background investigation employs a combination of methods.

A number of source documents are used to provide information for the background investigation. These include: (1) the employment application; (2) local, state, and federal criminal history files; (3) state and local driver's license files; (4) military records; (5) medical records; and (6) prior employment records. In addition, the background investigator might wish to interview past and present friends and associates of the applicant, his family, his neighbors, past employers and supervisors.

The purpose of the background investigation is to provide a balanced, objective, and accurate picture of the applicant's character and suitability for police work. While conducting the background investigation, it is important that both *negative* as well as *positive* aspects of the applicant's history be recorded and evaluated. Too often, background investigators tend to focus merely upon the negative factors in a person's background, overlooking positive factors. Throughout the process, fairness to the individual must be a prime consideration.

A candidate's prior arrest record, if any, should be carefully evaluated. Arrests for minor offenses, particularly if they did not result in conviction, should usually not be the sole basis for rejection of the applicant. The person's age at the time the arrest occurred should also be considered. Crimes committed early in life are not always indicative of future criminal behavior. The circumstances surrounding past offenses should also be carefully weighed, particularly if there are indications that no criminal intent on the part of the person existed, or that the individual's participation in the offense was minimal. Disqualification from police service for such reasons may be unfair to the individual and may not be in the interests of the police agency.

The Psychological Examination

The police officer in modern society is subjected to many emotional stresses and pressures that are unknown to the average worker. Police work is rigorous and demanding, both emotionally and physically. Police officers must be able to withstand unusual strains. Therefore, it is imperative that the emotional stability of the candidate be determined through suitable psychological and psychiatric examinations.

> The emotional stability to withstand the stresses of police work must, of necessity, be a requisite of police personnel. Officers must rationally cope with violence, verbal abuse, resentment, and emergencies. The emotionally unfit cannot meet these stresses. Although a comprehensive character investigation will eliminate many socially mal-adjusted applicants, personality defects in some of the applicants will be latent and not easily discernible.[35]

Various types of psychological and psychiatric tests have been employed by police agencies to assess emotional stability in police applicants.[36] Unfortunately, however, there have yet been developed no tests which have proven to be valid predictors of successful police performance.[37] This fact was noted by the National Advisory Commission on Criminal Justice Standards and Goals:

> The current usefulness of psychological techniques, however, is limited to the elimination of those who are grossly unfit for the police service. Current psychological techniques lack the validity necessary to support any refined prediction of the level of future performance or success within the police organization.[38]

There has been reluctance in the past among police administrators to use psychological or psychiatric tests in the selection process. The police administrator (dogmatic, pragmatic, and conservative) has been traditionally hesitant to accept the notion that such "pseudo sciences" as psychiatry and psychology can be of any value in the selection process. More and more, however, police agencies are turning to the "pseudo sciences" as a standard part of the selection process. Incompetent, brutal, and socially inept police officers, however few in number, can seriously jeopardize the image and reputation of a police department. Psychological and psychiatric techniques offer the police practicioner the opportunity to reduce the likelihood that such persons will be admitted to the force. There is a growing recognition of the need to develop more effective measures to screen out candidates who will later become problems. The National Advisory Commission on Criminal Justice Standards and Goals recommended that by 1975 every police agency should retain the services of a qualified psychiatrist or psychologist to examine police applicants and to screen out those who are emotionally unfit for the police service.[39] In addition, a number of studies that attempt to develop much more reliable means of predicting police performance through psychiatric and psychological means are underway or have been conducted.[40]

The Oral Interview   Candidates who successfully pass other phases of the selection process may be asked to appear before an oral interview board. The board may be composed of police officers, civilians, or a combination. The oral interview may be conducted by the local civil service board, if there is one. The purpose of the oral interview is to obtain information about the applicant that cannot be obtained through other means. It also gives representatives of the prospective employer an opportunity to meet the candidate and to evaluate such intangible qualities as poise, bearing, presence of mind, and the ability to express oneself.[41]

Prior to the oral interview, members of the panel should review the individual's original application, college transcripts (if there are any), prior work history, military service records, and other documents. At the same time, members of the panel should determine which questions they intend to ask the applicant. They should also be aware of what types of questions are not legally permissible during the oral interview.[42] The interview may last from thirty minutes to one hour. At the conclusion of the interview, a final score is determined, usually by summing or averaging the score determined by each member of the panel. Seventy percent is normally considered passing.

Eligibility

Once all phases of the selection process have been completed, an eligibility list must be established. This is usually done by ranking the candidates in descending order, based the scores obtained on one or more examinations given during the selection process. Usually, the scores obtained on the written and oral examinations will be combined in some fashion to determine an eligibility score. Raw scores may be weighted in order to determine the final score. For example, the written score may be weighted heavier than the score obtained on the oral interview, or vice versa.

Vacancies will usually be filled by selecting from the highest names on the eligibility list. In some cases, the police administrator may have a certain degree of flexibility and may select one candidate from the top three or four names on the list. In other cases, each candidate on the list must be selected on the basis of his or her overall standing.

An eligibility list should be retained for twelve months, during which time the candidates whose names appear on the list remain eligible for appointment to the force. At the expiration of the list, individuals whose names were on the list and who were not selected must go through the selection process again.

Joint Selection Procedures

The recruitment, testing, and selection of police applicants is an expensive and time-consuming process. It is especially difficult to conduct thorough selection and testing programs in small- and medium-size police departments that cannot afford a full-time staff to attend to such matters. In such cases, the police department may be forced to abbreviate the selection process in order to cut costs and manpower requirements. However, the results may be contrary to the best interest of the department.

Joint selection procedures, whereby a number of police agencies participate in the selection process and share the costs, offer many advantages to the small- and medium-size police department. First, by pooling their resources, police departments can significantly enhance the quality of the selection process and thereby improve the calibre of candidates who are selected. In addition, joint selection procedures are normally conducted several times each year, so that the participating agencies will always have a sufficient number of candidates to fill vacancies. As a result, they do not waste valuable time in setting the selection process in motion, and can fill vacancies sooner. A third advantage is that the applicant will only need to undergo certain phases of the selection process once, rather than several times, in order to be qualified for employment by one of several agencies. Thus, he stands a much better chance of getting selected by any one of the participating agencies.

Joint selection procedures may be accomplished in several ways. First, several police agencies may combine their resources and allocate sufficient funds for the employment of a professional personnel agency to conduct the examinations. In other cases, several police departments may pool resources and alternate conducting the selection process among them. A third alternative is for a smaller agency to rely upon another unit of government, such as a county or state personnel unit, to conduct all or part of the selection process.

Joint selection procedures do not necessarily relieve the individual agency of the responsibility of conducting its own testing procedures in addition to those employed in the joint selection process. For example, one agency may wish to administer psychological examinations or other screening devices that are not included in the joint selection procedure. Indeed, the final responsibility for selecting qualified personnel lies with the individual agency, and the joint selection procedure is only designed to minimize some of the costs associated with that task.

Probationary Service   Despite the extensive selection procedures employed by most police agencies, the real test of a person's suitability for police work begins with his appointment to the force. Many who are appointed to the police service soon discover that they are dissatisfied with the nature of the work. Still others seem to lack the innate ability to satisfactorily perform the rigorous duties expected of them. Others fail to attain passing grades at the police academy. Most police agencies, therefore, require new appointees to undergo a probationary period ranging from six months to one year in order to fully evaluate their aptitude for police work. During the probationary period, an officer may be dismissed from the police service if he fails to meet expected standards of performance.

> No selection device is foolproof. Even the best investigation can fail to detect the candidate who will not live up to his potential. The probationary period is therefore a trial period, during which his supervisors can evaluate his performance. In most circumstances it is easier to separate a probationary employee than one who has passed probation.[43]

The line supervisor plays a key role in the evaluation of probationary officers. It is he who has the opportunity to view personally the new officer's performance in the field and to determine whether or not the officer is performing as expected. The supervisor also should consult periodically with his subordinates to discuss the progress of probationary officers. Those that are progressing slower than expected may need remedial training. Particular care should be taken to detect signs of sloppy work habits, inability to follow instructions, insubordination, and poor attitudes toward the public.

Monthly evaluation reports should be completed on probationary officers by their immediate supervisors. When appropriate, senior patrol officers should be consulted before these evaluation reports are prepared so that their comments and observations can be included. Evaluation reports should be complete and accurate. They will provide the basis for subsequent decisions as to the suitability of a candidate for permanent appointment.

Shortly before a probationary officer nears the end of his probation, his personnel file should be carefully reviewed and all evaluation reports should be examined. A final evaluation report should be made, indicating whether or not the officer merits permanent appointment. In some borderline cases, probation may be extended by as much as six months to allow further evaluation and to give the officer every chance to prove his competency. However, in cases where the candidate is clearly unsuitable for the police service, he should be terminated as soon as possible, to protect both his own interests as well as those of the agency. The probationary period should be extended only in extraordinary circumstances.

Police Training

If asked, most police administrators in small- and medium-size police departments would probably agree that providing training is one of the most pressing needs of their departments—a need that has not been satisfactorily met in the past. Limitations in personnel, financial resources, and physical facilities restrict the ability of many police administrators to provide suitable training for their personnel. While nearly every state now requires a minimum level of pre-service training, some officers are forced to wait several months after appointment before attending the basic police academy. In other states where there are not enough centralized training facilities, some officers are required to complete their basic training in two and three-day periods, often on weekends and on their days off, and sometimes without compensation. Even where adequate training resources are available, some police administrators are handicapped by a lack of sufficient funds and by personnel shortages. Officers are sometimes forced to attend in-service training programs on their days off and at their own expense.

Police Training in Perspective

August Vollmer, the first Chief of Police in Berkeley, California, and one of the earliest authorities on law enforcement, was perhaps the first practicing police administrator to recognize the value of a broad program of professional training for police officers. He established the first regular school for police officers in the United States during the first decade of the twentieth century.[44] Among the courses taught at Berkeley were physics, chemistry, criminology, police organization and administration, and criminal law. According to Vollmer:

A school for the specialized training of police officers is a
requirement of the times. Those authorized and empowered
to enforce the laws, rules and regulations which are intended
for the better protection of the public should have some
knowledge of the fundamental principles underlying human
actions, more especially those actions which are commonly
designated as criminal or contrary to law and order.[45]

While the level of training offered to police officers has
risen dramatically in recent years, it still lags far behind the
training programs received by members of other professions

Courtesy of the Berkeley California Police Department

August Vollmer, the Father of American Law Enforcement.

and occupational groups. In 1967, for example, the International Association of Chiefs of Police reported that the average police officer in the United States received less than 200 hours of formal training. This can be compared with 11,000 hours for physicians; 9,000 hours for lawyers; 7,000 hours for teachers; 5,000 hours for embalmers; and 4,000 hours for barbers.[46]

Pre-Service Training

Pre-service training is that training a police officer receives before assuming regular police duties. Under normal circumstances, a police officer will be sent to a police academy prior to being assigned to police duties. In some cases, however, police officers may wait several months after appointment before being sent to a police academy. By this time, the value of the training program is questionable because the police officer may have already learned many bad habits as a result of his exposure to street duty. In most cases, states only require that a police officer complete the required training program within one year of appointment to the police department. Sometimes, however, this standard is not even observed with regularity.

Pre-service training is usually conducted at a central police training academy, which may be operated by the individual police agency or by another police agency that provides pre-service training for members of other departments. In southern California, for example, a number of smaller departments use the training academies of the Los Angeles Sheriff's Department, the Los Angeles Police Department, the Long Beach Police Department, and the Riverside County Sheriff's Department. In less urban parts of the country, regional police training academies have become popular. These regional academies are usually supported by a number of police and sheriff departments. Regional training academies can usually provide more efficient training at lower cost than individual departments could provide.

States and municipalities vary as to the duration of the minimum number of hours of training required in the pre-service training program. The lowest requirement is about 200 hours, with a few states now requiring as many as 400 hours. Most large city police departments have their own pre-service training program requirements that considerably exceed this figure. For example, in 1973, the Dayton, Ohio, Police Department required 960 hours; Chicago, Illinois required 1,040 hours; and Seattle required 880 hours.[47]

Courtesy of the Dallas Police Department

Recruit officers are required to undergo extensive physical training.

If training is to be effective, its influences must be carried over into the working environment of the police officer. Too often, however, the classroom training received by the police recruit at the academy is negated or diluted by early experiences in the field. Frequently, a new police officer is induced to forget what was learned in the classroom and to concern himself with the "real" business of policing as it is conducted on the street. The transition from the idealism of the police training academy to the real world of law enforcement causes a subtle but definite change in his orientation toward his job, and has been referred to as the "detraining syndrome."[48]

One basic criticism of pre-service police training programs is that they often do not take into consideration the expanding role of the police officer in society. Police work has become a complex blend of duties oriented toward healing many of the social ills of community life. More and more, police officers are being pressed into service in areas only indirectly related to law enforcement. As this occurs, it is important that pre-service police programs be restructured accordingly. Although it is certainly important that a police officer know how to investigate a traffic accident or a crime scene, it is equally important that he be capable of dealing with the mentally ill, the intoxicated, and the bully. Although it is necessary that a police officer be qualified to use a firearm when required, it is perhaps more important that he knows when *not* to use it.

The National Advisory Commission on Criminal Justice Standards and Goals recommended several broad areas that should be included in the basic pre-service police training curriculum and the approximate amount of time that should be devoted to each.[49]

1. *Introduction to the Criminal Justice System* (8 percent)—an examination of the foundations and functions of the criminal justice system with specific attention to the role of the police.
2. *Law* (10 percent)—an introduction to the development, philosophy, and types of law: criminal law, criminal procedure and rules of evidence, discretionary justice, application of the U.S. Constitution, court systems and procedures, and related civil law.
3. *Human Values and Problems* (22 percent)—public service and non-criminal policing, cultural awareness, the changing role of the police, human behavior and conflict management, psychology as it relates to the police function, causes of crime and delinquency, and police-public relations.
4. *Patrol and Investigation Procedures* (33 percent)—the fundamentals of the patrol function including traffic,

juvenile, and preliminary investigation; reporting and communication; arrest and detention procedures; interviewing; criminal investigation and case preparation; equipment and facility use; and other day-to-day responsibilities and duties.

5. *Police Proficiency* (18 percent)—the philosophy of when to use force and the appropriate determination of the degree of force necessary; armed and unarmed defense; crowd, riot, and prisoner control; physical conditioning; emergency medical services; and driver training.

6. *Administration* (9 percent)—evaluation, examination, and counselling; department policies, rules, regulations; organization; personnel procedures.

While it is not generally desirable to assign a police recruit to regular field duty prior to the completion of the basic training program, some departments combine basic training with field experience in order that the concepts taught in the classroom assume practical meaning to the young officer. For example, in Dayton, Ohio, each police recruit spends 120 hours engaged in community service activities as part of his basic academy training. In Oakland, California, police trainees actively participate in a number of local community service organizations in order to gain a better understanding of the public's attitude toward government agencies.[50]

The environment in which the police recruit is taught the basic principles of law enforcement is of critical importance and bears directly on his future performance. In the past, police agencies have relied basically on a program of "stress" training, similar to that used by the military. Under a stress training program, discipline and obedience to orders is of paramount importance, while learning to think for oneself is rarely emphasized, if at all.

In recent years, however, the trend has been away from this type of authoritarian, punitive, pre-service training. Police agencies have begun to develop more humanistic training models that encourage creative, goal-oriented, problem-solving approaches to law enforcement problems.

In 1972, the Columbus, Ohio Police Division initiated a "guidance method approach" training program to replace the controlled environment that had prevailed in the recruit training academy. The purpose of this experimental program was to determine whether or not alternative training methods could prove more effective in preparing police officers for the rigors of their duties than the traditional methods usually found in the highly structured, controlled environment.

The objectives of the Columbus training projects were to provide—[51]

1. an opportunity for the recruit to think for himself and to act upon his own jundement;
2. a method of developing self-discipline on the part of the individual officer;
3. a means of revealing his leadership potential and facilitating the decision-making process;
4. an opportunity to further develop leadership abilities once they have been recognized;
5. a method of making the transition from police recruit to police patrolman smoother and more efficient.

While the new program has yet to be fully evaluated, early indications are that its objectives have been at least partially achieved and that it has been proven an improvement over traditional pre-service training techniques.

In-Service Training   In-service training is that training offered to police officers on a regular basis throughout their police careers. In-service training may consist of formal classes of instruction, weekly drills and training exercises, or short periods of instruction prior to, during, or after the regular tour of duty. In-service training, however, should not be confused with briefings during which routine information on operational matters is disseminated to officers before going on duty.

In-service training is vital to the continuing efficiency and effectiveness of the police agency. There is no point in a police officer's career at which training is no longer useful or necessary. Changes in the law and evidentiary matters, technological developments, and the evolving nature of society and the police officer's role all require that a police officer remain contemporary in his thinking and in his actions.

> Continuing education enables us to re-evaluate our habits of thought, concepts and ideals in the light of these changing times. It prepares us to face any change or chance, so that we are not easily thrown into a panic. It assures us of where we are, indicates where we are going, and tells us what we had better be doing under these circumstances.[52]

In all too many cases, in-service training programs are perfunctory, shallow, and ritualistic. They are often performed with little attention given to their purpose or expected results. Too frequently they are not goal-oriented. As a result, benefits are negligible and difficult to measure.

To be truly effective, in-service training programs should be logically planned and developed. They should be an integral component of the agency's career development program. They should be designed with the intent of improving the overall efficiency and effectiveness of the agency, as well as the performance of individual officers. Developing and conducting an in-service training program for police should be the responsibility of a designated officer or unit within the police department. In smaller departments, this may be someone appointed to this duty on a part-time basis, while larger departments will have a number of persons involved in conducting the training program. In addition, regional law enforcement training academies may offer a number of police refresher courses for the members of participating agencies.

In order to provide satisfactory in-service training, a police department should have a training budget with sufficient funds to allow officers to attend necessary training courses. Personnel schedules should also be flexible enough so that officers can be allowed to attend training courses in lieu of their regular duties, rather than on their own time. The National Commission on Criminal Justice Standards and Goals recommended that each police agency should provide a minimum of forty hours of in-service training for each officer annually.[53] While larger police departments will normally exceed this goal, many smaller departments will be hard-pressed to meet it unless local officials can be convinced of the need to continually upgrade the proficiency of law enforcement personnel through the provision of up-to-date in-service training programs. This should a primary goal of the police administrator.

Specialized Training   In addition to pre-service and in-service training, police departments require specialized training programs specifically designed for those persons in the agency who are assigned to special duties. Investigators, juvenile specialists, criminalistics technicians, traffic officers, and crime prevention specialists, for example, all perform duties that require specialized forms of training beyond that received by the general law enforcement practitioner.

A number of excellent specialized courses of instruction are available to law enforcement officers. Among these are the Northwestern University Traffic Institute, the Southern Police Institute, the National Crime Prevention Institute, and the Delinquency Control Institute. In addition, most colleges and universities with law enforcement or criminal justice education programs offer a variety of seminars and training institutes on subjects ranging from organized crime to police-community relations to homicide investigation.

The individual or unit responsible for the in-service training program in the police department should also assess the need for specialized courses of instruction and attempt to obtain sufficient funds to make such training available. Due to the shortage of funds and resources, such specialized training should be appropriate. Officers who have an actual need for specialized courses of instruction should be given priority over others who merely want to attend to satisfy their own personal interests. At the same time, every officer assigned to specialized duties should be required to periodically attend courses of instruction that will enhance proficiency in their duties.

The assessment of police training needs should be a continual process. Long-range plans should be developed that will accurately predict the future training needs of the department in terms of subject matter, available resources, and estimated costs. These projections should be incorporated into the annual budget request for the police department, and should be periodically updated.

Summary

The police department must recruit and select the most qualified candidates it can find if it is to provide an acceptable level of public service. At the same time, it must ensure that its entrance requirements and selection procedures are job-related and non-discriminatory. While the individual police administrator may not be actively involved in the recruitment and selection process, he will ultimately be held accountable for its results. He should therefore be allowed to participate in the decision-making process that culminates when an individual is appointed to the police service.

Ensuring adequate and appropriate training is another responsibility of the police administrator. Pre-service, in-service, and specialized police training programs should be continually reviewed to ensure that they are appropriate to the demands of the police service. Police training budgets should be adequate to provide sufficient training at all levels in the police department. Long-range training programs should be developed to assist the police administrator predict future training needs and prepare annual budget requests.

Discussion Questions

1. What is a police agency's most valuable resource? Why?

2. What are the four basic steps involved in the recruitment process?

3. Define affirmative action.

4. What are some reasons why police departments have not been fully successful in recruiting minorities?

5. Give two problems posed by raising the educational requirements of police officers. Can you think of others?

6. List several source documents that can be used when conducting a background investigation.

7. What is the purpose of the probationary period?

8. What is meant by "detraining syndrome?"

9. How does the "guidance method approach" differ from traditional police pre-service training methods?

10. Why is the in-service police training program so important?

References

1. O.W. Wilson and Roy C. McLaren, *Police Administration*, 2d ed. (New York: McGraw-Hill, 1972), p. 245.

2. For a detailed discussion of police recruitment techniques and programs, see Joseph Kimble, "Recruitment," in Richard Blum, ed.,

Police Selection (Springfield, Ill.: Charles C. Thomas, 1964), pp. 71-84.

3. National Advisory Commission on Criminal Justice Standards and Goals, *Police* (Washington, D.C.: U.S. Government Printing Office, 1973), p. 320 (Subsequently referred to as National Goals Commission).

4. See Philip Ash, *Meeting Civil Rights Requirements in Your Selection Program* (Chicago: International Personnel Management Association 1974); Carmen D. Saso and Earl P. Tanis, *Selection and Certification of Eligibles: A Survey of Policies and Practices* (Chicago: International Personnel Management Association, 1974).

5. 401 U.S. 424 (1970).

6. For an analysis and interpretation of the Duke Power Company case, see Albert H. Arondon, "The Duke Power Company Case," *Public Employment Practices Bulletin No. 1* (Chicago: Public Personnel Association, 1971); for a synopsis of other cases relating to discriminatory practices in public employment, see National Civil Service League, *Judicial Mandates for Affirmative Action* (Washington, D.C.: National Civil Service League, 1973).

7. Horace G. Bussell, "Result-Oriented Affirmative Action," in *The Municipal Year Book 1975* (Washington, D.C.: International City Management Association, 1975), pp. 163-70; see also, Richard E. Biddle, "Discrimination: What Does it Mean?" *Public Employment Practices Bulletin No. 5* (Chicago: International Personnel Management Association, 1973); W. Ed Mansfield, "An Affirmative Action Program Proposal," *Public Employment Practices Bulletin No. 6* (Chicago: International Personnel Management Association, 1974); Jacque K. Boyer and Edward Griggs, *Equal Employment Opportunity Program Development Manual* (Washington, D.C.: Office of Civil Rights Compliance, Law Enforcement Assistance Administration, U.S. Department of Justice, 1974).

8. Boyer and Griggs, *Equal Employment Opportunity*.

9. President's Commission on Law Enforcement and Administration of Justice, *Task Force Report: The Police* (Washington, D.C.: U.S. Government Printing Office, 1967), p. 167 (Subsequently referred to as President's Commission, *Task Force Report*).

10. *Report of the National Advisory Commission on Civil Disorders* (New York: Bantam Books, 1968), p. 316.

11. National Goals Commission, *Police*, p. 330.

12. For a discussion of the minority recruitment efforts of some police departments, see Richard J. Margolis, *Who Will Wear the Badge?* (Washington, D.C.: U.S. Civil Service Commission, 1971).

13. Urban Data Service, Laurie S. Frankel, *Personnel Practices in Municipal Police Departments* (Washington, D.C.: International City Management Association, November, 1973), p. 5.

14. National Goals Commission, *Police*, p. 343.

15. Peter Bloch, Deborah Anderson, and Pamela Gervais, *Policewomen on Patrol (Major Findings: First Report, Vol. I)* (Washington, D.C.: Police Foundation, 1973).

16. For a review of the development of state law enforcement training commissions, see Dennis Coltin and Larry T. Hoover, "Role of Law Enforcement Training Commissions in the United States," *Journal of Criminal Justice*, 1 (Winter, 1973), pp. 347-52.

17. National Goals Commission, *Police*, p. 335.

18. Urban Data Service, Laurie S. Frankel, *Personnel Practices*, p. 1.

19. Donald E. Clark and Samuel G. Chapman, *A Forward Step: Educational Backgrounds for Policemen* (Springfield, Ill.: Charles C. Thomas, 1966).

20. President's Commission Report, *Task Force Report*, p. 126.

21. National Goals Commission, *Police*, p. 369.

22. For a review of the development of programs of higher education for police officers, see Jack Kuykendall and Armand P. Hernandez, "A University's Administration of Justice Program," *Journal of Police Science and Administration*, 2 (September, 1974), pp. 297–307.

23. James W. Sterling, "The College Level Entry Requirement: A Real or Imagined Cure-All," *The Police Chief*, 41 (August, 1974), pp. 28–31.

24. Bernard Cohen and Jan M. Chaiken, *Police Background Characteristics and Performance—Report prepared for the National Institute of Law Enforcement and Criminal Justice* (New York: The Rand Institute, 1972), p. x.

25. See, for example, James O. Finckenauer, "Higher Education and Police Discretion." *Journal of Police Science and Administration*, 3 (December, 1975), pp. 450–57.

26. President's Commission, *Task Force Report*, p. 130.

27. Urban Data Service, Laurie S. Frankel, *Personnel Practices*, p. 2.

28. President's Commission, *Task Force Report*, p. 131.

29. For a useful guide, see *Your Employment Application: Bridge or Barrier to Public Employment* (Washington, D.C.: Bureau of Intergovernmental Programs, U.S. Civil Service Commission, 1975).

30. Wilson and McLaren, *Police Administration*, pp. 262–63; V.A. Leonard, *Police Personnel Administration* (Springfield, Ill.: Charles C. Thomas, 1970), pp. 11–12.

31. Cohen and Chaiken, *Police Background Characteristics*, p. 27; see also Melany E. Baehr, John E. Furcon, and Ernest C. Froemel, *Psychological Assessment of Patrolman Qualifications in Relation to Field Performance* (Washington, D.C.: U.S. Government Printing Office, 1968); National Goals Commission, *Police*, pp. 337–338.

32. National Goals Commission, *Police*, p. 501.

33. Ibid., p. 499.

34. William J. Bopp, *Police Personnel Administration* (Boston: Holbrook Press, 1974), p. 167.

35. President's Commission, *Task Force Report*, p. 129.

36. Joseph C. Kulus, Robert A. Lorinskas and Rebecca Byrne, eds., *Psychology and the Police: A Bibliography and Summary of Findings* (Chicago: The Chicago Police Academy, 1972).

37. David H. Smith and Ezra Stotland, "A New Look at Police Officer Selection," in John R. Snibbe and Homa M. Snibbe, eds., *The Urban Policeman in Transition: A Psychological and Sociological Review* (Springfield, Ill.: Charles C. Thomas, 1973), pp. 5–24.

38. National Goals Commission, *Police*, p. 338.

39. Ibid., p. 337.

40. Baehr, et al., *Psychological Assessment.*

41. Wilson and McLaren, *Police Administration*, p. 269.

42. Practical tips on conducting pre-employment interviews can be found in Richard A. Fear, *The Evaluation Interview* (New York: McGraw-Hill, 1973); see also, Lipman G. Feld, "Fifteen Questions You Dare Not Ask Job Applicants," *Management Review*, 63 (November, 1974), pp. 34–36.

43. George D. Eastman and Esther M. Eastman, eds., *Municipal Police Administration*, 6th ed. (Washington, D.C.: International City Management Association, 1969), p. 180.

44. The New York City Police Department had developed at least a rudimentary training program as early as 1853. *Police Training and Performance Study* (Washington, D.C.: National Institute on Law Enforcement and Criminal Justice, Law Enforcement Assistance Administration, U.S. Department of Justice, 1970), p. 7; Raymond B. Fosdick, *American Police Systems* (New York: The Century Company, 1920), p. 299.

45. August Vollmer and Albert Schneider, "The School for Police as Planned at Berkeley," *The Journal of the American Institute of Criminal Law and Criminology*, 7 (March, 1917), pp. 877-98.

46. National Goals Commission, *Police*, p. 380.

47. Ibid., p. 393.

48. Donald G. Webb and Gene F. Westergren, "The Detraining Syndrome," *The Police Chief*, 40 (November, 1973), pp. 36-40.

49. National Goals Commission, *Police*, p. 394.

50. Ibid., p. 395.

51. Robert L. Ruddock, "Recruit Training: Stress v. Nonstress," *The Police Chief*, 41 (November, 1974), pp. 47-49.

52. "Lifelong Learning," *The Royal Bank of Canada Monthly Letter*, 55 (December, 1974), p. 1.

53. Wilson and McLaren, *Police Administration*, pp. 308-9; National Goals Commission, *Police*, p. 405; Eastman and Eastman and Eastman, *Municipal Police Admin.* 6th ed., p. 184.

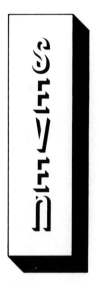

Police
Personnel
Management

General
Observations . . .

Direct and indirect personnel costs (salaries, insurance premiums, retirement benefits, etc.) consume between 75 and 90 percent of the total police budget. By the time an individual has been appointed to the police department and has undergone the necessary pre-service training, the employing jurisdiction has already made a substantial investment. The longer the employee remains with the agency, the more benefit the jurisdiction will realize from its initial investment. On the other hand, high employee attrition rates, low morale, and substandard performance largely negate the investment that a local unit of government makes in its personnel. Proper personnel management practices can increase the dividends that municipal governments realize from their investments in police personnel.

Over two decades ago O.W. Wilson emphasized the importance of sound police personnel management practices.

> Of all the knotty problems that confront the police executive, none transcends in complexity and importance the problems related to the management of personnel. Personnel administration is important because the quality of police service is strongly influenced by the manner in which policemen are selected for appointment and promotion, trained in the effective performance of their duties, and otherwise managed.[1]

Personnel Management Responsibilities

Ultimately, the chief of police is responsible for the actions of the police department and its personnel. Accordingly, the police executive must be involved in the personnel management process. In smaller agencies, the police executive may become directly involved in a number of personnel management functions, while in larger departments the police executive will delegate many personnel management responsibilities to a number of individuals or units within the police agency.

In most cases, the police executive shares the responsibility for personnel management with other local officials. The division of authority and responsibility for personnel management between the police executive and other officials will depend largely upon the form of government under which the police department operates (council-manager, mayor-council, commission) and the size of the jurisdiction. For example, many personnel management responsibilities, such as initial selection, promotion, discipline, and dismissal, may be performed by an independent police commission, appointed by the chief executive of the unit of government. Under the council-manager form of government, however, the chief administrative officer may assume many of the personnel management functions for the police department. In smaller jurisdictions, it is likely that the police executive will play a major role in police personnel management. Whatever the size of the jurisdiction, and regardless of the form of government under which it operates, the police executive is responsible ultimately for the performance of police personnel and the operational effectiveness of the police agency. Therefore, it is important that the police administrator know and practice proper personnel management techniques.

The Merit Principle

Most police agencies in the United States today are under some form of civil service system, based upon the merit principle. A merit system usually consists of the following practices.[2]

1. Hiring and promoting employees on the basis of ability, with open competition in initial employment.
2. Fair and equitable compensation.
3. Retention of personnel on the basis of performance; correcting inadequate performance wherever possible; and separating those employees whose performance cannot be corrected.

4. Fair treatment of all employees, without regard to race, sex, color, national origin, or religion.

5. Employee freedom from political pressures.

Origins of the Merit Principle

President Andrew Jackson has been credited, perhaps undeservedly, with instituting the "spoils system," under which government employment depended more upon allegiance to the political party in power than upon ability to do a particular job. Actually, public employees in the federal service had been hired and fired on the basis of political faith for many years before Jackson came into office. Only under Jackson's administration did political patronage come into full bloom.

Jackson's concept of grass roots democracy was contrary to the traditional beliefs that only the "most fit" (i.e., those of great wealth and social prominence) were qualified to hold public office. During Jackson's administration, the ideal of social equalitarianism emerged, and with it, the spoils system. The unfortunate result was frequent turnover in public office, incompetent and inexperienced public officials, inefficient government, and political patronage at all levels of government. These shortcomings led to a movement to reform public employment practices, and resulted ultimately in the creation of the National Civil Service Reform League (later the National Civil Service League).[3] Impetus to reform public employment practices was further stimulated in 1881 with the assassination of President Garfield by a dissapointed office seeker. Finally, in 1883, Congress passed the Pendleton Act, which provided for appointment to government service on the basis of competitive examinations. Even though the Pendleton Act originally applied to only a comparatively few federal positions, it has been amended several times to include nearly all civilian federal employees. Most states have enacted similar legislation. As a result, the majority of all public employees in the United States at the federal, state, and local level are protected by some form of merit system.

Merit Systems and the Police

The police, due to their special position of authority in society, have always been subject to corrupting influences and political pressures to a greater extent than other public employees. Indeed, during the late nineteenth century it was not uncommon for individuals to buy their appointments to the police force or to gain promotions and comfortable assignments

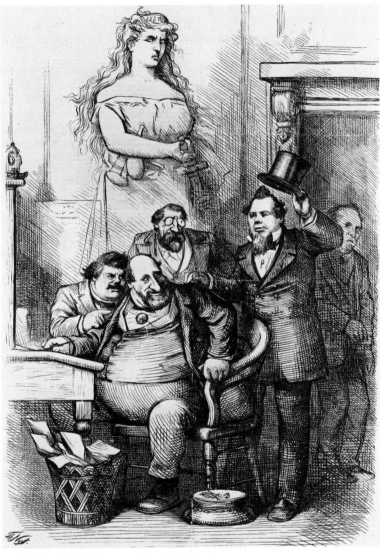

Courtesy of the Library of Congress

Boss Tweed, for years the ruler of machine politics in New York City, gained much of his power through corrupting police and other officials.

within the police department as a result of granting valuable favors to the political party in power. As late as the 1920s it was not unusual to find police departments in some American cities completely dominated by the political party in power.

Changes in political parties in city hall were often accompanied by mass discharges and appointments in the police department. As Fosdick observed during this period:

> Without civil service, appointments to the police department are generally a matter of political faith, involving allegiance to the local boss and fidelity to the party machine. Consequently, in such departments, the boss rather than the commissioner has the loyalty of the force, for commissioners are temporary creatures, birds of passage, subject to sudden political decapitation and retirement . . . while the boss, representing the permanency of the party machine, is always in a position to provide jobs.[4]

The implementation of some form of merit system for most police employees has tended to minimize, although not eliminate completely, political manipulation of the police and to ensure fair and equitable treatment of police employees. In general, merit systems have done much to improve the quality of police service in America.

At the same time, merit systems pose real problems for the police administrator. For example, when the responsibility of the police executive to ensure the selection, appointment, and promotion of only the most qualified individuals within the police department is nullified or negated by the overdominance of independent civil service boards or commissions, his ability to effectively manage the affairs of the department is seriously impaired. Even Fosdick, who praised the overall impact of the merit principle on the police service, recognized its weaknesses. He argued that, once admitted into the police service, an officer who was too well protected by inflexible rules and regulations might tend to become lazy and incompetent, realizing that the police administrator was virtually helpless to do much about his conduct. Fosdick also noted that, in many cases, civil service systems operating under the merit principle were actually bulwarks for neglect and incompetence, and that:

> Too often does the attempt to protect the force against the capricious play of politics compromise the principle of responsible leadership, so that in trying to nullify the effects of incompetence and favoritism, we nullify capacity and intelligence too.[5]

There is a growing awareness among public administrators and government officials that large-scale reform of traditional civil service laws is required. A number of U.S. cities have initiated plans to modify or abolish civil service requirements altogether. In 1976, Chicago became the largest city in the country to eliminate its Civil Service Commission, transferring its powers to a central personnel agency.[6]

While the merit principle is a useful means of insulating police employees from political pressures and corruptive influences, if applied too strictly it may jeopardize the police administrator's ability to ensure individual accountability and operational responsiveness. In some instances, major modifications in existing civil service systems may be necessary to effect this purpose.

Personnel Classification and Compensation

Many police departments today suffer from inadequate budgets, low salaries, and inequitable distribution of salaries among different classes of employees. To correct the latter two defiencies, a police department must have a sound classification plan upon which to base adequate and equitable salaries for all classes of police employees. While the typical police administrator will not usually be involved directly in the preparation of a classification plan or in the establishment of police salary scales, it is useful for him to have a working knowledge of the fundamental principles involved in the development of such plans.

Position Classification   The purpose of classification is to bring about a semblance of order and logic from potential confusion and disarray. With respect to personnel, position classification assists in allocating available resources, distributing work assignments, and making more logical decisions regarding the transfer, assignment, and promotion of personnel.

It is reported that the ancient Chinese were the first to apply classification principles when allocating personnel resources. The Chinese developed and employed three basic principles of classification.[7]

1. Separate the person from the job and determine the value of the work in relation to other jobs.
2. Assign the right person to the right job.
3. Reward better performance with higher compensation.

These principles remain largely applicable today. For example, modern classification plans are typically developed by following three basic steps:

1. the analysis of duties and responsibilities attached to the positions within the organization;
2. the establishment of classes of positions, the selection of appropriate class titles, and the preparation of written descriptions of the work and requirements of each class;
3. the allocation of individual positions to the classes established.

A position classification plan is usually designed to group together those jobs in an organization which are essentially similar with respect to nature of work, have approximately the same level of difficulty and responsibility, require similar training and experience, and which may be compensated for by the same general levels of pay. It is important to keep in mind that it is the job or position, not the individual, that is classified.

In a comprehensive personnel management program, the classification plan should be used—

1. to assure that equal pay is provided for equal work;
2. to establish education and experience qualifications and standards for employee selection;
3. to provide administrators and supervisors with a means of analyzing work distribution, areas of responsibility, lines of authority, and other relevant relationships between individual positions and groups of positions;
4. to assist authorities in determining personal service costs and in projecting such costs for annual budget requirements;
5. to provide a basis for developing standards of work performance;
6. to establish lines of promotional and career opportunities;
7. to indicate employee training needs and career development requirements;
8. to provide consistent and meaningful titles for all positions.

Personnel classification plans are normally prepared for local units of government and for state employee systems by professional personnel consulting firms. Owing to the continuing evolution of the police role and the rapid growth and development of many police agencies, position classification plans should be periodically updated to ensure that they adequately meet contemporary demands.

**Police Personnel
Compensation**

There remains today a serious need to upgrade the quality of
the police service through the promotion of professional
standards and increasing police salaries. One of the most
significant barriers to achieving professionalism in law enforcement today is the low salaries offered to police personnel in many parts of the United States. This is particularly true in those small, rural agencies where governmental
budgets are simply not sufficient to meet the demands made
upon them.

While police salaries in major urban centers have increased
dramatically in recent years, they continue to lag behind those
enjoyed by members of other professional and occupational
groups. In many instances, skilled laborers, such as bricklayers,
electricians, and plumbers receive higher salaries than police
officers.

The National Advisory Commission on Criminal Justice
Standards and Goals reported that in 1972, nearly 90 percent
of all police officers employed in cities having more than
100,000 inhabitants received starting salaries lower than the
median income for an average family of four in the United
States.[8] The situation in smaller cities is undoubtedly worse.
According to data compiled by the International City Management Association, the average starting salary for police officers
in U.S. municipalities as of January 1, 1974, was $9,523, and
cities with populations between 250,000 and 500,000 paid
the highest starting salary for police officers, an average of
$10,807. Overall, maximum salaries for police officers averaged
$11,438, with cities of populations in excess of 500,000 show-
ing the highest average maximum salary level of $13,258.[9]
Those figures are shown in Table 7–1.

The problem of inadequate police salaries is often a reflection of general economic trends and pressures which are felt
keenly in municipal finances. Inflation and recession combine
to shrink the available finances of government bodies and to
reduce the level of services that can be obtained for budgeted
expenditures.

At the same time, taxpayers have become increasingly
cost-conscious and mindful of economy measures. They want
to cut the costs of government in every possible way. Local
politicians are elected to office on platforms promising to
control or reduce government expenditures. Once in office
they begin seeking ways to fulfill their campaign promises.
All too often, employee salaries, which represent the biggest
single item in the municipal budget, become their targets.

Table 7-1   Mean Entry Level and Maximum Salaries and Longevity Pay Data for Police
Officers in U.S. Cities by Population Category

Population Category	Mean Entry Salary	Mean Maximum Salary	Mean Maximum Salary With Longevity	Mean Number of Years to Attain Longevity
All Cities	$ 9,523	$11,438	$12,250	17
Over 500,000	$10,304	$13,258	$14,624	19
250,000-499,999	$10,807	$13,086	$13,348	21
100,000-249,999	$10,181	$12,395	$13,323	21
50,000-99,999	$10,232	$12,396	$13,004	18
25,000-49,999	$ 9,787	$11,922	$12,479	18
10,000-24,999	$ 9,132	$10,833	$11,688	16

Source: Carol A. Pigeon, "Personnel, Compensation, and Expenditures in Police, Fire, and Refuse Collection and Disposal Departments, *Urban Data Service Reports* (Washington, D.C.: International City Management Association, April 1975), p. 3.

As a result, a basic conflict develops between the need to reduce operating expenditures through budget cuts and salary ceilings, and the need to provide an increased level of public service to meet growing demands. As Stahl has observed:

> Taxpayers want economy, but they also want public services. Economy of program, the reduction of activities to their bare essentials, is one thing; an attempt to secure a wide variety of public services cheaply is something else. Taxpayers *should* want the kind of pay policy and levels that will secure and retain an able staff, public employees who can give service.[10]

In some cases, local units of government will never be able to provide the level of police salaries needed to attract and retain competent and professional police personnel. The National Commission on Criminal Justice Standards and Goals has recommended that, where necessary, states should assist local units of government in upgrading police salaries.

> Every State and local government should establish and maintain salaries that attract and retain qualified sworn personnel capable of performing the increasingly complex and

demanding functions of police work. Every State should set minimum entry-level salaries for all State and local police officers and reimburse the employing agency for a portion of the guaranteed salary.[11]

It is unlikely that local government agencies ever will be able to compete effectively with private industry in providing salaries and fringe benefits to attract the most qualified personnel. Private firms need only to raise the price of their commodities or services in order to raise salaries, while government agencies must rely upon taxes and other sources of revenues, which are unpredictable at best. Nevertheless, local units of government must recognize that equitable salaries are essential to the recruitment of qualified personnel. If a municipality expects to have a high level of police professionalism, it must be prepared to pay the costs necessary to attract and retain the most qualified personnel possible.

The Compensation Plan Compensation plans are related to position classification plans in that they are designed to equate the job requirements of a position, the abilities of a person assigned to that position, and the compensation to which that person is entitled. To put it simply, a compensation plan attempts to ensure equal pay for equal work. Since not all jobs in a police department are the same in terms of required training, duties, and responsibilities, compensation plans are needed to bring a sense of equity to personnel compensation.

Police compensation plans should provide the following:

1. a framework to ensure equal compensation for work involving similar duties and responsibilities;
2. a means for compensating employees for continuing or outstanding service;
3. a means for establishing compensation rates that compare favorably with those of employees performing similar duties in other departments or in private industry and which aid in the recruitment and retention of qualified personnel.

Several interrelated factors must be considered when developing a police compensation plan. None of these factors should be considered in isolation; rather, they should be considered in the context of their contribution to the overall plan. These factors include:

1. the relative difficulty and responsibility of the work involved;
2. independence of action and initiative required or expected, nature and extent of guidelines provided for the job, extent and nature of supervision required or provided, consequence of error;
3. responsibility for contacts with other governmental agencies and levels of government and with public groups and officials;
4. required knowledge, skills, and abilities;
5. comparative pay practices of private and public employers;
6. recruitment and retention potential;
7. internal administrative and hierarchic relationships among positions and the extent to which they vary within the organization;
8. the financial policies of the organization.

The Salary Schedule

A salary schedule is simply a table or chart that systematically arranges the pay grades or levels for all positions in an organization.[12] Usually, a salary schedule will provide for minimum, maximum, and intermediate salary steps for all positions in the organization. Incremental salary increases, commonly called "merit" increases, are normally included in the salary schedule to provide for periodic salary increases upon proof of advanced competency. The number of merit increases in the salary schedule may vary from three to six, each representing an approximate five percent increase over the previous step. Merit increases usually continue during the first three to four years of service. Maximum salaries for a police officer at the lowest grade are normally between twenty and twenty-five percent higher than entrance level salaries. Normally, there should be a ten to fifteen percent difference between the top salary for one position and the beginning salary for the next highest position. In other words, a patrol officer at top salary range will receive ten to fifteen percent less than a sergeant at the basic salary step. In addition to merit increases, most police salary schedules provide for longevity pay increases at five, ten, fifteen, and twenty years of service.

The Salary Survey

The question of what is an equitable salary for police employees continues to be a nagging one for police administrators and public officials. Obviously, budget limitations often play an important part in determining the salaries that police officers will receive. In addition, however, local units of government need to ensure that, to the extent possible, salaries paid to police employees are on a par with those paid by neighboring jurisdictions. One method of accomplishing this is through a salary survey.

A salary survey is nothing more than a survey of the compensation practices of a representative sample of comparable and/or neighboring jurisdictions. A salary survey may be conducted by an employee organization, a private individual, or by a firm hired for that specific purpose. Normally, a salary survey will be conducted in conjunction with the preparation of a position classification plan. In some cases, the municipality may conduct its own salary survey.

Four basic tasks are normally involved in the salary survey; these are—[13]

1. identification and selection of a representative set of positions that are typical of the duties performed by the agency and that are likely to be found in comparable agencies;
2. preparation of brief written descriptions of these positions in order to help identify them in other agencies;
3. gathering, through personal contact and/or mail surveys, information about pay rates, work hours, fringe benefits, and related factors;
4. systematically arranging the accumulated data in a manner that reflects the central tendency or prevailing compensation practices among the agencies being surveyed.

Once these steps have been accomplished, it is then possible to construct a salary schedule based upon prevailing wage conditions and compensation practices in the survey area. The salary survey thus enables the public administrator to develop a compensation plan which is competitive with those of comparable agencies, thereby placing the agency in a better position to attract and retain qualified employees.

Sources of Salary Information   In addition to the salary survey, it is also possible and often desirable to obtain more global figures of wage rates and trends. The following are a number of sources that can provide this information.

International City Management Association
1140 Connecticut Avenue, N.W.
Washington, D.C. 20036
Publication: *The Municipal Year Book* (annual)

U.S. Bureau of Labor Statistics
U.S. Department of Labor
14th and Connecticut Avenue, N.W.
Washington, D.C. 20210
Publications: *Current Wage Developments* (monthly); *National Survey of Professional, Administrative, Technical and Clerical Pay* (annual); *Employment and Earnings* (monthly).

International Personnel Management Association
1313 E. 60th Street
Chicago, Illinois 60637
Publications: *Pay Rates in the Public Service* (semiannual).

Labor-Management Relations Service
National League of Cities,
U.S. Conference of Mayors, and
National Association of Counties
1620 Eye Street, N.W., Suite 616
Washington, D.C. 20006
Publication: *A Spotlight on City Employee Benefits: National Survey of Employee Benefits for Full-time Personnel of U.S. Municipalities* (annual).

Compensation Practices

Compensation practices vary from one police agency to the next. Some departments offer a number of generous benefits in addition to the basic salary; others do not. Such additional benefits may mean the difference between attracting and retaining highly qualified or marginally qualified personnel.

Overtime. The demands of police work are such that overtime work is often a necessary part of the job. A police department must maintain a minimum number of personnel on duty at all times to respond to citizens' needs. Vacations, illnesses, and absences due to training frequently reduce the number of personnel available for duty beyond an acceptable level. In such cases, it is often necessary to assign police personnel to work beyond their regular duty hours.

Normally, overtime for police personnel will be compensated either by direct wages paid to the employee or by compensatory time, in which case the employee may take time off at some later time proportionate to the overtime worked. Overtime may be compensated at time and one-half or on a straight-time basis. The trend appears to be toward rewarding all overtime on a time and one-half basis, as is the general practice in private industry.

Different types of overtime may be compensated in different ways and at different rates. Extra shifts beyond the employee's regular tour of duty are normally compensated at time and one-half. Training sessions and court time, on the other hand, are sometimes compensated at straight time. In still other cases, the jurisdiction may award either time and one-half in direct wages or straight time reimbursable in compensatory time. This is done to keep the compensatory time accruals to a minimum, since mounting compensatory time accruals present a nagging problem to the police administrator in terms of future scheduling.

It is often useful to limit both the amount of compensatory time that can be accrued by an employee and the amount of compensatory time that may be used at any given time. Otherwise, the police administrator will be constantly faced with the problem of trying to fill shifts left vacant.

Shift differential. Some police departments have adopted policies whereby individuals assigned to less desirable shifts (e.g., early morning shifts) are awarded a higher rate of compensation. There are several reasons to question this policy.

First, since many police departments rotate shifts, most officers will be required to work all shifts at one time or another. Paying shift differential to officers on a particular shift in such circumstances would pose an additional problem for the police administrator.

Second, most police officers, under normal circumstances, tend to gravitate toward those shifts they like best where shift rotation is not practiced. Younger officers, for example, who are more "action-oriented," tend to choose the late evening and early morning shifts since they are the ones that usually generate the most exciting police incidents. Older, more seasoned officers usually will favor the day shifts, which allow them to be home with their families more often. In such cases, shift differential would be of questionable value.

Finally, shift differential is basically contrary to the principle of equal pay for equal work, the foundation of any compensation plan. While the nature of police work varies from one shift to the next, there is no logical reason to expect that officers assigned to one shift will be expected to perform at different levels than officers on other shifts. Thus, while shift differential may be an attractive benefit to some police employees, it is not considered to be an equitable compensation practice and should be avoided if possible.

Police-fire wage parity. One problem that continues to plague the police administrator is that of wage parity between members of the police and fire services. Maintaining police-fire parity has become a hallowed tradition in municipal governments. In 1969, more than two-thirds of all cities in the United States maintained wage parity for police and fire personnel.[14] A more recent survey places the number of cities maintaining police-fire parity at just under 50 percent, with the most frequent use of police-fire parity being found in the northeastern United States (69.0 percent of the cities surveyed) and in cities having more than 250,000 inhabitants (66.7 percent of the cities surveyed).[15] There are many justifications for discontinuing such practices. Among these are the following:[16]

1. The duties of the police and fire service are basically dissimilar. Police officers work in an environment and under conditions which are more demanding, in terms of individual judgement, discretion, initiative, and sensitivity to human and social problems, than those of firemen. The duties of firemen, moreover, can be much more narrowly prescribed than those of police officers. At best, the role of the police officer is often ambiguous, while the job of the fireman is more clearly defined in terms of duties and responsibilities.
2. While very little of the fireman's time is spent actually fighting fires and related tasks, the police officer is constantly engaged in duties for which he was trained. Even while on routine patrol, a police officer is observing his physical surroundings, alert to the potential of criminal behavior and other incidents requiring his attention. Much of the fireman's time, on the other hand, is spent eating, sleeping, and performing station and equipment maintenance.
3. The police officer, in most cases, works almost entirely free of direct supervision and thus must rely heavily upon his own judgement and initiative in deciding what action to take in any given situation. This is notwithstanding the fact that his actions will later be subject to careful scrutiny and sometimes criticism by his superiors who were not there when decisions had to be made. Firefighters, however, perform most of their work under direct supervision and can usually rely upon the advice and instructions of their superiors in difficult situations.
4. The actions of police officers are subject to review and possible criticism by authorities and individuals outside the police department (e.g., the news media, private

citizens, the courts, and other officials), while the actions of firemen usually will be judged only by members of their own department.

5. Whereas the police are often held accountable and brought to task for increasing crime rates and other problems over which they have no control, firefighters are rarely blamed for outbreaks of fires or for their failure to contain them.

6. While the police are often hard-pressed to recruit and retain qualified employees, vacancies in the fire service are rare by comparison. Many police departments conduct year-round recruiting campaigns to fill vacancies, while fire departments usually have long lists of eligible applicants waiting to be appointed. As Lewin noted, positions in the fire service "are rationed among an excess supply of applicants."[17]

There would undoubtedly be many hurdles to overcome in any attempt to discontinue police-fire parity. Well-organized groups of firefighters and fire employee unions could bring great pressures to bear on public officials attempting to curtail such practices.[18] Nevertheless, police-fire parity is not an equitable compensation practice and should be avoided wherever possible.

Specialist pay. Specialist pay, sometimes called premium pay or hazardous duty pay, is sometimes awarded to selected individuals or positions in the police department. It is common practice, for instance, to award specialist pay to traffic officers, investigators, and others whose assignments require specialized training, skills, and expertise. It is important, however, that specialist pay be associated with the *position*, rather than the individual filling a position. That is, an individual is entitled to specialist pay only so long as he remains in a position to which specialist pay has been attached. Upon leaving that position, the individual is no longer entitled to specialist pay.

This sometimes creates problems when individuals become so accustomed to specialist pay that they resist efforts to have them transferred or reassigned to positions in which they would no longer be entitled to specialist pay. This problem can be avoided if provisions are included in personnel rules and regulations clearly reserving the right to the police administrator to make whatever personnel transfers and assignments are necessary for the good of the police service. Individuals occupying positions to which specialist pay is attached should be mindful of the fact that they are only entitled to specialist pay as long as they occupy those positions and that they are subject to transfer or reassignment at any time if the police administrator determines that such transfer or assignment is warranted.

Education incentive plans. In recent years, local units of government have recognized the importance of increasing the educational level of police personnel and have implemented education incentive plans to accomplish this purpose. As of January 1, 1972, one-third of all cities serving populations of 50,000 or more offered some form of education incentive plan to police employees.[19] There is little variation between cities of different sizes in this respect.

Table 7-2   Police Education Incentive Plans for Cities Over 50,000 Population, 1972

Population Category	Total Number of Cities	Cities Reporting Education Incentive	
		Number	Percent
All Cities	289	111	37.1
Over 500,000	23	6	26.1
250,000–499,999	26	8	30.8
100,000–249,999	79	30	38.0
50,000–99,999	171	67	39.2

Source: Laurie S. Frankel, "Personnel Practices in Municipal Police Departments" *Urban Data Service Reports* (Washington, D.C.: International City Management Association, November, 1973), p. 16.

Types of education incentive programs differ greatly. While some cities offer a flat salary differential based upon level of college achievement (e.g., $25 for a two-year degree; $50 for a four-year degree; etc.), others award a percentage of the individual's base salary for educational achievements (e.g., 2.5 percent for one year of college; 5.0 percent for two; etc.). Still other cities have combined college education with in-service training credits in the education incentive plan.

In such cases, an officer may combine non-academic technical training (fingerprint classification, accident investigation, etc.) with college courses to qualify for an education incentive award.

The following are a few examples of the education incentive plans offered by some cities:[20]

1. Atlanta, Georgia: 4.5% salary increase for two years of college; $970 for four years of college.
2. Cambridge, Massachusetts: 3% of base pay for 10 college credits; 6% of base pay for 25 college credits; 10% of base pay for 40 college credits; 15% of base pay for 60 college credits; 20% of base pay for a bachelor's degree; and 30% of base pay for a master of laws degree.
3. Los Angeles, California: a police officer who has completed 60 college units begins at the second step of the salary range; a police officer with a bachelor's degree in a pertinent field begins at the third step of the salary range.
4. Milwaukee, Wisconsin: $275 per year for 16 college credits, up to $750 per year for a bachelor's degree.
5. Oklahoma City, Oklahoma: 5% of base salary for an associate degree; 10% for a bachelor's degree; and 15% for a master's degree.

In addition, other cities award salary incentives for the achievement of intermediate and advanced certificates awarded by the state peace officer standards and training commissions.

Education incentive plans are expensive to maintain, but they offer the advantage of increasing the opportunity of recruiting and selecting highly qualified personnel. Police departments without education incentive plans will find themselves at a disadvantage when competing with other departments for qualified personnel.

Fringe Benefits Fringe benefits represent a substantial investment in the personal health and welfare of an agency's employees. In 1973, fringe benefits represented 35.5 percent of total direct personnel costs.[21] In other words, a police employee being paid $10.00 an hour was actually earning $13.36 an hour when fringe benefits were included in his salary.

Fringe benefits are those indirect costs to the employer for contributions to unemployment insurance, health and life insurance, and retirement plans.[22] Between 1970 and 1973, fringe benefits for police and fire personnel increased by 8.5

percent a year, compared with annual salary increases averaging 6.4 percent.[23]

Fringe benefits, although costly, represent three distinct advantages to the municipal employer:

1. the creation of an atmosphere of better employer-employee relations;
2. a decrease in personnel attrition rates;
3. protection of employees from hazards associated with their work.[24]

Traditional fringe benefit plans are often too restrictive and do not offer the individual employee the flexiblity to choose those benefits which best suit his own needs. More flexible plans may permit the employee to arrange his own benefit package to suit his own needs. For example, younger employees may be more interested in direct wages, while senior employees may wish a greater share of their salary to go into health and life insurance or retirement plans. In addition, as employees grow older and as their domestic situation changes, they may desire to restructure their benefit plans.

While flexible benefit plans have not yet been employed to any extent in public employment, they have been successfully implemented in several major American corporations. They might find equal acceptability in public employment.[25]

Police Performance Appraisal

Appraising performances of personnel, organizations, activities, and programs is a fundamental function of management and supervision.[26] Performance appraisals must be conducted periodically to ensure that goals and objectives are being met, that resources are being efficiently used, and that individuals and units within the organization are working up to their capability.

Since people represent the single most important resource of any organization, it is important that their performances be periodically reviewed and evaluated. When deficiencies or discrepancies between expected and actual performance are discovered, corrective action should be initiated. Thus, performance appraisals represent an attempt to detect and correct minor problems before they become major ones.

Many police officers, including first-line supervisors, regard performance appraisal with distrust, misapprehension, and suspicion. Performance appraisals often assume a negative image in the police organization. In too many cases, performance appraisals are viewed merely as an attempt to exact retribution against any employee who, for one reason or another, has incurred the disfavor of his superior officers. In addition, the performance appraisal process is sometimes viewed with skepticism because it may be influenced by personal biases and subjective feelings.

Police performance appraisal procedures are frequently criticized because they (1) do not accurately portray the true ability and performance of the employee; and (2) they can be manipulated by supervisors to punish officers who may have a personality conflict with a superior officer. In addition, some supervisors are often reluctant to make harsh or critical judgements of their subordinates, even when their performance is clearly below standard. Finally, performance appraisal is often inconsistent, changing from one supervisor to the next. ". . . Raters frequently are biased; some raters are harder to satisfy than others; employee morale can be adversely affected by a poor rating; ratings are not scientific; raters are unwilling to tell the truth if the truth hurts."[27]

While it may not be possible to eliminate entirely the subjective elements of the performance appraisal process, certain guidelines can be developed to ensure that gross inequities are at least minimized. Such guidelines should ensure, to the extent possible, that the performance appraisal process is conducted fairly and impartially, and that it is based upon objective standards of performance which are clearly understood and measurable.

Performance appraisal procedures are usually based upon either quantitative or qualitative measures. Ideally, both quantitative and qualitative measures should be included in performance appraisal. **Quantitative measures**, which are perhaps the easiest to use, utilize performance standards to which numerical values have been attached. Rating scales, ratios, and percentages are examples of quantitative performance measures. For example, an officer may be rated in comparison with other officers on his overall productivity, such as arrests, citations, field interviews, convictions, clearances, and so forth.

The danger of quantitative performance measures is that they place too much emphasis on quantity, or numbers, and not enough on quality, or substance. Officers may feel obligated to compete against each other in a numbers game, in which high-producing officers are believed to be superior to low-producing officers. Unfortunately, some police departments encourage this attitude, either intentionally or otherwise, by posting the track record of individual officers, units, and shifts in order to point out those who are responsible for the most arrests, traffic citations, and so forth.

Performance appraisal procedures based upon production records do little to improve the police image or to promote professional police conduct. Performance appraisal measures based solely upon numbers, ratios, and similar criteria are too mechanical and superficial to be effective. They perpetuate the existence of quota systems that have been imposed upon many police officers in the past. "The use of production records as a major or sole criterion in the evaluation process should be discouraged. Police work by its nature is not an assembly-line type of occupation and such records only indicate quantity as opposed to quality work performance."[28]

Measures of quality should be an integral part of any performance appraisal system. The quality of an individual's work is difficult to measure, in comparison to quantity, but it is nevertheless essential. Attitudes, professional bearing, judgement, discretion, forbearance, initiative, and ethical conduct are all indications of work quality in the police profession, but they do not lend themselves to easy measurement or appraisal.

There are relatively few police performance appraisal systems in effect today that have been received with enthusiasm and that have proven effective. Moreover, no one system can meet the needs of all agencies. However, when developing appraisal systems, a few basic guidelines are applicable.

1. The purpose of the performance appraisal process should be clearly understood by all involved. Individuals being evaluated should know the intent of the appraisal process and what objectives it is intended to accomplish.
2. Performance standards should be clearly understood by supervisors and subordinates alike. The need for uniformity should be stressed. Variations between raters should be kept to a minimum. Evaluations should be consistent from one supervisor to the next.
3. Supervisors should be trained in the techniques of performance appraisal. Peer group training sessions, in which a number of supervisors collectively evaluate their own percormance and that of their colleagues, can be used to

instruct supervisors in the techniques and criteria to be used in the performance appraisal process.

4. Individuals whose performance is being evaluated should be allowed to discuss the evaluation with their immediate supervisors. Indications of substandard performance should be thoroughly explained by the supervisor. The positive nature of the appraisal process, as a means of correcting deficiencies and improving performance, should be emphasized.

5. Performance appraisal should be conducted on a regular basis. Probationary officers should be evaluated every month; tenured officers should be evaluated once every six months. It is also a good idea for an officer's performance to be appraised each time he is transferred to a new assignment so that the new supervisor will have an up-to-date performance record.

6. The performance appraisal process should include a provision for officers to appeal their ratings to higher authority if they feel they are being treated unjustly. Standard grievance procedures should be implemented for this purpose.

Thus, while the performance appraisal process is complicated and not easy to administer, it is necessary to ensure the continued operational effectiveness of the organization and its members. Therefore, it should be approached with objectivity and fairness to the individual.

The Promotion Process

The process of promoting police employees to positions of higher authority and responsibility is a particularly rewarding task for the police executive; it enables him to enhance the quality of the organization by surrounding himself with persons in whom he has confidence. At the same time, the promotion process has many inherent pitfalls and hazards. Errors made during the promotion process may haunt the police administrator for years to come and may cast an unfavorable light on the police organization itself.

The basic problem in the promotion process is one of determining which individuals in the police department are the most capable of assuming positions of higher responsibility and authority. There have been many techniques devised to select those individuals with potential, but few have demonstrated any degree of predictive validity.

Too often, individuals in the police service are promoted to higher ranks simply on the basis of tenure and past performance. Seniority and superior performance in subordinate positions, however, do not necessarily qualify a person for advancement to a higher rank. Because an officer has performed superbly as a patrolman, for example, does not mean that he has the unique qualifications necessary to perform well as a supervisor.

Traditional police promotion systems are commonly based upon a number of criteria, including the following:

1. successful performance at a lower grade for a specified number of years;
2. completion of a written examination with a minimum passing score (usually 70 percent);
3. appearance before an oral examining board and the attainment of a minimum passing score (usually 70 percent).

In some cases, consideration is given to an officer's educational background. Approximately one-third of all police departments surveyed by the International City Management Association indicated that they considered educational achievement as a factor in the promotion process.[29]

Candidates for promotion are usually selected on the basis of a composite score derived from a number of factors, the written test and the oral interview usually contributing heaviest to the final score. These factors may be weighted in various ways. In some cases, the written score may carry the greatest weight, while in others the oral examination score will be more important.

Once a final score is determined, the names of the successful candidates are then placed on an eligibility list. The appointing authority, which may be the chief of police, or the city manager, or the chairman of the Civil Service Commission, will then make appointments from the list of eligibles. In some cases, the person with the highest overall score must be appointed first, followed by the person with the next highest score, and so on. In other cases, the appointing authority may be allowed to choose from among the top two or three names on the list. This allows greater flexibility in the selection of candidates for promotion, but sometimes causes hard feelings among those who are not chosen.

In any case, it is preferable that the police executive be allowed to make the final decision determining who will be promoted. While the promotion process may be the responsibility of a central personnel office or civil service board, the police executive alone will be faced with accounting for the actions of his subordinates. Therefore, it is reasonable and proper that he should have the final decision.

The Assessment Center   Traditional promotional policies leave much to be desired. Promotion criteria are often arbitrary and unreliable. Techniques used in the promotion process do not adequately predict future performance in positions of responsibility and authority. An element of bias is usually unavoidable. Past performance and tenure tend to overshadow more realistic considerations. At best, traditional promotion policies and procedures are based on guess work and speculation.

The result of the deficiencies inherent in traditional police promotion systems is that some individuals are promoted to positions for which they are not qualified and in which they will not perform satisfactorily. Thus, organizational performance is adversely affected, causing many police officers to lose confidence in the entire promotion system.

> Employees in the uniformed service complain, with much justification, that existing examination procedures do not give them a fair chance to demonstrate their leadership or the human skills which are needed at supervisory levels.[30]

The skills and attributes needed in supervisory positions are much different than those required of a patrolman. Traditional promotion procedures do not adequately assess these skills and attributes. Supervisory, management, and leadership potential can best be demonstrated through practical application. One method of accomplishing this is through the **assessment center technique** which is beginning to be used more frequently in the police service.

Assessment centers, or "assessment laboratories," as they are sometimes called, were first used by the German Army to select officers during World War I. In the late 1940s, the British Civil Service Selection Board adopted the assessment center technique for the selection of candidates for civil service positions.[31]

"An assessment center is a method, not a place. It involves multiple evaluation techniques, including various forms of job-related simulations, and may sometimes include psychological tests. . . . The exercises are selected to bring out behavior related to the dimensions identified by research as important to job success in the target-level positions for which the participants are being considered."[32]

The assessment center technique is perhaps the most thorough and effective method yet devised to determine suitability for selection, assignment, and promotion. It is a process which may take several days to complete, and it can be very expensive, depending upon the nature and difficulty of the position or assignment for which a candidate is being considered.

In the assessment center, a candidate's aptitude or potential for an assignment or position is judged on a number of job-related dimensions, or criteria, which are carefully selected beforehand by a team of assessors who are highly skilled and trained in the evaluation process. Job-related criteria are determined through a systematic analysis of the skills and aptitudes necessary to perform the job in question in a satisfactory manner.

Assessors may be members of a professional group outside the one in which the assessment is being performed or they may be well-trained members of the same profession.

The duties of the assessors consist of (1) observing the actions of the candidates as they perform various job-related exercises; (2) recording their observations on specially prepared forms; and (3) discussing the relative merits of each of the candidates with other members of the assessment team at the conclusion of the exercises. A profile of each candidate's individual strengths and weaknesses is then developed. Finally, the assessors, both individually and as a group, judge the overall potential of each candidate for the positions for which they are being considered.

The unique feature of the assessment center technique is that it employs situational exercises that closely approximate the circumstances that will confront the candidate in the position or assignment for which he is being considered. As a result, promotion potential is more effectively determined. Typical exercises used in the assessment center process are shown in Figure 7–1.

Assigned Role Group Discussion

In this leaderless group discussion, participants, acting as a city council of a hypothetical city, must allocate a one-million-dollar federal grant in the time allotted or make other judgments on the varying proposals offered. Each participant is assigned a point of view to sell to the other team members and is provided with a choice of projects to back and the opportunity to bargain and trade off projects for support.

Non-assigned Role Group Discussion

This exercise is a cooperative, leaderless group discussion in which four short case studies dealing with problems faced by executives working in state government agencies are presented to a group of six participants. The participants act as consultants who must make group recommendations on each of the problems. Assessors observe the participant's role in the group and the handling of the content of the discussion.

In-basket Exercise

Problems that challenge middle- and upper-level executives in state government are simulated in the in-basket exercise. These include relationships with departmental superiors, subordinates and peers, representatives of other departments, representatives of executive and legislative branches, the public, and the news media. Taking over a new job, the participant must deal with memos, letters, policies, bills, etc., found in the in-basket. After the in-basket has been completed, the participant is interviewed by an assessor concerning his/her handling of the various in-basket items.

Speech and Writing Exercises

Each participant is given a written, narrative description of a policy, event, situation, etc. and three specific situational problems related to the narrative, each requiring a written response. The participant is also required to make a formal oral presentation, based upon the background narrative description, before a simulated news conference attended by the Capitol Press Corps and interested government officials and citizens (assessors).

Analysis Problem

The analysis problem is an individual analysis exercise. The participant is given a considerable amount of data regarding a state agencies' field operations, which he/she must analyze and about which he/she must make a number of management recommendations. The exercise is designed to elicit behaviors related to various dimensions of managerial effectiveness. The primary area of behavior evaluated in this exercise is the ability to sift through data and find pertinent information to reach a logical and practical conclusion.

Paper and Pencil Tests

Three different commercially available objectively scoreable tests are included in the assessment: a reading test used for self-development purposes, a reasoning-ability test, and a personality test. The latter two are being used experimentally at present, and as with the reading test, are not made available during assessor discussions.

Source: William C. Byham and Carl Wettengel, "An Introduction and Overview," *Public Personnel Management*, 3 (September-October, 1974), p. 355. Reprinted by permission of the International Personnel Management Association.

Figure 7-1. Description of Typical Assessment Center Exercises.

Results of the assessment center technique are considered to be generally more reliable than those derived from conventional promotion procedures. As a result, individuals promoted to advanced positions through the assessment center technique are more likely to perform well than those selected for promotion through conventional methods.

Application to Law Enforcement

A number of police departments have begun to utilize the assessment center technique in recent years, both in selecting candidates for promotion and for entry level positions as well. In New York City, the police department has utilized the assessment center technique to identify potential managerial candidates and to provide training for the rank of captain and above.[33] In Palo Alto, California, a modified version of the assessment center technique has been used for selecting candidates for police sergeant.[34] Both the Fort Collins Police Department and the Colorado State University Police Department have employed a modified version of the assessment center technique for selecting police recruits.[35] In Orem City, Utah, the assessment center method has been successfully used for selecting candidates for promotion in the fire department; plans are underway to use similar methods in the police department. The International Association of Chiefs of Police has conducted a number of assessment centers for municipal police departments on a contract basis.

The assessment center method may not be the panacea of the promotion process, but it does offer a number of advantages over traditional methods. There is every likelihood that it will be used increasingly by police departments in the years to come, both for the promotional process and for selecting police recruits.

Assuring Professional Conduct

Misconduct by police officers erodes the public's confidence in the police and in the system of criminal justice. The police possess awesome power over their fellow citizens. When that power is misused or abused, the integrity of our system of social justice is threatened. Maintaining professional and ethical conduct is a primary responsibility of the police executive.

There are three essential elements that must be included in any system intended to ensure professional and ethical conduct. These are: (1) a system of internal directives; (2) a disciplinary system; and (3) a system of internal investigation. In addition, every police department should have some formal means of receiving, investigating, and adjudicating citizen complaints against the police.

Internal Directives   Police officers, like other employees, have a right to know which actions are expected of them and which are prohibited. A system of internal directives accomplishes this purpose.

Rules and regulations are specific directives that deal with specific issues. They state clearly actions that are required and prohibited of police officers. Violations of rules and regulations are usually dealt with by disciplinary action. An example of a rule is the following:

> 404.10. *Alcoholic Beverages.*   Officers are not to report for duty intoxicated, nor are they to report for duty within four (4) hours after consuming any alcoholic beverages.

Vague or ambiguous rules, such as *conduct unbecoming an officer* should be avoided wherever possible. If rules are to be enforced, they should lend themselves to easy interpretation.

Rules and regulations should be included in a manual that is logically organized, including a table of contents and an index. Each member of the department should be given a copy of the manual upon appointment, and he should be responsible for keeping it up to date by entering any additions, deletions, or revisions that may be issued for it. Each officer should acknowledge in writing that he has received a copy of the manual, that he is familiar with its contents, and that he understands that he is to be held accountable for its provisions.

A **policy** is a broad statement of purpose or intent. Policies form the guidelines against which we measure our progress toward particular objectives. Policies embody the values and principles which underly our activities.

Police departments need policies to guide them in their actions. Police officers need policies to assist them in developing solutions to a variety of complex problems and situations. The Los Angeles Police Department has developed a comprehensive policy manual which has served as a guide to many other law enforcement agencies. Following is an excerpt from the Los Angeles Police Department's *Policy Manual.*

> 580.40 *Enforcement of Parking Regulations.* Street parking is restricted in various areas of the City to ensure fair access to parking and to expedite the flow of vehicular traffic. All existing parking regulations will be enforced with reasonableness and impartiality in all areas of the City.[36]

A **procedure** is more specific than a policy, but less restrictive than a rule or regulation. A procedure is designed to assist officers in accomplishing a particular purpose or objective. Police procedure manuals usually include instructions governing such matters as arrests, death notifications, patrol operations, use of police equipment, testifying in court, care and custody of prisoners.

General orders consist of a combination of policies, rules, regulations, and procedures. They usually are long-term in nature. Moreover, they may deal with administrative matters, such as personnel rules and vacations, rather than strictly operational matters.

Special orders may be either administrative or operational in nature, but usually are issued to cover special events or situations and for a specified period of time. For example, a temporary change in hours for officers' court appearances would be published in a special order.

Maintaining Discipline

Discipline is essential in a police organization. This is partially due to the very nature of police work. Police officers are often thrust into situations in which they may be tempted to use their official authority to personal advantage. In addition, police officers hold a position of trust. Corrupt, brutal, and incompetent police officers can easily ruin a reputation of honesty and fairness that a department has worked for years to establish. A thorough and uniform system of discipline can help to ensure that such occurrences, if not avoided altogether, are, at least, the rare exception.

Police discipline has undergone a radical change in the past decade. It was only a few years ago that chiefs of police ruled their departments with an iron hand. Even small infractions were dealt with quickly and, sometimes, harshly. Police disciplinary measures, although somewhat arbitrary and heavy-handed, were generally quite effective.[37]

Today, the police discipline system bears little resemblance to that of years gone by. Police disciplinary proceedings have become much more formal and have incorporated at least the rudiments of the same constitutional safeguards that have played such an important role in the evolution of criminal proceedings. This change is due largely to three historical developments. First, the law enforcement profession came under intense criticism during the 1960s from many segments of the community. Anti-war demonstrators, civil rights advocates, and student radicals, to name but a few, found the police an easy target upon which to vent their dissatisfaction with the establishment. In many cases, the police response to the militant tactics of such groups served merely to heighten tensions and prove the inadequacy of police internal control measures. Cries were heard around the country for civilian review boards and other similar means to exercise greater control over the police. Police departments were forced to overhaul their own review procedures or risk having outside supervision thrust upon them.

A second development was the rapid and tumultuous emergence of the police labor union which occurred during this same time period. Police officers, often confused and frustrated over their loss of public support, eagerly sought some means to protect themselves from what they perceived to be unwarranted attack and criticism. Police labor unions quickly asserted themselves as the protectors of the rights of individual officers. Police administrators soon found their authority over police disciplinary matters considerably diminished. (For a more detailed discussion of the effect of the police labor movement on personnel administration, refer to Chapter 8.)

A third factor, more subtle than the previous two, has been the emergence of the spirit of humanism in the police organization. Autocratic control measures have given way to methods more sensitive to the needs of individuals. Police administrators have come to rely upon reason and understanding when dealing with subordinates.

As a result of these key developments, the nature of disciplinary procedures has changed dramatically. What was once a simple, straightforward process, has become, in many instances, more formal and complicated. The net effect of these changes, however, has not lessened the importance of a firm but fair disciplinary system. Indeed, a comprehensive police disciplinary system is more important now than ever before. Uneven administration of discipline, as a matter of fact, is one of the most frequent causes of internal strife and poor morale in police departments today.

A sound disciplinary system should include several elements.

1. *Written Foundation.* Police personnel must know what is expected of them. In addition, they must know in advance the penalties for wrong-doing. Policies, rules, and regulations must be firmly established in writing.

2. *Established Procedures.* Procedures for enforcing rules and regulations must be established and promulgated. Police officers must know which procedures will be followed when an infraction is committed. In addition, they must know their rights and responsibilities under the disciplinary system.

3. *Uniform Punishments.* Arbirtary application of discipline should be avoided. Punishments for infractions should be applied equally, without regard to rank, age, sex, or seniority. Written directives should establish prescribed penalties for specific violations, allowing for sufficient latitude in the administration of discipline. Generally, punishments may include oral or written reprimand, transfer, suspension from duty (with or without pay), demotion, and dismissal. The authority of the police administrator to effect these levels of punishments will normally depend upon established civil service regulations and state and local laws.

4. *Trial Review.* In cases of serious misconduct for which the penalty is dismissal or reduction in rank, a trial review board comprised of representatives of all ranks should be established to determine guilt and recommend appropriate punishment. The chief of police, however, is not normally bound by the findings of the trial board.

5. *Right of Appeal.* In cases resulting in suspension, demotion, or dismissal, the officer should be afforded the right of appeal to higher authority, which may be automatic or optional. The final review authority, depending upon local requirements, may be the city manager, the Civil Service Commission, the city council, or some other authorized body.

Internal Controls   To ensure that the highest standards of conduct are maintained in a police department, the police administrator must have the capability to detect and investigate unlawful or inappropriate conduct by police personnel. In small departments, this function is normally performed rather informally by either plain-clothes investigators or by someone appointed by the chief of police to handle such cases when they arise. In larger departments, internal affairs units are normally established to conduct such investigations. In either case, it is an important function that should not be neglected.

The procedure used to seek out evidence of misconduct by police officers in the Chicago Police Department may serve as an example.[38] In Chicago, incidents involving police misconduct may be handled in one of three ways.

1. Complaints regarding unlawful use of force are automatically referred to the Office of Professional Standards (OPS). The OPS is commanded by three lawyer-administrators who oversee four supervisors and forty civilian investigators. The lawyer-administrators report directly to the superintendent of police. Complaints of unlawful force by police may originate from citizens or from supervisors and other members of the department. In addition, the OPS reviews all reports involving the discharge of weapons and, depending upon the circumstances, may initiate an investigation. An investigation is conducted automatically whenever a citizen is killed or injured by a police officer. Once an investigation by OPS has been completed, it is referred to the commanding officer of the unit in which the officer works. From there it passes upward through the chain of command for appropriate action. Since its establishment in August 1974, the OPS has handled over 3,000 such investigations.
2. All complaints not involving excessive use of force are directed to the department's Internal Affairs Division, where they are recorded. The Internal Affairs Division (IAD), which had an authorized strength of 119 personnel in 1976, received 6,664 complaints in 1974, and in excess of 6,000 in 1975. If the complaints are relatively minor and involve a single officer, they are normally referred to the commanding officer of the unit in which the officer is assigned for investigation and disposition.
3. Cases involving major infractions or in which officers from more than one command may be involved are usually handled by IAD. In addition, IAD initiates its own investigations whenever there is any indication of wrongdoing by a member of the department.

Investigative Findings   Once an investigation into possible police misconduct has been completed, a finding as to guilt or innocence must be established. Generally, one of several findings may be made.

1. *Unfounded.* The investigation conclusively proved that the incident did not occur, or that the officer named in the complaint was not involved.
2. *Exonerated.* The investigation revealed that the act which provided the basis for the complaint did occur, but that it was justified, legal, and proper, and that no misconduct was involved.
3. *Not Sustained.* The investigation failed to disclose enough evidence to clearly prove or disprove the allegation.
4. *Sustained.* The investigation disclosed sufficient evidence to prove that the incident did occur and that the individual named in the complaint was responsible and was culpable.

Criminal Misconduct   In the more serious types of police misconduct, violations of criminal law may be involved. In such cases, investigations may also be conducted by authorities outside the police department, such as state's attorneys or grand juries. In cases involving violations of civil rights, the Federal Bureau of Investigation may intervene.

Even though investigations may be conducted by agencies outside the police department, the police administrator has a responsibility to conduct internal investigations of all cases involving police misconduct. Actions that may result in a finding of not quilty or a failure to prefer criminal charges may nonetheless be grounds for disciplinary action within the department.

Citizen Complaints   The police have a responsibility to serve the public honestly and fairly. When they neglect that responsibility by the unlawful use of their authority or some similar action, the public has a right to expect that appropriate remedial measures will be taken against the offending officer. To do otherwise surely means the erosion of public confidence in the police.

All police departments should encourage citizens to bring forth complaints about what they believe to be unlawful or inappropriate police conduct. In many cases, the complaints arise merely from misunderstandings and can be easily resolved. In other cases, the grievances may be actions of a more serious nature that require a formal investigation. In all cases, the public must be made confident that the police are capable of arriving at a fair and reasonable solution.

Many citizens are reluctant to make complaints against the police. Sometimes, this is due to a belief that the police will not take appropriate action and will attempt to cover up instances of wrongdoing in order to protect themselves. In other instances, some people are afraid that they will incur the wrath of the police and will be subjected to harrassment and subtle forms of persecution if they suggest that the police acted improperly. Both of these fears must be eliminated.

Specific guidelines for accepting, recording, and investigating citizens' complaints against the police should be incorporated into the policies and procedures of the police department. A formal register of such complaints should be kept, indicating the name of the complainant, the date received, who received it, the actions involved, the officer(s) involved (if known), and the disposition of the complaint.

When such complaints arise out of relatively minor infractions of regulations, or involve misunderstandings between the police officer and the citizen, every attempt should be made to reconcile the matter early and simply. Complaints involving more serious allegations, however, should be forwarded to the chief of police or his designated representative for a full and complete investigation.

In every case, the citizen should be convinced that the police will act responsibly on their complaint. The citizen should be informed as to the eventual results of the investigation, as well as to the disposition of the complaint. While the citizen may not always be satisfied with the results taken by the department, he will rest comfortably with the knowledge that at least some action was taken. At the same time, officers will know that the department will not tolerate misconduct on the part of its members.

Summary

Local units of government invest heavily in the personnel they select to enforce the law and protect citizens. This investment may be wasted if the personnel management policies and procedures of the police department are not soundly conceived and administered. The police administrator usually has an indirect role in such matters as personnel classification and compensation. On the other hand, he should play a key role in the evaluation and promotion process. Finally, he must take positive steps to ensure that professional conduct is maintained by his subordinates. This can be accomplished by a system of internal directives, a system of administering discipline, and conducting internal investigations into allegations of police misconduct. A formal system of receiving and investigating citizen complaints is essential if public confidence in the police is to be maintained.

Discussion Questions

1. *What percent of the police budget goes toward personnel costs?*

2. *Give a brief definition of the merit principle.*

3. *Explain what is meant by the "spoils system."*

4. *Explain how the merit system jeopardizes the police executive's management responsibility.*

5. *What are the basic purposes of the position classification plan?*

6. *What factors should be considered when developing a compensation plan?*

7. *Give several reasons why police-fire wage parity is considered to be inequitable.*

8. *What are the three basic advantages of fringe benefits?*

9. *Describe the differences between quantitative and qualitative performance measures. Give examples of each.*

10. *Describe the assessment center technique and its advantages over traditional promotion methods.*

11. *Define (1) rules and regulations; (2) policies; (3) procedures; (4) general orders; (5) special orders.*

12. *What are the four findings that may result from investigations of police misconduct? Give definitions of each.*

References

1. O.W. Wilson, "Problems in Police Personnel Administration," *Journal of Criminal Law, Criminology and Police Science*, 43 (March-April, 1953), p. 840.

2. Robert E. Hampton, "Rededicating Ourselves to Merit Principles," *Personnel Administration/Public Personnel Review*, 1 (July-August, 1972), p. 58.

3. O. Glenn Stahl, *Public Personnel Administration*, 6th ed. (New York: Harper & Row, 1962), pp. 32-33.

4. Raymond B. Fosdick, *American Police Systems* (New York: The Century Company, 1920), pp. 271-72.

5. Ibid., p. 284.

6. For a review of the process leading to the abolishment of civil service in Chicago, see Jean L. Couturier, "The Quiet Revolution in Public Personnel Laws," *Public Personnel Management*, 5 (May-June 1976), pp. 150-67.

7. Carl F. Lutz and James P. Morgan, "Jobs and Rank," in O. Glenn Stahl and Richard A. Staufenberger, eds., *Police Personnel Administration* (Washington, D.C.: Police Foundation, 1974), p. 20.

8. National Advisory Commission on Criminal Justice Standards and Goals, *Police* (Washington, D.C.: U.S. Government Printing Office, 1973), p. 357. (Subsequently referred to as National Goals Commission.)

9. Carol A. Pigeon, "Personnel, Compensation, and Expenditures in Police, Fire, and Refuse Collection and Disposal Departments," *Urban Data Service Reports* (Washington, D.C.: International City Management Association, April, 1975), p. 3.

10. Stahl, *Public Personnel Administration*, p. 79.

11. National Goals Commission, *Police*, p. 354.

12. William J. Bopp, *Police Personnel Administration* (Boston: Holbrook Press, 1974), p. 99.

13. Stahl, *Public Personnel Administration*, p. 86.

14. David Lewin, "Wage Parity and the Supply of Police and Firemen," *Industrial Relations*, 12 (February, 1973), p. 77.

15. Laurie S. Frankel, "Personnel Practices in Municipal Police Departments," *Urban Data Service Reports* (Washington, D.C.: International City Management Association, November, 1973), p. 11.

16. James T. McCutcheon, "Should Police and Fire Salaries be Equal?" *The Tax Journal*, 42 (Fourth Quarter, 1974), p. 135.

17. Lewin, in *Industrial Relations*, p. 78.

18. For a discussion of the problems associated with breaking police-fire wage parity, and an explanation of how one such situation was eventually resolved in a major U.S. city, see William F. Danielson, "Should Policemen and Firemen Get the Same Salary?" *Public Personnel Report No. 641* (Chicago: Public Personnel Association, 1964).

19. Frankel, in *Urban Data Service Reports*, p. 16.

20. Ibid., p. 11.

21. "Municipal Worker Fringe Benefits Grow Faster Than Pay Scales," *Nation's Cities*, 13 (February, 1975), p. 27.

22. For a general discussion of public employee fringe benefits, see "Fringe Benefits for Public Employees," *Public Management*, 55 (October, 1973), entire issue.

23. *Second National Survey of Employee Benefits for Full-Time Personnel of U.S. Municipalities* (Washington, D.C.: Labor-Management Relations Service, National League of Cities, U.S. Conference of Mayors, and National Association of Counties, 1974).

24. Bopp, *Police Personnel Admin.*, p. 125.

25. Thomas E. Wahlrobe, "The Cafeteria Approach to Employee Benefits," *Administrative Management*, 35 (December, 1974), pp. 48-52.

26. For a more detailed discussion of the performance appraisal process, see Bopp, *Police Personnel Admin.*, pp. 205-30; see also, Frank J. Landy and Carl V. Goodin, "Performance Appraisal," in Stahl and Staufenberger, *Public Personnel Admin.*, pp. 165-84.

27. George D. Eastman and Esther M. Eastman, eds., *Municipal Police Administration*, 6th ed. (Washington, D.C.: International City Management Association, 1969), p. 186.

28. Joseph C. DeLadurantey and Lyle Knowles, "The New Management Team," *The Police Chief*, 40 (October, 1973), p. 23.

29. Frankel, *Urban Data Service Reports*, p. 12.

30. A.N. Paulionis, "The Value of Practical Promotional Examinations in the Police and Fire Ranks," *Public Personnel Management*, 2 (May-June, 1973), p. 179.

31. William C. Byham and Carl Wettengel, "An Introduction and Overview," *Public Personnel Management*, 3 (September-October, 1974), p. 358.

32. Ibid., p. 353.

33. Paul F. D'Arcy, "Assessment Center Program Helps to Test Managerial Competence," *The Police Chief*, 41 (December, 1974), pp. 52-53, ff; see also, William J. Kearney and Desmond D. Martin, "The Assessment Center: A Tool for Promotion Decisions," *The Police Chief*, 42 (January, 1975), pp. 31-33.

34. James C. Zurcher, Dale Miller, and Jay C. Rounds, "Selecting Effective Police Sergeants," *The Police Chief*, 42 (January, 1975), pp. 28-30.

35. James F. Gavin and John W. Hamilton, "Selecting Police Using Assessment Center Methodology," *Journal of Police Science and Administration* 3 (June, 1975), pp. 166-76.

36. National Goals Commission, *Police*, p. 610.

37. Bopp, *Police Personnel Admin.*, p. 300.

38. Information regarding the Chicago Police Department's Office of Professional Standards and Internal Affairs Division were obtained in telephone interviews with Supervisor Letman (OPS) and Sergeant Salewski and Lieutenant Sloan (IAD) 2/11/76. Their assistance is gratefully acknowledged.

EIGHT

Police-Labor Relations

General
Observations . . .

Until the 1960s, labor relations, as a formal process involving collective bargaining, grievance procedures, and impasse resolution, was virtually unknown in the police service. Since then, however, the labor relations process has become increasingly important to the police administrator. While some police executives tend to shy away from their responsibilities in the area of labor relations, most have recognized that the ability to manage the operations of the police department depends, to a certain extent, upon their willingness to enter into the labor relations process with a knowledge of and appreciation for its purpose.

The progressive police administrator has come to realize that police labor relations is a growing part of his job, and that it is a responsibility he cannot neglect. Poor labor relations in a police department can have disastrous consequences on the operational effectiveness and internal harmony of the organization. This chapter focuses on the basic principles and processes of police labor relations, and the role of the police executive in the process.

Police Labor Unions and Employee Associations

Police labor unions and employee associations have experienced phenomenal growth in recent years, and their activities have become a cause of concern by police executives. Since the early 1960s, police employee associations have evolved from informal fraternal groups, created to foster fellowship and harmony among their members, to highly organized and powerful groups whose primary mission has been to gain for their members higher wages, increased benefits, and more favorable conditions of employment. In addition, some of these groups have attempted (with success, in many cases) to gain control over administrative decisions that were once the exclusive prerogative of the chief of police.[1]

The rapid growth and development of police labor unions and representative associations has been paralleled by a similar increase in labor unions in other parts of public sector employment. Since the end of World War II, unionization of public employees has far surpassed the growth of labor unions in private employment. The American Federation of State, County, and Municipal Employees (AFSCME), which includes several thousand police employees among its membership, is the fastest growing labor union in the AFL–CIO. In 1970, membership totalled nearly 500,000.[2]

The rapid growth of public employee unions and the aggressive tactics employed by those groups to gain more benefits for their members have had adverse effects upon the ability of police executives to control and administer their departments properly. Internal conflicts have arisen concerning terms and conditions of employment. Escalating costs brought about by higher employee wages and fringe benefits have forced the tightening of fiscal controls in other programs and activities. Entire police departments in major U.S. cities have been crippled by mass strikes by police employees.[3]

There are a number of reasons for the dramatic growth in number, size, and activities of police labor unions and employee associations.[4] First, police employees began to realize several years ago that their salaries were far below those of members of other professional and occupational groups. Second, police departments have come to be recognized by union officials as fertile grounds for expanding membership. Third, police officers during the 1960s became increasingly bitter due to public accusations of brutality and unethical conduct by the police. Riots, civil rights marches, and antiwar demonstrations brought the police into the public spotlight, often with negative results. Consequently, the police became frustrated and were alienated from the public.

Fourth, a number of national commissions have been created to study the police mission and role. The National Commission on Causes and Prevention of Violence; the National Commission on Campus Unrest; the President's Commission on Law Enforcement and Administration of Justice; and the National Advisory Commission on Criminal Justice Standards and Goals have all published widely distributed reports on the weaknesses of the law enforcement systems of this country and have proposed means of improving them.

Finally, arbitrary, unfair, and sometimes discriminatory personnel practices have created a void between the police manager and the police employee. Attempts to fill this void have resulted in formal machinery for collective bargaining, redress of grievances, and, in some cases, erosion of management prerogatives. All have been chiefly the result of increased activity by police unions and employee associations.

Development of the Police Labor Movement

The development of the police labor movement dates back to the latter part of the nineteenth century.[5] It was during this period that police officers in many cities began to experience a sense of isolation and alienation from fellow citizens. As a result, they formed social clubs and benevolent societies to promote fellowship and social harmony among themselves. During this same period of time, labor unions emerged as a powerful force in American industry. Organized labor began to make substantial gains in its struggle to represent the interests of the working man and woman. This fact did not go unnoticed by police officers, who decided that what worked well for the steel worker or coal miner should work equally as well for the police officer. In 1897, a group of police officers applied for a charter from the American Federation of Labor (AFL), and were promptly refused. Within 20 years, however, the AFL reversed its long-standing practice of not chartering police unions. By 1919, thirty-seven police locals had been granted AFL charters.[6]

Almost as soon as police officers gained entrance into labor unions, tragedy erupted in the form of a massive strike by policemen in Boston in 1919. When leaders of the Boston police local asked city officials for union recognition and bargaining rights, they were refused; and, charges were brought against union leaders. Most of the police department went out on strike, and the city was left virtually defenseless. Violence and social disorder ensued, and local authorities prevailed upon Calvin Coolidge, then Governor of Massachusetts, to intervene. Samuel Gompers, the AFL president, asked Coolidge to intercede on behalf of the union leaders. Coolidge refused, declaring that "there is no right to strike against the public safety by anybody, anywhere, anytime." This historic statement attracted national attention and helped Coolidge gain the Presidency of the United States. It also effectively broke the back of the striking workers, who were fired from their jobs. As a consequence, the AFL was forced to revoke all its police charters, and police unionism in the United States quickly withered on the vine.

The Period of Transition

Until the 1960s, organized police employee activity remained essentially a local issue. Police officers in most departments formed employee associations and fraternal groups which were concerned mostly with working unobtrusively within the confines of the department to promote the interests of their members. These efforts were largely unorganized and spontaneous. There were no formal procedures for collective bargaining or grievance resolution. Public officials and police administrators tolerated such activities, but were not threatened by them.

Due to low pay, public criticism, grievances over personnel policies, and so on, police employee associations became increasingly aggressive and militant in their tactics. At the same time, the entire field of public sector labor relations was gaining the interest of lawyers, legislators, and labor leaders, who recognized the need to develop more formal machinery to deal with the needs of public employees. State and federal legislation and several executive orders were enacted to expand the rights of public employees, and a vast legal apparatus has emerged to make the entire public employee labor relations process a complex management problem.

Present Conditions

Today there are a proliferation of police unions and employee associations, including a number that are affiliated with national labor unions. A recent study disclosed that national police organizations represent nearly 300,000 police employees, and that local police associations include several thousand more.[7]

Despite the increased enrollments of national police unions and employee associations, local police groups continue to dominate the police labor movement. Many police officers are wary of national labor organizations that may not have the best interests of local members at heart. In addition, police officers are reluctant to pay high dues to support an administrative staff thousands of miles away when there is no guarantee that they will receive an equitable return on their investment. Finally, local police employee associations have become increasingly successful in imitating the tactics employed by national labor unions in their negotiations with public managers, so they have not found a need to become affiliated with national labor unions. Nevertheless, a number of national police organizations continue to be quite active in promoting the collective interests of police officers. Of these, the Fraternal Order of Police (FOP) is the oldest and one of the largest. A recent survey indicated the FOP had more than 1,000 lodges around the nation with a combined membership of 150,000.[8] The FOP constitution specifically prohibits strikes or concerted job actions by police employees, thus limiting the scope of its influence in the police labor movement.

In terms of total membership, the International Conference of Police Associations (ICPA), probably represents more police personnel than any other association. As its name implies, the ICPA is an umbrella organization and its members are state and local police associations, rather than individuals. The ICPA claims to represent more than 175 police employee organizations, representing some 200,000 police officers.[9] Consequently, the ICPA does not participate directly in the police labor relations movement.

In addition, there are several national police unions that are directly affiliated with national labor unions. These are the American Federation of State, County, and Municipal Employees (AFSCME); the National Union of Police Officers (NUPO), which is affiliated with the Service Employees International Union (SEIU); and the International Brotherhood of Police Officers (IBPO), which is affiliated with the National Association of Government Employees (NAGE).[10]

Strikes, Job Actions, and Work Stoppages

Strikes by police employees are on the increase, representing a serious threat to the welfare and safety of the public. They also seriously impair the ability of the police executive to provide efficient and effective police services. Strikes by police employees, however, are not new. According to Bopp, the first recorded police strike occurred in Ithaca, New York, in 1889, thirty years before the national scandal of the Boston police strike.[11]

In the forty years following the Boston police strike, strikes by police employees were relatively rare. Since 1960, however, the threat of a police strike has become more imminent, and nearly every major U.S. city has suffered the effects of a police strike or some similar type of work stoppage or job action by its police employees. The job actions and work stoppages assume a variety of forms.

The **blue flu** has stricken a number of cities with disastrous consequences. Scores of police officers have reported sick and unable for duty, leaving the city protected only by a skeleton force. As a result, routine calls have gone unanswered, emergency calls have become backlogged, and police operations have virtually halted.

Police officers in some cities have engaged in **work slowdowns** as a means of pressuring city officials into accepting their demands. Under work slowdowns, police officers write no parking or traffic tickets, make only those arrests which are absolutely required to protect the public safety, and allow calls to backlog by responding slower than normally. A variation of the work slowdown is the **work speedup**, in which all minor traffic and parking infractions are ticketed in order to clog up the machinery of the system.

The public has a right to expect uninterrupted essential public services and to feel secure that they will be protected from criminal acts by an alert and aggressive police force. When police services are withdrawn intentionally as a result of a labor dispute, citizens began to lose confidence in the integrity of the men and women who have taken an oath to uphold the public interest. Rarely do citizens appreciate the conditions that prompted the police to take such actions. They are more concerned over their own safety and security. Even though such actions may gain increased salaries and fringe benefits to which the police are entitled, they may lose much of what they have strived to achieve in the eyes of the public in terms of respect, confidence, and support.

While most states now permit strikes by some classes of public employees, none yet permit organized work stoppages by police officers.[12] Moreover, organized work stoppages by police are specifically prohibited in most states and local jurisdictions. Even when upheld by the courts, such laws have had little success in deterring strikes and similar job actions by the police. It is likely that strikes and work stoppages will continue to plague the police administrator and other city officials.

The Role of the Police Executive

The police executive is in an extremely awkward and troublesome position insofar as strikes and work stoppages by the police are concerned. In many cases, he may sympathize with the plight of his subordinates, and may support their efforts to gain increased work benefits. At the same time, his ultimate responsibility is to the public. He cannot tolerate any threat to the public safety; he must know the proper action to take when such threats become manifest.

First, the police executive should ensure that policies, rules, and regulations are adopted that specify, in clear and unequivocal language, those types of organized activities that will not be tolerated. Such policies should be reasonable, and should allow for sufficient flexibility in their application, but their intent should be clear. Members should know in advance exactly what they are and are not permitted to do with respect to organized activities. Penalties for violating such rules and policies should be clearly stated.

Second, appropriate contingency plans that will provide for the continuation of necessary emergency services in the event of a strike or similar work stoppage should be developed in advance. Formal arrangements should be made with neighboring police agencies, sheriff's departments, and state police or highway patrol departments to supplement the remaining police force. Such plans should set forth which services may be curtailed during a work stoppage and those services that will receive the highest priority. Supervisory and administrative personnel will probably be required to respond to calls for service and perform other routine patrol duties. Extended work schedules should be planned to make optimum use of remaining personnel.

Third, the police executive should be prepared to deal promptly and firmly with those who participate in work stoppages once normal operations have resumed. This is a difficult task, and one that engenders considerable disagreement. Police administrators who have not come face to face with such situations generally favor strict enforcement of existing rules and regulations, recommending that full disciplinary measures be initiated against employees who intentionally violate rules. Such a course of action was taken in Battle Creek, Michigan, where over half the police officers were dismissed for engaging in a concerted work stoppage.[13]

At the other extreme, some police authorities suggest that no disciplinary action be taken because large scale dismissals, suspensions, or other punishments could seriously affect the operational performance of the agency, and that selective enforcement against only a few principal employees would be discriminatory and unfair.

The third course of action open to the police executive is to impose limited disciplinary action against all those involved in the work stoppage, giving full consideration to the factors that gave rise to the stoppage in the first place. This is a difficult decision for the police executive; it requires good judgement and discretion. Over-reaction on his part can be just as bad as too little reaction, and neither will be in the best interests of the agency.

Police Employee Rights

Even though most of the efforts of police labor unions and employee associations have been directed toward gaining higher wages and better fringe benefits for their members, such groups have also been active in promoting expanded employee rights in the police organization.[14] At one time police officers suffered from a kind of second class citizenship; when they became police employees they automatically forfeited some of their rights. Police labor groups have attempted to change this state of affairs and gain more liberal management policies.

The Right to Organize   Most states and local jurisdictions now formally recognize the rights of police employees to organize for the purpose of engaging in collective bargaining and for the resolution of grievances. Unfortunately, some labor unions have attempted to create "union shops" in police departments—requiring all members of certain ranks to be members of the union. Police officers have the same right not to join unions as they have to join them. Membership in a labor union should not be a condition of employment.

Freedom of Speech

Traditionally, police officers have been prohibited from making certain types of public statements concerning their work or their departments, usually for good reason. The work of the police department could be jeopardized, or the rights of citizens threatened, if police officers were allowed to make irresponsible public statements. It has long been believed that police officers give up a portion of their civil liberties when they accept the role of the police officer. In 1892, a decision by the Supreme Court (*McAuliff v. Mayor of New Bedford*) supported this principle and held that "the petitioner may have a constitutional right to talk politics, but he has no constitutional right to be a policeman."[15]

The situation is changing. Many police departments are being forced, through court decisions, to relax their policies on public statements by their employees. While police departments may continue to make rules regarding public statements, such rules must not be arbitrary or capricious, but must be reasonably designed to protect the interests of the agency. In general, public statements by police employees can be prohibited if they are (1) defamatory; (2) obscene; (3) unlawful (under the doctrine of clear and present danger); or (4) likely to disrupt the efficiency and morale of the department.[16]

If police departments fail to ease restrictions on the right of their employees to make public statements, it is likely that they will be forced to do so by the courts. A number of courts have taken the position that police employees should, within reasonable limitations, enjoy the same constitutional freedoms as other citizens. One such case involved a police officer in Washington, D.C. who had been dismissed after making public statements in support of a "sick out" by police officers. A lower court ruling supported the department's action in dismissing the officer, but a U.S. Court of Appeals disagreed and reversed the lower court's decision, stating that "policemen, like teachers and lawyers, are not relegated to a watered-down version of constitutional rights . . . ," and that only matters of the greatest urgency "can justify restrictions on the freedom of speech by police officers." (*Tygrett v. Washington*, 1974).[17]

Political Activities   Civil service rules and the merit system were designed to protect public employees from illegitimate political pressures. In many cases, however, these same rules have worked to the disadvantage of public employees by denying them the right to engage in many political activities considered essential to the democratic process.

Prohibitions on the political activities of public employees stem generally from the Hatch Act (Public Law 352), enacted in 1939. The Hatch Act, which originally applied to only federal employees, has been extended to include all state and local employees who are employed by agencies financed, in whole or in part, by federal funds. In addition, several states have enacted versions of the Hatch Act to regulate the political activity of state and local public employees. Because public employees represent a significant portion of the total voting population of the United States, and due to the changing public attitude toward the rights and responsibilities of public employees, there has developed a tendency toward easing state and local restrictions on political activities of public employees.[18]

Prohibited Activities   Under the Hatch Act and similar state laws, a public employees is generally prohibited—

1. from using official authority or influence for the purpose of interfering with or affecting the result of an election, or directly or indirectly coercing or attempting to coerce another employee to lend or contribute anything of value for political purposes;
2. from taking an active part in a political campaign, which includes, but is not limited to, the following activities:
   a. being a candidate for, or campaigning for, a partisan elective office;
   b. participating in the management of a political campaign for a partisan elective office;
   c. soliciting votes for or against a partisan candidate for an elective public office;
   d. directly or indirectly soliciting contributions for a partisan political purpose;
   e. endorsing or opposing a partisan candidate for an elective political office in a political advertisement, campaign literature, or similar material;
   f. serving as an officer of a political party or club; a member of a national, state, or local committee of a political party; or be a candidate for such position.[19]

Permitted Activities   Public employees are generally free to—

1. register and vote in any election;
2. join a partisan party or political organization;
3. express a private opinion on a political subject;
4. attend a political party, rally, convention, fund-raising function, or other political gathering;
5. sign a political nominating petition as an individual;
6. contribute funds to a political party or purpose;
7. actively take part in non-partisan elections, such as local school boards and the like.[20]

It appears that the trend is definitely toward expanding the rights of public employees to participate in political activities, and that state and local statutes will reflect this trend. At the same time, public officials must be vigilant to detect and curtail any political activities by public employees that threaten the integrity of the public service. While state and federal laws should protect the interests of public employees, they must also protect the interests of governing jurisdictions.

Bill of Rights for Police   Police unions and employee associations have also attempted to expand the rights of police employees faced with departmental investigations. In the past, police officers accused of a crime or a violation of departmental regulations were denied many of the rights enjoyed by private citizens accused of crimes. Police officers became frustrated and embittered when they were denied the same rights they were required to extend to criminals. Police trial boards and investigative proceedings sometimes resembled kangaroo courts in which the accused was not given a chance to prove his innocence. Police labor organizations have taken actions to have these rights restored to police employees.

A case in point is the struggle of the Buffalo, New York, Policemen's Benevolent Association (PBA), the bargaining unit for the rank and file members of the Buffalo Police Department, to include a police bill of rights clause in its labor contract with the city. After much debate and discussion, the PBA convinced the city to incorporate into its contract ten conditions designed to protect police officers from possible unfair and arbitrary methods in the investigation and disposition of internal investigations.

The police bill of rights included in the Buffalo contract provided for ten conditions that must be met when internal investigations into allegations of police misconduct are conducted. These included, for example, the time, place, length and manner of interrogation of police officers suspected of wrongdoing. Officials were also required to warn police officers of their constitutional right to remain silent, and to have an attorney present during investigations involving criminal charges.[21]

Police officers suspected of wrongdoing should be extended every reasonable opportunity to prove their innocence. Internal investigations into allegations of police misconduct should be thorough and impartial, intended neither to prove an officer's guilt nor innocence. Police officers should, wherever possible, be given advice and assistance from within the department, and should fully understand their rights and responsibilities during an investigation into their conduct. At the same time, police administrators should do everything in their power to prevent police labor organizations from encroaching upon their rights and responsibilities to detect, investigate, and properly dispose of instances of police misconduct. The right of the public to high standards of police conduct transcends the rights of police employees when the two are in conflict.

Grievance Procedures

In the advanced and turbulent state of police labor relations, employee grievances are likely to occur.[22] Grievances usually result when there are differences in opinion concerning the interpretation or application of provisions in the labor contract. Or, if there is no labor contract involved, employee grievances may result from conflicts regarding management practices or personnel policies, such as those involving personnel transfers, assignments, or promotions.

When grievances do occur, the police executive should act quickly and positively to resolve them. To accomplish this, the police agency should include in its policy manual or personnel rules a formal grievance procedure. The process of grievance resolution usually involves several steps.[23]

1. The aggrieved employee may orally present his complaint to his immediate supervisor. In all cases, the chain of command should be preserved. Employees should not violate the chain of command unless they are convinced that their immediate supervisor is unable or unwilling to take proper action. The grievance should be presented within a reasonable length of time from its occurrence. An employee who wishes to file a grievance should not wait until several days after the incident to contact his supervisor. In addition, the supervisor should be required to take some action on the grievance within a reasonable period of time after it has been presented to him. Whenever possible, the supervisor should try to resolve the grievance.

2. If the grievance is not satisfactorily resolved by the employee's immediate supervisor, it should be forwarded in writing to the next in command. The employee's immediate supervisor should endorse the grievance, explaining why he could not or would not take action himself. He, in turn, should recommend a course of action to his own supervisor.

3. If the grievance is not satisfactorily resolved at the second stage, it should be forwarded to the chief of police, or to his designated representative.[24] The comments of the employee's supervisor and the next in command should be included, explaining why the grievance could not be resolved at an earlier stage.

4. If the chief of police cannot or will not resolve the grievance to the satisfaction of the employee, the matter should be referred to the chief administrative officer of the jurisdiction, who may wish to appoint a committee to review the grievance and report its recommendations. Some cities have standing committees comprised of department heads or other city officials who are designated to review grievances and report their recommendations to the city manager. After a full review of the matter, the city manager should make a decision.

5. If the city manager fails to take action on the grievance to the satisfaction of the employee, it may be referred to the Civil Service Commission, if there is one in the jurisdiction. In some cases, a police and fire committee of the city council or board of trustees may be designated as the final authority for resolving grievances. These boards may choose to hold formal hearings at which parties to the dispute will be allowed to explain their positions and to offer evidence on their own behalf. The action of these boards will normally be final. Most police employee grievances, however, are resolved before reaching the final stages of the process.

Grievance resolution procedures should not be too formalistic, but should provide for a maximum degree of flexibility throughout the entire proceedings. Police administrators should be given, and should use, every opportunity to resolve grievances before they go beyond their control. The earlier in the process that a grievance can be resolved, the more satisfactory it will be for all concerned. Supervisors and middle managers should be encouraged to resolve grievances at their own levels when possible. Too often, lower level supervisors shirk their responsibility and merely forward grievances to avoid making decisions. This should not be encouraged.

> Research indicates that a major problem with the grievance system lies in the lower and middle management levels of police agencies. In many cases these managers fail to make a decision on the issue in question and, instead, simply refer it to the next higher level. Police executives should establish firmly the amount of responsibility that lower level managers should assume on grievances.[25]

Collective Bargaining

A few years ago the term collective bargaining had little meaning in the police service. Collective bargaining today is a commonly accepted practice in the police service, and it is an element of police personnel administration that occupies an increasing share of the police executive's time. Many states now guarantee the right of police employees, through their designated representatives, to enter into collective bargaining agreements with their employers. Collective bargaining is now an inevitable consequence of the advanced state of the police labor relations process.[26]

Bopp defines collective bargaining as the process whereby "representatives of a political entity meet in conference with representatives of their employees to agree upon the terms under which labor will be performed. . . ."[27]

Newland offers a more encompassing definition:

> Collective bargaining is a relationship between management and the representative of organized employees. It is characterized by periodic negotiations resulting in written agreement on a basic rule system to govern the work relationship and

organized arrangements for resolving disagreements and problems as they arise day-to-day.[28]

Collective bargaining, then, is a process whereby representatives of management and labor meet to decide upon the terms and conditions of employment and to agree upon methods of resolving differences that may arise out the interpretation and application of those agreements. In some cases, these agreements are formalized by means of a labor contract.

Collective Bargaining Principles

Police administrators are likely to become involved in the collective bargaining process, and they should be familiar with the basic principles that are fundamental to that process. These include the following:[29]

The management team.   Collective bargaining requires a team approach, and should be a joint responsibility of those in management positions in the local unit of government. The chief of police or his designated representative should be included on the management team when police employees are involved in collective bargaining. In addition, the police executive should seek the advice and assistance of his principal subordinates in resolving issues arising out of the collective bargaining process.

The bargaining unit.   Clear procedures should be established for determining the bargaining unit and defining its constituency. Normally, public employee bargaining units should be organized according to a "community of interests," in which employees with similar jobs, skills, duties, and working conditions are represented by the same bargaining unit. Clerk typists, for example, would not normally be represented in the same bargaining unit as police officers.[30] At the same time, management should seek to avoid a proliferation of bargaining units that may produce endless and needless competition for wages and increases in benefits. To determine lawful representation of employee interests, bargaining units should be selected by written ballot, preferably supervised by some outside party.

Know the issues.   One of the chief weaknesses of public management in the past has been its failure to be adequately prepared to enter into the collective bargaining process. To be prepared, the public official must be armed with sufficient information about the issues to be discussed during collective bargaining sessions. Management should be aware of trends in the public employee–labor relations process. It should be able to anticipate union demands and to offer appropriate responses and counter offers. Public managers should have time and accurate data available to support their positions on all issues likely to be raised. Finally, they should have available to them accurate information on the costs and financial impact on the city of the union's wage demands.[31]

Negotiate in good faith. Negotiations with public employee labor representatives must be conducted in a spirit of good faith, even though the parties represent opposing interests. The negotiations should involve a two-way exchange of views and information. Union and management should be prepared to share in a give-and-take process. Negotiators must be firm but fair in their approach to the issues under consideration. Proposals and counter offers must be carefully deliberated, and both sides should endeavor to fully understand the position of the other.

Management rights. Public managers should strongly oppose any attempt to bargain away their management prerogatives. Generally, the collective bargaining process should be confined to "terms and conditions of employment," and should not extend to managerial rights. In some cities, police labor unions have successfully negotiated such matters as one-man versus two-man patrol units, shift assignments, and staffing levels. These are clearly management decisions which should not be negotiated. Public managers who fail to exclude such issues from the bargaining table will find themselves faced with mounting problems in attempting to ensure efficient and effective delivery of police services.[32] The labor contract or bargaining agreement should include a clause that stipulates that all conditions and terms not specifically covered in the agreement are the exclusive province of management.

Impasse resolution. In some cases, it may not be possible for management and labor representatives to satisfactorily resolve all issues through the collective bargaining process. In such instances, provisions should be made for resolving the impasse. Impasse resolution may take one of several forms.

1. *Mediation.* Through mediation, a neutral third party is brought in to offer advice and assistance to both labor and management concerning the disputed issues. Neither party, however, is required to accept the advice of the mediator.
2. *Factfinding.* An independent source may be requested to gather information on the unresolved issues and to present recommendations to the parties involved in the dispute. The parties are free to either accept or reject the findings of the factfinder.
3. *Arbitration.* Final arbitration may be required to resolve the disputed issues. By local ordinance or state law, arbitration may be either voluntary or compulsory. **Compulsory arbitration** requires the party to accept the decision of the arbitrator. Under **voluntary arbitration**, neither side is required to accept the aribtrator's ruling. **Binding arbitration** is usually not desirable from the standpoint of management, since local governments may be forced to accede to demands with which they cannot live.

The Labor Contract

The labor contract is simply a written instrument that formally records the issues agreed upon during the collective bargaining process. The labor contract will usually contain the following provisions.[33]

1. *Fixed Provisions* are relatively stable and remain unchanged throughout the life of the contract. Fixed provisions usually include such items as wages, fringe benefits, dues, and union security.
2. *Contingent Provisions* are those that govern the conduct of labor and management in coping with conditions that arise during the effective period of the contract. Such matters as layoff procedures, promotional policies, discipline, and employee discharges would be included in this category.
3. *Dispute Resolution Provisions* are those that govern the conduct of labor and management in their attempts to resolve difficulties that arise in the application or interpretation of the contract. Formal grievance procedures would be included in this category.

Collective Bargaining and the Merit Principle

A basic conflict has arisen as a result of the activities of police labor unions and employee associations concerning the collective bargaining process and the merit system. In the past, police executives, city managers, civil service commissions, and other public officials wielded great power in the selection, promotion, and assignment of police personnel. That power has been somewhat eroded as a result of the encroachment of labor leaders into those areas traditionally considered to be the exclusive concerns of management. Indeed, the police personnel management system has evolved from one of "unilateralism," in which labor leaders and police employee representa-service commissions was nearly absolute, to one of "bilateralism," in which labor leaders and police employee representatives have gained increased influence in personnel management decisions.[34]

Some authorities believe that the collective bargaining process is incompatible with the merit principle, since the former encroaches upon the sovereignty of the latter.[35] Labor unions disagree, however, and argue that collective bargaining and the merit system can coexist without serious difficulties.[36] In any event, there does appear to be a definite conflict between the aims of union leaders engaged in the collective bargaining process and the basic purposes of merit systems.

The merit system reserves, to certain public officials, the right to make decisions regarding the selection, assignment, promotion, and dismissal of public employees. Labor leaders claim that although such processes are theoretically based upon the principle of merit, what constitutes "merit" cannot be clearly defined. As a result, many deserving employees ("deserving" in the sense of long years of service to the agency) are often bypassed in order to provide for younger members with less seniority. As a result, labor officials are often critical of what they characterize as unfair, arbitrary, and capricious personnel policies and procedures.

If the police labor movement is to be conducted in a manner conducive to harmonious relations between management and labor, these problems must be resolved. Police labor unions have a right and a duty to protect the interests of the constituents and to guard against unfair labor practices. Public officials, on the other hand, have an even greater responsibility to the public to ensure that the police operate in a professional manner and with optimum effectiveness. Perhaps if each side understands the rights and the responsibilities of the other, the police labor movement will gain the respect and support it seeks.

Collective bargaining has been found to be of great value in advancing the interests of public employees who have gained higher wages, fringe benefits, and more favorable conditions of work. Public managers, on the other hand, have found collective bargaining to be at best a nuisance and at worst a threat to their managerial capabilities. If nothing else, collective bargaining has created a conflict between labor and management in the public sector. A more important question, however, remains unanswered: is public employee collective bargaining in the public interest? Authorities disagree on this issue.

Most police officers who have participated in the collective bargaining process or who have enjoyed the benefits of collective bargaining point with satisfaction to the advantages they have gained over the last two decades. Public managers, on the other hand, regard collective bargaining by public employee groups as detrimental to the provision of public services and a threat to local government prerogatives. It cannot be denied that collective bargaining has created many problems for local government officials.

Police strikes, work stoppages, and related job actions by police officers (all too often the end result of the collective bargaining process) obviously do not benefit the public. Often, more problems are created than are solved. Indeed, a strike or work stoppage by the police is nothing more than a negative reflection of the inability of labor and management to reach an equitable solution to their common problems. No one really wins when the collective bargaining process ends in a work stoppage by public employees.

Even though they may gain concessions from city officials through pressure tactics, police officers probably lose more than they realize. Strikes and work stoppages cannot help but erode the public's confidence in the police as upholders of the law and public servants. Militant actions by police officers are basically inconsistent with the oath that police officers take to protect and serve the public interest. As Gammage and Sachs have pointed out, the seemingly callous and self-serving actions of police officers engaged in pressure tactics to win concessions from public officials are "certainly not within any 'ideal of service,' and [are] an arrogant expression of contempt for [the] public interest." [37]

Do the interests of police officers or other public employees come before those of the community? Obviously, they cannot. But the actions of police labor unions and employee associations seem to reject this notion. Unyielding demands for higher salaries and fringe benefits, even in the face of shrinking municipal revenues and higher costs of government through inflation, place an unacceptable and unnecessary burden on public officials who are obliged to provide the highest level of public service possible for the lowest reasonable cost. Attempts to gain control over management prerogatives are an unnecessary interference with the authority and responsibility of police administrators and public officials. Finally, self-serving actions on the part of police officers violate the public service ethic to which professional police officers must subscribe if they are to be true to their oaths of office.

Public needs, after all, must come before those of public servants. This is a point that is often ignored by police labor leaders who are determined to gain for their constituents certain concessions from management at all costs. This point is emphasized by Wellington and Winter who argue that public employee collective bargaining, as it has been conducted in the past, is detrimental to sound government operations and a threat to the welfare of the public.

> We believe that in the cities, counties, and states there are other claimants with needs at least as pressing as those of public employees. Such claimants can never have the power that unions will win if we mindlessly impart into the public sector all the collective bargaining practices developed in the private sector. Make no mistake about it, government is *not* 'just another industry.'[38]

Collective Bargaining and Police Productivity

Improving productivity in the police service has gained increased importance in the minds of public officials in recent years and is likely to emerge as an important issue in the collective bargaining process in the years to come. (Refer to Chapter 10 for a discussion of police productivity.) Many public officials have arrived at the conclusion that police employee representatives must enter into the collective bargaining process with something to offer in return for their demands. Public managers are no longer content to participate in the collective bargaining process without some positive indication that the public will derive some benefit from the agreement reached during the negotiating session.

One of the first cities on record to formally negotiate police productivity in the collective bargaining process was Orange, California. Police representatives agreed to accept salary increases contingent upon reductions in selected types of crimes. If the police failed to reduce those crimes during the period the contract was in effect, they would receive no salary increase. On the other hand, the more the reduction in crime, the more would be the salary increase. During the time the contract was in effect, the city experienced a significant decrease in crime in the categories specified in the agreement, and police officers received proportionate pay increases. The experiment contained a number of provisions to ensure that decreases in crime were not merely the result of negligent reporting or manipulation by the police department.

A number of prominent organizations and institutions, including the Police Foundation, the Urban Institute, the National Commission on Productivity, the International City Management Association, and the International Association of Chiefs of Police have studied individually and collectively, the issue of increased police productivity. In addition, a number of federally and privately financed studies have been initiated to determine in what ways productivity in the police service may be improved.

Police labor leaders, however, are somewhat skeptical of attempts by management to implement productivity improvement programs, particularly when these efforts neglect the human needs of the individual police officer, or when they ignore what union officials believe to be basic safety considerations. For this reason, police labor leaders are opposed to one-man police units, even though they may represent increased police productivity.

The responsible police executive should recgonize that increased productivity in the police service cannot be achieved without the endorsement and support of rank and file police officers and their labor representatives. Unilateral attempts by police managers to implement police productivity improvement programs will doubtlessly be met with resistance by police labor leaders and will have little chance of success. For this reason, administrators should attempt to work with labor leaders to develop programs designed to improve police productivity.

Police employee representatives are not necessarily opposed to the concept of improved police productivity, and will often lend their support to such efforts, providing they do not neglect the basic needs and welfare of police officers. As one national police union leader remarked, ". . . once police management gets rid of the idea that we are anti-productivity, they are going to be very surprised when they propose some of the issues as to how readily acceptable they are to the guys in the union."[39]

Improving police productivity should be on the minds of every police executive and city administrator. Improved police productivity is one means of increasing the level of police service with little or no increase in expenditure of limited resources. Police productivity programs should be developed and implemented through the collective efforts of police management and labor leaders.[40]

Police Labor Relations: The Public Management Perspective

Public managers have become increasingly concerned over the issue of public employee labor relations, and for good reason. Undoubtedly, a breakdown in the labor relations process will create many problems for the public administrator, and will jeopardize his ability to effectively control the delivery of essential public services. For this reason, public officials have carefully studied the subject of public employee labor relations. Among the organizations that have devoted attention to the subject is the International City Management Association (ICMA).

On January 10, 1975, the ICMA Executive Board, after careful study and deliberation of the issues involved, declared its position on public sector labor relations. In so doing, the Board recognized—

- that the regulation of local government labor relations is an issue of growing concern to public managers;
- that the costs of local government are increasing dramatically due to escalating demands made by public employee unions;
- that the tendency of public employee unions to engage in work stoppages, strikes, and other forms of job actions are a growing threat to the operational effectiveness of local units of government.

The statement on labor relations in the public sector included the following declarations.[41]

1. *Federal Regulation.* Public employee labor relations is essentially a local problem and federal regulation would be constitutionally inappropriate and contrary to the best interests of local units of government.

2. *Unit Determination.* Supervisory and management personnel should be excluded from bargaining units for the purpose of collective negotiations.

3. *Scope of Negotiations.* Collective bargaining agreements should be limited to (a) wages, hours, and conditions of employment; and (b) grievance resolution procedures.

4. *Impasse Resolution.* Laws governing local government labor relations should (a) prohibit strikes by local government employees that either directly or indirectly affect the public health, safety, or welfare; (b) permit the use of fact-finding, mediation, and voluntary arbitration; and (c) prohibit compulsory binding arbitration.

5. *Employer Rights.* Laws governing local government labor relations should reserve to management the exclusive right to (a) direct, supervise, hire, promote, suspend, discipline, transfer, assign, schedule, and retain employees; (b) relieve employees from duties due to lack of work, insufficient funds, or other conditions which dictate that such actions are necessary in the public interest; (c) determine what services are to be rendered, which operations are to be performed, what technology is to be utilized, and overall budgetary considerations; (d) maintain and improve the efficiency and effectiveness of governmental operations; and (e) take whatever other steps are necessary to serve the best interests of the public.

6. *Employee Rights.* Public employees should have the right to (a) form, join, and participate in employee organizations; and (b) refrain from joining or participating in employee organizations if they should so choose.

The ICMA Executive Board's policy statement is clear and to the point. Undoubtedly, it will be opposed by the leaders of most public employee unions and representatives, since it denies to them many of the privileges they have been seeking for so long. Nevertheless, it does provide a basic guideline for public managers to follow when negotiating with public employee groups.

Labor Relations and the Police Executive

If there was a time when the police executive could afford to leave the worries of police employee labor relations to someone else, that time is no more. Even though the police executive may not become directly involved in the collective bargaining process, he must nevertheless assume an active role in police labor relations. The success or failure of police labor relations is a direct reflection of the police executive. He cannot delegate this responsibility to someone else, nor can he afford to simply pass the buck to higher authorities. He must be directly involved.

The increased militancy of police labor unions and their growing tendency to engage in work stoppages requires that the police executive fully understand his role, duties, and responsibilities in the labor relations process. The police executive must become actively involved in police labor relations and should take positive steps to avoid conflicts that may escalate into serious labor problems. There are several things he can do.

First, he can do everything in his power to ensure that grievances are settled quickly and equitably. He should take steps to avoid conflict situations that may result in formal grievance procedures. This can be achieved by creating within the police organization an environment that is conducive, at all ranks and levels, to harmonious relations between management, supervision, and employees. He can act quickly to resolve minor conflicts before they escalate into larger ones. He can also ensure that supervisors and middle managers have the authority to resolve disputes within their respective spheres of authority and command.

Second, he can establish open lines of communication between his office and police labor representatives. He must recognize his role, as the executive officer of the department, to represent the best interests of the department, the jurisdiction, and the community. At the same time, he should recognize the rights and duties of the police labor union or employee association to preserve and protect the interests of its constituency. The police executive must endeavor to deal firmly but fairly with police labor leaders, respecting their positions, and demanding respect for his obligations.[42]

Third, the police executive must become knowledgeable in the art and process of police labor relations and collective bargaining. He should know and understand the extent and limits of his rights and responsibilities in the labor relations process. He should keep abreast of current developments and latest court decisions regarding public sector labor relations.[43] He should have available to him, and not hesitate to consult, legal counsel concerning his duties and responsibilities in the labor relations process.[44]

Fourth, the police executive should recognize the fact that labor relations has become, and will probably remain, an important element in police personnel management. As such, it is his responsiblity to ensure that police labor relations is conducted with a minimum of conflict and disharmony.

The police executive can do much to ease the strain engendered by the labor relations process if he will recognize the legitimate interests of police labor unions and employee representatives and attempt to facilitate, rather than obstruct, their efforts. He can do this without jeopardizing his own position as the chief executive of the police organization if he approaches the task with a positive point of view.[45]

The respective goals and objectives of labor and management in the police service need not be incompatible or irreconcilable, even though they may at times be in conflict. What is needed is an underlying spirit, on the part of both labor and management, of compromise, cooperation, and conciliation. If this can be achieved, the police labor relations process can be conducted with a minimum of friction and discord. As Miewald has observed, both labor and management must be prepared to give and take.

> Of course it will be hard for employee organizations to give up their new-found powers; of course it will be hard for managers to relinquish the prerogatives of high office. Unless the attempt is made, however, the public has little to look forward to but an endless series of crises. Unless a new direction is begun, perhaps future historians will note that, while international politics entered the 'Era of Negotiations,' domestic politics fell prey to those archaic power confrontations that once characterized foreign affairs.[46]

Summary

Police labor relations is rapidly becoming a focal point in the police personnel management field. The police executive has a key role to play in ensuring that police labor relations are conducted with a minimum of friction and disruption to the efficient delivery of police services. Many of the efforts of police labor leaders are legitimate attempts to improve the working conditions of the police employee. On the other hand, some of the tactics employed by organized police employee groups create additional burdens for the police administrator. Continual efforts by police executives and police labor leaders must be made to ensure that police labor relations does not affect the interests of the police organization, the jurisdiction, and the community in negative ways.

Discussion Questions

1. *What is the fastest growing labor union in the AFL-CIO?*

2. *Name several reasons for the rapid growth and development of public employee labor unions.*

3. *About how many police employees are represented by national police unions and organizations?*

4. *Describe (a) the blue flu; (b) a work slowdown; and (c) a work speedup.*

5. *Describe the steps a police executive should take when dealing with a work stoppage.*

6. *Under what conditions can public statements by police employees be prohibited?*

7. *List several political activities in which police officers may and may not participate.*

8. *What is the purpose of the Policeman's Bill of Rights, as implemented in Buffalo, New York?*

9. *Define collective bargaining.*

10. *Define a bargaining unit.*

11. *Describe the basic conflict between the merit principle and collective bargaining.*

12. *List several reasons why collective bargaining by the police either is or is not in the public interest.*

13. *How can police productivity be included in the collective bargaining process?*

14. *According to the ICMA Executive Board, what should be the rights of public managers in the labor relations process?*

15. *What are several things the police executive can do to avoid serious labor problems in the police organization?*

References

1. For an excellent case study of the evolution of a police employee organization from a fraternal group to a highly organized and militant labor organization, see Rory Judd Albert, *A Time for Reform: A Case Study of the Interaction Between the Commissioner of the Boston Police Department and the Boston Police Patrolmen's Association*, Technical Report No. 12-75 (Cambridge, Mass.: Operations Research Center, Massachusetts Institute of Technology, 1975); see also, Stephen C. Halpern, *Police-Association and Department Leaders: The Politics of Co-Optation* (Lexington, Mass.: Lexington Books, D.C. Health Company, 1974).

2. Robert Booth Fowler, "Normative Aspects of Public Employee Strikes," *Public Personnel Management*, 3 (March–April, 1974), p. 129.

3. In New York City alone, nearly two million man-hours were lost due to work stoppages by public employees between 1964 and 1968 (Fowler, op. cit., p. 130); in 1971, strikes by public employees at the federal, state, and local level accounted for more than 900,000 idle man days (U.S. Bureau of Labor Statistics,

Handbook of Labor Statistics, 1973 (Washington, D.C.: U.S. Government Printing Office, 1973), p. 363.

4. Generally, police employee associations are local groups with only loose affiliations with national police organizations, whereas police unions are usually affiliated with a recognized national labor union.

5. For a detailed discussion of the police labor movement, see William J. Bopp, *Police Personnel Administration* (Boston: Holbrook Press, 1974), pp. 320–39; Allen Z. Gammage and Stanley L. Sachs, *Police Unions* (Springfield, Ill.: Charles C. Thomas, 1972).

6. Hervey A. Juris and Peter Feuille, "Employee Organizations," in O. Glenn Stahl and Richard A. Staufenberger, eds., *Police Personnel Administration* (Washington, D.C. Police Foundation, 1974), p. 204.

7. Hervey A. Juris and Peter Feuille, *The Impact of Police Unions—Summary Report* (Washington, D.C., National Institute of Law Enforcement and Criminal Justice, Law Enforcement Assistance Administration, U.S. Department of Justice, 1973), p. v.

8. John A. Grimes, "The Police, the Union, and the Productivity Imperative," in Joan L. Wolfle and John F. Heaphy, eds., *Readings on Productivity in Policing* (Washington, D.C.: Police Foundation, 1975), p. 56.

9. Juris and Feuille in Stahl and Staufenberger, *The Impact of Police Unions*, pp. 210–11.

10. Ibid., pp. 210–12; Grimes, in *Readings in Productivity*, pp. 56–63.

11. Bopp, *Police Personnel Admin.*, p. 362.

12. For a review of state legislation governing public employee strikes, see Antone Aboud and Grace Sterrett Aboud, *The Right to Strike in Public Employment* (Ithaca, New York: School of Industrial and Labor Relations, Cornell University, 1974).

13. National Advisory Commission on Criminal Justice Standards and Goals, *Police* (Washington, D.C.: U.S. Government Printing Office, 1973), p. 467. (Subsequently referred to as National Goals Commission.)

14. For an analysis of public employee rights generally, see Daniel H. Rosenbloom, "Citizenship Rights and Civil Service: An Old Issue in A New Phase," *Public Personnel Review*, 31 (July, 1970), pp. 180–84.

15. National Goals Commission, *Police*, p. 451.

16. Ibid.

17. Prentice-Hall, *Public Personnel Administration Bulletin*, 2 (December 17, 1974), pp. 5–6.

18. Phillip L. Martin, "The Hatch Act: The Current Movement for Reform," *Public Personnel Management*, 3 (May-June, 1974), pp. 180–84.

19. "The Hatch Act: Civil Servants Watching for a Break," *Congressional Quarterly Weekly Report*, 30 (September 9, 1972), p. 2297.

20. Ibid.

21. Halpern, *Police-Association and Dept. Leaders*, pp. 53–54.

22. *Labor Relations for Supervisors: A Manual For Day to Day Living with Employee Organizations* (Washington, D.C.: Labor Management Relations Service, pp. 15–17.

23. Bopp, *Police Personnel Admin.*, pp. 388–89.

24. It should be noted that the administrative levels through which a grievance may proceed will vary with the size and complexity of the organization. The present typology assumes a small- to medium-size police department with few administrative levels.

25. National Goals Commission, *Police*, p. 450.

26. Thirty-seven states, including the District of Columbia, either require or permit public employees to engage in collective bargaining or to meet and confer with public employers. Carlton Lewis, "State Regulation of Local Government Labor Relations," *Public Management*, 57 (February, 1975), p. 7.

27. Bopp, *Police Personnel Admin.*, p. 340.

28. Chester A. Newland, "Collective Bargaining Concepts: Applications in Governments," *Public Administration Review*, 28 (March-April, 1968), p. 118.

29. *What You Need to Know About Labor Relations: Guidelines for Elected and Appointed Officials* (Washington, D.C.: Labor Management Relations Service, 1975).

30. For a detailed discussion of the bargaining unit, see Thomas P. Gilroy and Anthony C. Russo, "Bargaining Unit Issues: Problems, Criteria and Tactics," in Arvid Anderson and Hugh D. Jascourt, eds., *Trends in Public Sector Labor Relations: An Information and Reference Guide for the Future* (Chicago: International Personnel Management Association and Public Employment Relations Research Institute, 1975), pp. 67–68.

31. In Covington, Kentucky, city officials have employed a computer to assist them in obtaining timely information for collective bargaining purposes. See Paul H. Royster and Harry J. Patterson, "The Computer as a Col-

lective Bargaining Tool," *Public Management*, 57 (April, 1975), pp. 13-14.

32. Gene Huntley, "Diminishing Reality of Management Rights," *Public Personnel Management*, 5 (May-June 1976), pp. 174-80; Edward A. Martin, "Critical Issues in Police and Fire Negotiations: A City Manager's Viewpoint," *Arizona Review*, 25 (April 1976), pp. 2-8.

33. James A. Craft, "Notes on the Administration of Collective Bargaining Agreements," *Personnel Administration/Public Personnel Review*, 1 (July-August 1972), p. 31.

34. David T. Stanley, "What Are Unions Doing to Merit Systems?" *Public Personnel Review*, 31 (April 1960), p. 109.

35. Muriel M. Morse, "Shall We Bargain Away the Merit System?" in Kenneth O. Warner, ed., *Developments in Public Employee Relations: Legislative, Judicial, Administrative* (Chicago: Public Personnel Association, 1965), p. 160.

36. Jerry Wurf, "Merit: A Union View," *Public Administration Review*, 5 (September-October 1974), pp. 431-34.

37. Gammage and Sachs, *Police Unions*, p. 121.

38. Harry H. Wellington and Ralph K. Winter, Jr., *The Unions and the Cities* (Washington, D.C.: The Brookings Institution, 1971), p. 202; for a similar view, see Emerson P. Schmidt, *Union Power and the Public Interest* (Los Angeles: Nash Publishing Corp., 1973).

39. Grimes, in *Readings on Productivity in Policing*, p. 73.

40. The concept of productivity bargaining in the public sector has not yet received widespread acceptance. A survey of 772 cities and counties published in 1975 by the National Commission on Productivity and Work Quality revealed that only five percent of the units of government responding either had tried or planned to implement productivity bargaining. See: John M. Capozzola, "Productivity Bargaining: Problems and Prospects," *National Civic Review*, 65 (April, 1976), p. 176.

41. "ICMA Statement on Management/Labor Relations," *Public Management*, 57 (March 1975), pp. 18-19.

42. This problem is discussed at length in Halpern, *Police-Assoc. and Dept. Leaders*, and in Albert, *A Time for Reform*.

43. A number of national organizations, including the International Association of Chiefs of Police and the International City Management Association, conduct periodic seminars and short courses on police labor relations.

44. See Anderson and Jascourt, *Trends in Public Sector Labor Relations*.

45. The role of the police executive in the labor relations process is discussed in Robert M. Igleburger and John E. Angell, "Dealing with Police Unions," *The Police Chief*, 38 (May, 1971), pp. 50-55; Mollie H. Bowers, "Police Administrators and the Labor Relations Process," *The Police Chief*, 42 (January 1975), pp. 52-59.

46. Robert D. Miewald, "Conflict and Harmony in the Public Service," *Public Personnel Management*, 3 (November-December 1974), p. 535.

Police Records
and Communications

General Observations . . .

Accurate, timely, and complete information about police activities is essential in a modern police department. A police administrator needs up-to-date, accurate information concerning the activities of his department if he is to be able to determine manpower requirements, allocate resources, evaluate past performance, and plan future operations. Police communication and records systems vary in complexity and sophistication depending upon the size of the police agency, its resources, and its particular needs. There is no standard for communication and records systems that can be applied universally to all police departments. A good communication and records system is one that meets the needs of the particular agency in an efficient manner.

Many police communication and records systems are characterized by duplication of effort, outmoded and inefficient procedures, and the collection of incomplete and inaccurate information. In such police departments, the ability of the police administrator to manage and control the affairs of the department is severely restricted.

This chapter focuses on those elements of police communication and records systems common to most police agencies, although they may differ substantially in many respects from one police department to the next. When evaluating any police communication and records system, the questions that must be asked are: (1) does it provide the police administrator and his staff with the information necessary to properly manage and control police operations; and (2) does the system operate with a minimum of duplication and a maximum of efficiency. As long as these questions can be answered satisfactorily, the exact nature of the communication and records system is irrelevant.

Police Communications

Speedy and accurate communication of information is vital to a police organization. Information is the life blood of a police department. Without effective communications, a police department operates in a vacuum, unable to provide those services necessary for the protection of the public interest. Police departments must communicate with many people and institutions by a variety of methods. A police communications system must facilitate the exchange of information between a police agency and the public; other public agencies (i.e., fire departments, schools, traffic departments, etc.); other law enforcement agencies; and other agencies within the criminal justice system (i.e., prosecutors, courts, probation, parole, etc.). In addition, a police department must maintain effective communications between its headquarters personnel and its operating units in the field.

Police Communication Systems

Police communication systems and the equipment employed by those systems have changed dramatically in the last decade. Communications technology has advanced rapidly in recent years, particularly during the age of space exploration. The manufacturers and distributors of communications equipment and systems have placed greater emphasis on the needs of police departments in recent marketing campaigns. In addition, the large sums of money available from state and federal funding sources have made it possible for police departments throughout the country to upgrade their communications systems considerably.

As a cumulative result of these several influences, the state of police communication equipment and systems has reached a high level of sophistication. It can be expected to continue to grow and develop in similar fashion during the next several years. Nevertheless, many problems remain unresolved, particularly in smaller agencies, whose resources to implement sophisticated communication systems remain somewhat limited.

Receiving Information

A police department receives most of the information upon which it bases its activities from the public. In a sense, the public is the eyes and ears of a police department. Crime victims, witnesses, complainants, and informants supply the police with various types of information needed to perform their mission. It is important that the police receive this information promptly. Delays in the receipt of information often result in crimes not being solved and criminals not being apprehended. In addition, the safety of citizens is placed in further jeopardy if communications between the police and the public are impeded.

The telephone is the most common means of communication between the police and the public. A large police department may receive several thousand telephone calls each day. Many of these telephone calls concern emergencies, requiring immediate police response. In addition, a police department receives many telephone calls from people requesting information and other calls which are non-emergency in nature.

Except in the very smallest police departments, it is a good practice to separate emergency from non-emergency telephone calls. This may be accomplished by publishing separate numbers in the telephone directory for emergency and non-emergency calls, thus reducing the delay that may otherwise result when a police switchboard becomes overloaded with non-emergency calls.

A number of jurisdictions throughout the country have converted to a universal emergency telephone number, such as the 911 system. Through the 911 emergency telephone number, all emergency services (police, fire, and ambulance) can be summoned by dialing a simple, easy-to-remember telephone number. In some cities, it is possible to dial the 911 emergency number from a pay phone booth without depositing a coin, further ensuring that emergency calls will not be unnecessarily delayed.

The installation of universal 911 systems is impeded in some localities due to the proliferation of telephone service companies. By 1973, however, there were 185 emergency 911 telephone systems in operation in the country.[1] This number is expected to increase during the next several years.

Summoning emergency assistance can be made even more efficient through the development of the Automatic Number Identifier (ANI) system, which can automatically indicate to the emergency switchboard operator the telephone number and location of a person dialing.[2]

Dispatching   Once information requiring a police response has been received at the police headquarters, it must be relayed promptly to a police unit in the field. This is usually accomplished through

Courtesy of IBM

The police dispatcher is a key link in the information chain, connecting the police officer with the public.

the police dispatcher or complaint officer. In larger cities, information receipt and dispatching duties are normally separated. An information officer or complaint officer will receive the original call, prepare a dispatch card showing the nature of the call and location, and pass the information along to the dispatcher. The police dispatcher will determine what type of response is required, will dispatch the appropriate units to the location, and will record further information on the complaint card, such as the time dispatched, the time of arrival by the patrol unit, the time the call is completed, and the disposition of the complaint. In smaller departments, complaint receipt and dispatching duties are often combined. In some cases, a records clerk may assume responsibility for both functions. Police departments which cannot afford their own full-time dispatching service may contract with another police or sheriff's department to provide either full-time or part-time dispatching.

The police dispatcher in the small department is often required to perform a number of duties not directly related to dispatching. These duties sometimes interfere with the prompt receipt of information and dispatching police units to required locations. Typically, a police dispatcher in a small police agency may be required to serve as public information officer and receptionist, accept bail money and fees for animals and bicycle licenses, answer telephone calls for other municipal departments after business hours, maintain a variety of logs and records, assist in booking prisoners, be responsible for persons in custody, and so on. Such extraneous duties often interfere with the dispatcher's principal duty of maintaining an information and communication link between the police officer in the field and the public.

To the extent possible, the dispatcher should not be required to perform clerical and bookkeeping functions which may interfere with his primary responsibility. In addition, the dispatch area should be located and constructed in a manner that will reduce outside noises and distractions. It is often desirable to place the police dispatcher in close proximity to the records section in order that he may have access to police records which may be needed by patrol units in the field.

Computer-Aided Dispatching

A number of large cities are now employing computers to increase the speed and efficiency of the dispatching function. One such system is employed in the Dallas, Texas Police Department. Telephone clerks located in a room adjacent to the dispatch center receive the initial telephone call and gather all pertinent information concerning the nature of the call, the location, and the name of the person making the call. This information is then entered into a computer via a visual display console equipped with a typewriter keyboard. The computer then automatically creates a service call record with a distinct service number.

The consoles used by the telephone operators flash a "questionnaire" format on the display screen, thus enabling the operator to enter necessary information in the blank spaces. In the case of emergency calls, the telephone clerk may transmit partial information to the dispatcher, enabling him to dispatch a patrol unit to the location while additional information is being obtained.

Courtesy of IBM

Visual display terminals connected to computerized files have revolutionized the police information system.

Almost instantly, the type of incident, complainant's name, and location are printed on the visual display device before the dispatcher, along with the units available for service within the district in which the incident is located. Calls for service are automatically routed by the computer to the dispatcher responsible for the district in which the incident is located.

Once a patrol unit has been dispatched to the location, the number of the patrol unit assigned, the time of arrival, the time the call is cleared, and the disposition of the call are entered into the memory file of the computer by the dispatcher. This information is later compiled by the computer and can be used to construct comprehensive reports of police activities.

Recording Devices   Police departments use a variety of methods of recording complaints, calls for service, and the communications between patrol units and the police dispatcher. Many departments use radio logs to show what messages are transmitted between the police dispatcher and police units in the field. These radio logs, however, are time-consuming and often do not serve the purpose for which they were intended.

Multi-track logging and recording devices can be installed, at nominal cost, to record not only radio transmissions but telephone communications also. Such devices can be used to compile a semi-permanent record of all radio and telephone messages received and made by the police dispatcher and complaint officer. They can also be used to show the exact date and time that a message was received or dispatched.

Such devices can be used to protect the department from unfounded allegations that a police dispatcher or complaint officer was rude, or that a police unit failed to respond promptly to a call for service. They can also be useful to the police administrator when periodically reviewing the message receipt and dispatching function to ensure that police services are being provided promptly and efficiently.

Portable Radios   One of the problems facing many modern police departments in the past has been that officers are often confined to their patrol units simply because they had no means of communicating with police headquarters once away from the police radio in the car. As a result, officers are often reluctant to leave their units to inspect possible insecure premises, or to visit with people along their beats. Portable radios allow officers to retain constant communications with police headquarters even while away from patrol units. Portable radios may be either self-contained units worn by the officers on their belts, or may be mounted within the police unit as an integral component of the mobile radio system. Unit-mounted radios have a distinct disadvantage, however. If an officer damages or loses the radio while away from the police unit, he is left without radio communications. It is therefore advisable to equip officers with self-contained portable radios that are independent of the mobile radio unit in the patrol vehicle.

Beeper Devices   It may not always be possible or practical for investigators and administrative personnel to carry portable radios with them when they are away from their vehicles. Nevertheless, they must remain in close contact with headquarters personnel. In such cases, they may carry paging devices that transmit tone-encoded electronic signals when activated by someone in police headquarters. These devices are used by businessmen and volunteer firemen as well, and allow them to remain in communication with their central offices.

Communications with Other Police Jurisdictions

Police departments and patrol units frequently need to communicate with neighboring jurisdictions regarding matters of mutual interest. This is particularly common when a patrol unit is engaged in a high-speed chase of a vehicle entering another city. It is common for police jurisdictions to have access to radio frequencies used by other police agencies.

A number of states have also developed statewide emergency communication systems whereby any number of police agencies or patrol units in various parts of the state can communicate directly with other agencies or police vehicles. Two examples of such systems are the Illinois State Police Emergency Network (ISPERN) and the California Law Enforcement Mutual Aid Radio System (CLEMARS). Such systems permit patrol units from two or more police agencies to conduct emergency tactical operations in a more efficient manner without disrupting regular radio frequencies.

The Police Records System

A police department cannot function effectively without an efficient police records system. Police records are needed for the following purposes:

1. to determine the nature and extent of crime and traffic problems;
2. to determine the need for additional personnel and financial resources;
3. to properly allocate available resources proportionate to actual service requirements;
4. to evaluate past performance;
5. to plan future manpower requirements, goals, objectives, and operational strategies;
6. to document police activities.

Some police administrators complain that they and their departments have become bogged down in a quagmire of paperwork that prevents them from accomplishing their real goals and purposes. To the contrary, however, a police department cannot function effectively without accurate records.

Police records systems differ greatly in complexity, extent, nature, accuracy of the information contained, and the amount of effort required to operate them. The information needs and resources of a large metropolitan police department are obviously different than those of a small rural agency. Therefore, no single type of records system can be designed to meet the needs of all police departments. Records systems must be tailored to meet the requirements of the particular agency.

Most police records systems, however, share one feature: they are frequently in need of improvement and updating. The information needs of a police department evolve slowly but surely over time, just as do the resources, needs, programs, and duties of the department. Changes in state law, new procedures, and the availability of modern time-saving equipment, such as microfilm systems and computers, all have an impact on the changing nature of a police records system.

Unfortunately, some police records systems fail to keep up with the changing times. Manual methods continue to be employed despite their obvious deficiencies and the availability of modern computer systems. Many police records systems are poorly organized and improperly managed. Information that should be maintained is not, while useless information that serves no purpose is recorded diligently and filed away. Duplication of effort created by decentralization of files and inefficient reporting systems are also common in many police records systems.

A number of factors should be considered when designing, installing, or upgrading a police records system.

1. The records system should meet the needs of the police agency. The records system should provide no less, and generally no more, information than the department requires. While manual records-retrieval systems are usually adequate for the small police agency, they are generally inadequate for a larger department.

2. The records system should be flexible and capable of future expansion and development. As a police department grows and assumes new responsibilities, its information needs will undoubtedly grow proportionately. The records system should be capable of growing with the agency. Too often, a police records system must be re-

designed periodically to adjust to the developing needs of the department. A carefully and logically designed records system should meet the needs of a police agency for several years.

3. The police records system should be centralized to minimize duplication of effort and to maximize efficiency. There should be no need to search through several different files in numerous offices, divisions, or bureaus to locate a record on a single person or incident. While auxiliary files may be maintained in separate offices within the police agency, all official records, reports, and documents should be centrally located in the records bureau.

4. The records-keeping operation is a clerical function and should be performed by well qualified civilian personnel. Sworn officers should not be relegated to clerical duties unless they are physically incapacitated and unable to perform field duties. The police records system should be under the direction of a trained professional records clerk who can ensure that all necessary records functions are performed in a competent and efficient manner.

5. The records system should be designed and maintained to support the line operations of the police department. Information contained in the records system should be readily accessible to line personnel. Procedures for obtaining records and reports should be simple so as not to obstruct the free flow of information within the department. At the same time, procedures should be developed to safeguard against the loss or destruction of police records through negligence and mistreatment.

Incident Reporting   A police records system should provide complete and accurate information on all police activities. This is usually accomplished through the preparation of a **police incident record (PIR)**. The police incident record is normally prepared by the police dispatcher at the time a call for service is received. In addition, it may be prepared each time an officer initiates some type of activity, such as issuing a traffic citation.

The location of the incident, along with the complainant's name, address, and telephone number are shown on the police incident record. Also shown are the date and time that the call is received, along with the time the call is dispatched, the time the officer arrives at the scene, and the time the call is completed. This information can be used later to determine response time and the amount of time required to complete certain types of service calls.

The police incident record should also reflect the nature of the incident, the officer(s) assigned to the call, and the disposition. When formal offense, arrest, or traffic reports are initiated, the case number of the report should be shown on the police incident record. If no formal report is required, the police incident record should provide sufficient information regarding the action taken by the officers, along with the final disposition. Completed police incident records should be checked for accuracy by the shift supervisor and then forwarded to the records bureau for processing.

The police incident record can provide the basis for the collection of detailed information on police activities with either manual or automated information systems. With auto-

Courtesy of IBM

Computers such as this have replaced many of the file cabinets and rotary files which once were used in police record rooms.

mated data processing, the information on the police incident record may be coded, keypunched on computer cards and stored on a disk or magnetic tape for retrieval and analysis, or it may be entered directly into a computerized information system through "on-line" terminals that allow computerized files to be continually updated and queried.

Smaller police departments without computers may manually tabulate the data contained on the police incident record through the use of tally sheets by which the time, location, nature, and time required to complete the calls are recorded. This information may be aggregated by day of the week, location, shift, or individual officer to construct a profile of how, why, where, and when police resources are being expended. This information can be of great value to the police administrator in determining manpower needs and in developing resource allocation strategies.

Building Case Files   It is important to know not only how much time was required to complete an initial investigation, but also the total amount of time expended on an incident until it is concluded. For this reason, the police records system should provide for the compilation of cumulative case file information, along with final disposition data. For example, in the case of a burglary, a patrol officer may be required to complete the initial investigation and offense report; an evidence technician may be summoned to the crime scene to collect evidence; an investigator will no doubt conduct a follow-up investigation and perhaps make an arrest in the case. All three officers may be required to appear in court one or more times before the case is finally concluded.

A carefully devised records system will provide the means whereby the amount of time expended by each officer involved in a case from its inception to its conclusion will be recorded in a single case file. In this way, a complete case record may be developed to show how much time was devoted to a particular case, by whom, and in what capacity. At the conclusion of a case, the police administrator may then have precise information concerning the manner in which police resources are being expended. This information may also be used to develop a comprehensive management information system, which will allow the police administrator to better evaluate the needs of the police agency.

Master Name Index   The master name index file provides the police agency with a central reference to all other police records maintained by the department, and is the core of a police records system. The master name index file is simply an alphabetical listing of all persons with whom the police agency comes into contact. Master name index cards should be prepared on victims of crimes (including businesses), witnesses, complainants, and persons suspected of committing crimes, as well as for persons arrested.

The master name index file usually consists of a series of 3" x 5" cards on which are typed the name, address, and telephone number of the individual, along with a brief notation as to the nature of the incident in which the person was involved and the case number. The master name index card should provide sufficient space for recording consecutive entries concerning an individual, thus providing a chronological history of police contacts with the same person. For easy reference, persons arrested should be indicated by typing the arrest or booking number in the upper right hand corner of the card.

Some police departments make the mistake of separating the master name index file into two or more files, depending upon the nature of the incident in which the person was involved. This only creates duplication of effort when files are being searched for a record on an individual. Such a practice should be avoided.

It is often useful to attach colored metal or plastic tabs to the master name index cards to identify missing or wanted persons, individuals suspected of committing crimes, or persons for whom warrants have been issued. These facts should be noted on the face of the card and should be updated as the status of a person changes.

Modus Operandi File   Police departments typically operate under the assumption that criminals, like most humans, are creatures of habit, and that peculiarities in personal traits are often reflected in the crimes they commit. This is the basis for the modus operandi (MO) file. The term, *modus operandi*, means method of operation.

The police MO file serves two important purposes. First, it permits the grouping of all crimes of a similar nature, thus allowing police planners and investigators to detect crime trends and patterns. Second, it provides the investigator with a useful tool with which he may link several crimes that may have been committed by the same person or persons. This information may lead to the eventual apprehension of the person(s) responsible and successful prosecution.

Police MO files may range from highly sophisticated to very simple, depending upon the resources and needs of the police agency. The availability of a computer allows the police agency to store, catalog, analyze, and retrieve large amounts of data concerning criminal activity, with a minimum expenditure of time and effort.

The most simple MO file consists of a listing of all offenses according to the basic offense category (i.e., homicide, rape, robbery, aggravated assault, etc.). As the MO file is expanded, it may be possible to add subclassifications, according to the type of weapon used, the type of premises upon which the crime occurred, the time of occurrence, the type of property stolen, the nature of the injuries sustained by the victim, and so on. For example, burglaries could be divided into commercial, residential, and manufacturing. Thefts could be categorized by the value and type of property stolen, such as cash, appliances, jewelry, furs, and so on. Crimes related to sex could be classified according to the age of the victim or the particular method of operation of the offender, such as voyeurism, exhibitionism, and so forth.

Stolen Property File   The stolen property file is an investigative tool that assists the police investigator in the identification and recovery of lost and stolen property. The stolen property file usually consists of two sections, one for numbered property and another for unnumbered property.[3]

In the numbered section are placed index cards describing the article and filed according to the identification number of the article. Since identification numbers on different types of property will vary considerably, it is useful to file the cards according to the last two or three digits of the identification number. In the event two or more articles have identification numbers with the same last two or three digits, the cards may be filed according to the type of property in alphabetical order.

For property with no known identification number, index cards should be filed in alphabetical order according to the type of property (i.e., billfold, men's; radio; snow skis; television; wristwatch, women's; etc.).

The stolen property file card should contain a complete description of the stolen property along with the identification number, if known, as well as the name of the victim, the date reported stolen, and the case file number. Stolen property file cards should be prepared on each identifiable item of stolen property reported to the police, if possible. In some cases, it may only be possible to prepare cards on major items of stolen property due to the time involved in the process. Reports of found or recovered property should be continually checked against the stolen property file. Once an item entered in the stolen property file has been recovered, the card may be removed from the file and destroyed.

Warrant Files Warrants of arrest may be issued for persons suspected of committing crimes or who fail to appear in court for trial or sentencing. Warrants may be issued for both criminal offenses (including felonies and misdemeanors) and for traffic and parking offenses. It is the duty of the police department to serve outstanding warrants, although this function may be performed by the county sheriff's department in some jurisdictions.

All warrants received by the police department should be recorded in the police records system. In larger police agencies, warrants may be entered into an automated information system, while smaller departments may record manually all outstanding warrants in a log designed for this purpose. The warrant log should state the name of the person for whom the warrant was issued, the offense, the date of the warrant, the case file or warrant number, the amount of bail set, if any, and the location and status of the warrant. If warrants are delivered to another police jurisdiction to effect service, this fact should also be noted in the warrant register. Similarly, warrants received from other police agencies should also be entered in the warrant log.

An index card should be prepared for each warrant received. The cards may be prepared by the court clerk at the time a warrant is issued, or they may be prepared by the police records clerk upon the receipt of a warrant. Warrant cards should also be prepared for warrants received from other police agencies for service.

Warrant cards should be kept in a file, arranged in alphabetical order according to the last name of the person for whom the warrant was issued. A complete listing of all outstanding warrants should be available to the police dispatcher in the event that police units in the field inquire about many out-standing warrants for persons they have stopped or have under surveillance.

A copy of the warrant card should be placed in the master name index file. Metal or plastic tabs may be attached to these cards to indicate that a warrant is outstanding for a person. These tabs may be color coded to reflect the type of warrant.

It is often useful to prepare warrant envelopes in which warrants may be enclosed to protect them from being soiled or damaged. These warrant envelopes may be prepared with space provided for showing information concerning attempts made to serve the warrant. With this information, it can be easily determined what attempts have been made to serve a warrant so that duplication of effort can be avoided.

Evidence Control   The receipt, care, and custody of evidence is a vital concern to any law enforcement agency. In view of the stringent legal constraints being placed upon the handling of evidence by police, it is important that adequate safeguards be incorporated into evidence handling procedures.

Proper evidence procedures are lacking in many police departments. Evidence storage spaces become rapidly inade-quate to accommodate the large volume of articles seized as evidence. Proper safeguards are not always established to ensure against evidence contamination. Often, procedures are not developed to ensure that evidence no longer needed is disposed of in a timely manner.

All police departments should have an evidence control system which includes the following elements:

1. a uniform system of receipt and control;
2. adequate storage facilities to ensure maximum security;
3. a systematic process for the disposition of items of evi-dence that no longer need to be retained.

All items of evidence seized by a police agency should be immediately marked and tagged and assigned an evidence control number by the officer seizing the evidence. An evidence report should be prepared to describe completely the item(s) of evidence seized, the case number, and the location stored. A copy of the evidence record should be attached to the offense or arrest report, and the original evidence record should be kept with the evidence in a safe place.

Departments that do not have a full-time evidence officer should provide temporary lockers in which individual items of evidence may be stored for a short time. The temporary evidence locker should be securely locked and the key placed in a secure lock box to which only the evidence officer has access. Each day the evidence officer should check the log box, remove the keys therein, and unlock all temporary lockers holding evidence.

All items of evidence should then be placed in permanent storage receptacles within a maximum security evidence storage room to which only the evidence officer has access. The evidence officer should enter all items of evidence in an evidence register showing the description of the evidence, the control number, and the date and time received. Suitable provisions should be made for storing items of a perishable nature, such as blood or urine specimens.

Officers requiring evidence for court or some other purpose should prepare a form designed for the removal of evidence from the evidence locker. These forms should be forwarded to the evidence officer who should be responsible for ensuring that the evidence is delivered to the officer initiating the request. The evidence officer should retain a copy of the evidence request form for control purposes.

Evidence that is released to the court, returned to the victim or suspect, or disposed of in some other fashion should be noted on the evidence request form. The evidence request form should be returned to the evidence officer, with any remaining items of evidence and with a notation showing the disposition of any items not returned.

It should be the ultimate responsibility of the officer entering the evidence into the system to ensure that proper disposition is made of all items of evidence over which he has responsibility. As soon as cases have been closed, the officer responsible should notify the evidence officer so that proper disposition can be made of any items of evidence. The evidence officer should maintain a tickler file showing what items of evidence remain in custody and should periodically check with the individual officers responsible for entering the evidence into the system to determine whether or not the evidence is still needed.

Evidence no longer needed should be disposed of in the manner directed by existing policy. Narcotics should either be destroyed or turned over to a state or regional criminalistics laboratory for destruction. Firearms should usually be destroyed.

Other usable items of evidence should either be returned to their rightful owner or auctioned by the police department along with other articles of found property. The evidence officer should maintain a permanent record of the final disposition of all items of evidence entered into the system.

Police Reports

Police reports are used to record criminal offenses, persons arrested, traffic accidents, and other police related incidents. Police reports are an integral part of the police records system and should be designed in such a way that they provide the necessary information to determine the nature and extent of crime, traffic, and other police problems. A police department should adopt a report system that effectively meets its own needs. Several factors should be considered in this regard.

1. Careful thought should be given to the design of police reports. Too often, one police department merely copies the report format used by another agency, even though the needs of the two departments are not the same. Instead, an effort should be made to survey the report formats used by a number of police departments and combine those elements which are particularly suited to the individual agency.
2. Elaborate report formats should be avoided wherever possible. Much of the patrol officer's time will be spent completing the report. This time should be kept to a minimum by eliminating unnecessary detail. At the same time, the police report should provide for the collection of all information that is needed by the agency.
3. Standard police reports should be used whenever possible. Some police departments tend to create a different report format for every type of police incident. This is generally unnecessary and merely complicates the report preparation and processing involved. Specialized report formats should be used only when absolutely necessary.
4. Police report forms should be designed in such a way that they can be completed expeditiously by the officer in the field. Some departments have adopted report formats that consist largely of a series of checklists which enable the officer to complete the report without resorting to a great deal of narrative.
5. Officers should not be required to type their own reports. Indeed, typewritten reports are generally not necessary except in a few instances. Neatly prepared hand-printed

reports usually should suffice. When typewritten reports are required, they should be typed by clerical personnel from a draft prepared by the reporting officer. A number of police departments provide their officers with minature tape recorders that allow them to dictate their reports in the field. The reports are later transcribed by a stenographer onto a regular report form. The principal drawback of this method is that the officer initiating a report often is not able to review his report before it is processed through the system.

6. Police reports should be subject to review and audit to ensure accuracy and completeness. Reports prepared by patrol officers in the field should be reviewed by their supervisors before being processed through the system. Likewise, reports should again be checked by records personnel to ensure that all necessary information has been provided and that the information is accurate. Erroneous entries and ommissions should be brought to the attention of supervisory personnel for proper corrective action.

Uniform Crime Reporting

For more than a hundred years, police officials have recognized the need to develop a comprehensive body of information on crime trends in order to better assess the need for police services. In 1871, police officials from a number of American cities met to discuss common problems. At this meeting, the officials expressed a desire to collect and analyze statistics on crime and police incidents for the purpose of devising more effective means of allocating police resources.[4]

The desire for a nationwide body of information on crime and related police activities continued to grow, and during the 1920s, the International Association of Chiefs of Police (IACP) began to actively solicit support for a national crime reporting system to meet the needs of all law enforcement agencies. The IACP was primarily responsible for the development of such a system and in generating Congressional support for a national crime reporting program. In 1930, Congress passed legislation authorizing the Federal Bureau of Investigation to act as a national clearinghouse for the collection and dissemination of crime information. The Committee on Uniform Crime Records of the IACP continues to serve in an advisory capacity to the FBI in the Uniform Crime Report Program.

The **Uniform Crime Report (UCR) program** is largely a local effort, supported by the active participation of some 10,000 law enforcement agencies in the United States. While the system is voluntary on the part of local agencies, several states have enacted legislation establishing state UCR programs and requiring the participation of all local police and sheriff's departments. In such states, UCR data are reported directly to the state, which in turn reports to the FBI. In those states where there is no state UCR collection agency, local departments report directly to the FBI.

Usually, crime data are collected and submitted on a monthly basis from local agencies that are provided with report forms, tally sheets, and self-addressed envelopes by the FBI to facilitate the collection of necessary data. States that have a central state agency responsible for the collection of UCR data often have a computer capability which enables them to compile large amounts of data from hundreds of police agencies into a single UCR format for the entire state, as well as for individual agencies within the state.

Several conditions must be met before a state agency is allowed to participate as a state clearinghouse for UCR data.

1. The state UCR program must conform to the national UCR standards, definitions, and information requirements. States may, however, collect statistical information beyond that required by the national program.
2. The state must have a proven, effective, mandatory statewide reporting program and must have instituted acceptable quality control procedures.
3. The state agency designated to collect UCR data must have an adequate field staff to assist local law enforcement agencies in developing proper record-keeping practices and reporting procedures.
4. The state must furnish to the FBI detailed data on a regular basis on offenses in the form of duplicate returns, computer printouts, and/or magnetic tapes.
5. The state must have the proven capability, tested over a period of time, to supply all statistical data needed to conform to national UCR publication deadlines.[5]

In August of each year, the FBI publishes a comprehensive report on offenses, offenders, and other police related information for the preceding year. In addition, quarterly announcements are published to provide a summary update on crime trends. The Uniform Crime Reports published by the FBI can be used to compare crime rates, arrests, and other activities between jurisdictions, as well to project trends in criminal offenses. Among the types of data contained in the Uniform Crime Reports are the following:

1. number and type of crimes reported to the police;
2. number and percent of crimes cleared by the arrest of the offender or by other means;
3. personal characteristics, including age, race, and sex, of persons arrested;
4. final disposition of charges placed against persons arrested;
5. information about officers assaulted and killed in the line of duty;
6. information about the use of one-man cars, foot patrols, plain clothes personnel, and other methods of deploying police resources;
7. information on the number of personnel, including both sworn and civilian, employed by police agencies in various population groups and in different sections of the country.

Care should be taken in comparing UCR data between police agencies, however. The incidence of crime may fluctuate due to a number of factors that are beyond the control of the police. Among other things, crime is a product of social inequality and economic disparity. High unemployment, poor housing, inadequate educational facilities, social disorganization, and poverty are all associated with crime. These are factors over which the police have little or no control and which vary considerably from one community to the next.

In addition, the physical, geographic, and socio-economic characteristics of the community must be considered when determining the appropriate level of police resources required to police a given community. A city of 10,000 residents located in a developing metropolitan area will require more police personnel than a community of approximately the same size in a rural environment. The needs of bedroom communities will be considerably different than those of a heavily industrialized community.

Victimization Studies   Recent studies have demonstrated that crime data collected through the UCR program are often inaccurate and do not reflect the actual incidence of crime. A national survey conducted by the University of Chicago in 1967 revealed that the actual incidence of crime is several times that reflected in UCR data. For example, it was estimated that the actual number of forcible rapes committed in the United States was three and one half times greater than the number reported to the police. Aggravated assaults and thefts of $50 and more occurred at a rate approximately double that reported to the police.[6]

The inaccuracy of the crime statistics generated through the UCR program is attributable to a number of factors, including the following:

1. Crime victims often fail to report offenses to the police.
2. Police departments sometimes fail to report crimes brought to their attention.
3. Deficiencies in police reporting systems sometimes result in the loss of crime information.
4. Some police departments (principally the smaller ones) fail to keep accurate records at all or to participate in the UCR program.

There are also a number of reasons why people fail to report crimes to the police. Among these are the following:

1. the belief by the victim that there is little the police can do to solve the crime and apprehend the offender;
2. dislike and/or mistrust of the police by some community residents, particularly in minority neighborhoods;
3. fear of reprisal by the offender;
4. the exorbitant costs and time delays in prosecuting a case through the criminal court system;
5. the feeling by the victim that the crime is not important enough to worry about;
6. the attitude by many that nothing will be done to solve the crime problem even if the offender is apprehended.

To a great extent, then, the underreporting of crimes by victims is a reflection of the inability of the various elements of the criminal justice system (police, prosecutors, courts, and corrections) to do the job expected of them. Unfortunately, it also reflects the general apathy of the public toward the problems of the police and other agencies of the criminal justice system. Nevertheless, it is important that more reliable information on the nature and extent of crime be obtained. For this reason, the Law Enforcement Assistance Administration

(LEAA) initiated in 1973 a series of victimization surveys which were conducted by the U.S. Bureau of the Census. The studies are the result of a National Crime Panel, which represents a new and improved method of measuring levels of crime both nationwide and in selected large cities. The crime panel utilizes scientific sampling procedures which determine the extent to which individuals age 12 and over, households, and commercial establishments have been victimized by certain types of crimes. Also examined are the personal characteristics of the victims and, when possible, the time and place of occurrence, the injury or loss suffered, and whether or not the offense was reported to the police.

Data generated by the crime panel studies differ from those compiled through the UCR program in that they are based upon victimizations rather than criminal incidents. Since one criminal incident, as reported through the UCR program, may involve more than one victim, the victimization rates will normally be higher than crime rates established by UCR data. In addition, the crime panel victimization rates for crimes against households and commercial establishments are based, respectively, on the number of households and businesses in the survey area. Crime rate data generated through the UCR program, on the other hand, are based upon the total population.[7]

Information derived from the National Crime Panel studies has revealed the expected—that crime, as reflected in the UCR program, is substantially underreported. For example, the crime panel studies have revealed that the total number of incidents of selected crimes reported by survey respondents in the nation's five largest cities was roughly double that reported to law enforcement agencies. Among the types of crime measured, auto theft was closest in relative terms to the number of offenses reported to the police. By contrast, larcenies were found to be four times greater than previously reported.[8]

The National Crime Panel studies are part of a comprehensive, ongoing effort to improve the reliability of crime statistics. They do not necessarily detract from the value of the Uniform Crime Report system, but merely reflect the inherent weaknesses in such a system. As more reliable information on crime becomes available, police agencies will be better able to determine their needs, evaluate their operations, and readjust their enforcement strategies and priorities.[9]

Criminal Justice Information Systems

Police departments across the nation generate thousands of reports each hour. The information contained in these reports must be sorted, indexed, classified, tabulated, compiled, and stored. In addition, it must be preserved in such a way that it is available for subsequent retrieval and analysis. The volume of information generated by a single large police agency usually exceeds the capability of a manual records system. For this reason, automated data processing systems and a multitude of computer systems have been developed to meet the particular needs of law enforcement agencies. Computer systems have begun to play an increasingly important role in police operations. Indeed, computers and computer technology have even found their way into the police patrol car, serving as the police officer's "silent partner."

As police departments began developing new and improved information systems to serve their individual needs, they recognized the developing need to share and exchange information of mutual interest. Crime and criminals know no boundaries and do not respect the jurisdictional limits of police departments. It is therefore important that police agencies develop the capability to quickly and efficiently share and exchange information regarding crime and criminals.

As early as 1963, law enforcement officials in California began to make plans for developing a comprehensive automated information system to serve police departments throughout the state. At this time it was recognized that the rapid advances being made in the field of automated data processing and computer technology could easily be applied to the problems of law enforcement agencies.[10]

As a result of these early deliberations, the California Law Enforcement Telecommunications System (CLETS), the nation's earliest statewide police information system, was formed. At the time of its initiation, CLETS represented the nation's largest and most sophisticated criminal information system. Its 20,000 mile communication network allowed more than 450 law enforcement agencies in the state to retrieve information in seconds on wanted persons, lost and stolen property, firearms, and stolen vehicles directly from computerized files in Sacramento. The CLETS computers also are linked directly to the FBI's National Crime Information Center

(NCIC) files in Washington, D.C. As a result, an officer in the field can have access to information in seconds that previously might have required several days to obtain.

CLETS is one of two primary components of the California Department of Justice Consolidated Data Center. The second component is the California Criminal Justice Information System (CJIS), which is a family of information systems operating as one program. Included in the CJIS are the Wanted Persons System, the Automated Property System, the Automated Firearm System, the Stolen Vehicle System, and the Criminal History System.

Combined, CLETS and CJIS constitute the largest law enforcement information system in use in any single state. More than 15 billion characters of data are contained in the two systems, which include more than 1500 terminals located in over 500 law enforcement agencies at federal, state, regional, county, and municipal levels.

More recently, a number of states, cities, counties, and metropolitan regions have developed information systems similar to CLETS and CJIS. These include—

- Washington Area Law Enforcement System (WALES) in the Washington, D.C. Metropolitan Police Department.
- Special Police Radio Inquiry Network (SPRINT) in New York City.
- Law Enforcement Automated Data System (LEADS) in the state of Ohio.
- Law Enforcement Information Network (LEIN) in the state of Michigan.
- Computer Assisted Bay Area Law Enforcement (CABLE) operated by the San Francisco Police Department.
- Automated Law Enforcement Response Team (ALERT) operated by the Kansas City, Missouri, Police Department.

Virtually every major city in the United States and most states and metropolitan regions today have some form of automated police information system to better serve the needs of the law enforcement agency and the individual police officer on the beat. Information technology is growing rapidly and promises to continue to accelerate in future years. The result hopefully will be continued improvement in the efficiency and effectiveness of law enforcement operations.

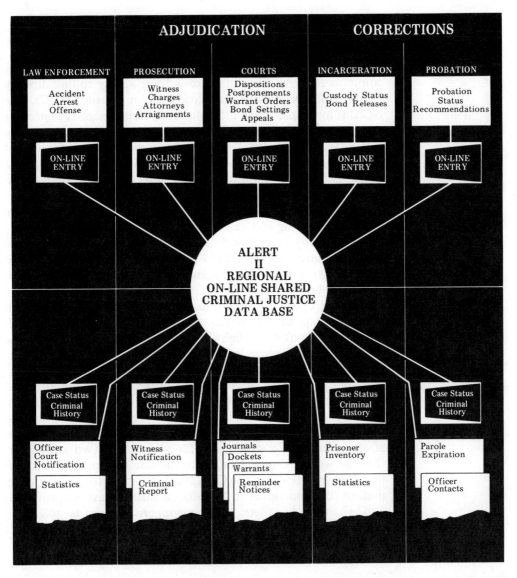

Figure 9-1. The ALERT II Information System, as Used in Kansas City, Mo., and Surrounding Agencies, Provides a Comprehensive Information Base for Police, Courts, and Corrections Agencies.

The National Crime Information Center (NCIC)

Automated law enforcement information systems share many common features. One of these is their ability to link directly to the FBI's National Crime Information Center (NCIC). The NCIC is a computerized information system designed to provide comprehensive, nationwide information on criminal activities and offenders to local, state, and federal law enforcement agencies. The system operates by means of computers, data transmission over communication lines, and telecommunication devices. The NCIC was established to improve the effectiveness of all law enforcement agencies through the more efficient handling and exchange of police information.

Originally composed of 15 law enforcement control terminals and one FBI field office terminal, the NCIC has expanded to include over 90 law enforcement control terminals, including terminals in all FBI field officers, all 50 states, the District of Columbia, and Canada. The first computer-to-computer link-up of the NCIC system occurred in April, 1967, when the California Highway Patrol became the first state agency to incorporate into the NCIC. Soon thereafter, the St. Louis Police Department entered the system.

The NCIC was originally composed of five computerized files: wanted persons, stolen vehicles, stolen license plates, stolen guns, and stolen identifiable articles. In 1968 the file was expanded to include stolen securities, snowmobiles, and aircraft. In 1969 a stolen boat file was added. Two years later, the file was further expanded to include Computerized Criminal Histories (CCH). The CCH file is designed to include information on individual offenders, arrests, court dispositions, and changes in their custody/supervision status following conviction.

Summary

This chapter has attempted to provide a broad survey of the records, communications, and information systems employed by police agencies today. Police information needs and capabilities are expanding rapidly, along with the developing technology of computers and communication devices. Police records, communications, and information systems must be continually updated to serve the growing needs of law enforcement agencies. Without a sufficient capability for change in these vital areas, the police administrator will be hard-pressed to effectively address the evolving problems facing the police.

Discussion Questions

1. *Give a brief definition of a good police records and communication system.*

2. *List several factors contributing to the rapid development of police communication systems and equipment in the last decade.*

3. *What is the Automatic Number Identifier system? Explain how it can be beneficial to law enforcement.*

4. *Describe briefly what is meant by "computer-aided dispatching."*

5. *List several purposes served by police records.*

6. *What information should be included on the master name index card?*

7. *Define modus operandi and explain its use in a police agency.*

8. *Name the basic elements of an evidence control system.*

9. *List several types of information published annually in the FBI's Uniform Crime Reports.*

10. *Give several reasons why people fail to report crimes to the police.*

11. *How does the information derived from the National Crime Panel studies differ from that collected through the Uniform Crime Report Program?*

12. *Briefly describe the purpose and function of the National Crime Information Center.*

REFERENCES

1. National Advisory Commission on Criminal Justice Standards and Goals, *Police* (Washington, D.C.: U.S. Government Printing Office, 1973), p. 549.

2. Ibid.

3. Federal Bureau of Investigation, *Manual of Police Records* (Washington, D.C.: U.S. Department of Justice), pp. 26-30.

4. Donna Brown, "The UCR Program: Development of a Standardized Audit," *The Police Chief*, 41 (December, 1974), p. 34.

5. Federal Bureau of Investigation, *Uniform Crime Reporting Handbook* (Washington, D.C.: U.S. Department of Justice, 1974), pp. 1-2.

6. President's Commission on Law Enforcement and Administration of Justice, *Task Force Report: Assessment of Crime* (Washington, D.C.: U.S. Government Printing Office, 1967).

7. *Crime in the Nation's Five Largest Cities: National Crime Panel Surveys of Chicago, Detroit, Los Angeles, New York, and Philadelphia: Advance Report* (Washington, D.C.: U.S. Department of Justice, Law Enforcement Assistance Administration, National Criminal Justice Information and Statistics Service, April, 1974).

8. Ibid., p. 1.

9. For additional information on victimization studies, see the following: Deborah Blumin, *Victims: A Study of Crime in a Boston Housing Project* (Boston: Mayor's Safe Streets Act Advisory Committee, 1973); John B. Cordrey, "Crime Rates, Victims, Offenders: A Victimization Study," *Journal of Police Science and Administration*, 3 (March, 1975), pp. 100–110; *Criminal Victimization Surveys in 13 American Cities: National Crime Panel Surveys of Boston, Buffalo, Cincinnati, Houston, Miami, Milwaukee, Minneapolis, New Orleans, Oakland, Pittsburgh, San Diego, San Francisco, and Washington, D.C.* (Washington, D.C.: U.S. Department of Justice, Law Enforcement Assistance Administration, National Criminal Justice Information and Statistics Service, June, 1975); *Crimes and Victims: A Report on the Dayton-San Jose Pilot Survey of Victimization* (Washington, D.C.: U.S. Department of Justice, Law Enforcement Assistance Administration, National Criminal Justice Information and Statistics Service, June, 1974).

10. V.A. Leonard, *The Police Records System* (Springfield, Ill.: Charles C. Thomas, 1970), p. 53.

Improving
Police Services

General
Observations . . .

The preceding chapters have examined the fundamental tasks involved in the organization, management, and administration of police operations. This chapter focuses on several related areas in which the overall quality of police services can be improved. These include planning, research, program evaluation, productivity improvement, and management by objectives. Together, they represent a comprehensive approach to the problems of (1) determining the needs of the police service; (2) utilizing existing resources in a more logical and efficient manner; and (3) enhancing citizen satisfaction in the level and quality of services provided by the police.

Planning

Systematic planning is essential to any organizational endeavor. Planning is necessary to set realistic goals for the organization, to develop objectives which lead to the accomplishment of those goals, to devise appropriate operational strategies to ensure goal attainment, to allocate available resources in the most effective and efficient manner, and to evaluate the impact of police operations and programs.

A police agency that fails to plan ahead is forced to operate from day to day, adjusting to new demands as new demands arise, but never undertaking long range projects to upgrade police service. The agency may appear effective, but it could be much more effective if it charted its course. Such an agency delivers less than maximum police service and short-changes its community.[1]

Planning is often done routinely in police organizations, but is not always given proper organizational identity and emphasis. As a result, the planning process is sometimes fragmented and uncoordinated, thus contributing little to operational effectiveness and efficiency. Careful planning should be an intergral component of police administration and management. Planning, for example, is required in the development and preparation of the annual budget; designing new police facilities or renovating old ones; hiring, training, and assigning personnel; developing work schedules; organizing and staffing; allocating resources; and many other related tasks.[2]

Responsibility for Planning

Responsibility for planning should be formally designated within the police department. In small police departments consisting of fewer than twenty-five personnel, the responsibility for planning will usually rest with the chief executive of the agency. He may designate one or two members of his command staff to assist him in certain functional planning areas, such as budget development and preparation and contingency plan formulation. In addition, each command officer should be responsible for planning within his respective organizational unit. The commander of the patrol division, for example, must plan to allocate resources according to predictable needs, by devising appropriate work schedules. The commander of the criminal investigation division, likewise, should plan the operations of his subordinates to ensure that appropriate investigative priorities are established and that investigative operations are conducted accordingly.

In police departments consisting of between twenty-five and fifty officers, planning may be formally assigned to one member of the department on either a part-time or full-time basis, depending upon the needs of the department. Departments consisting of more than fifty officers should probably have a full-time planner. Qualified noncommissioned personnel who possess a basic knowledge of law enforcement and have skills in operations research, budgeting, public administration, and evaluation, should be employed. Generally, sworn officers should not be assigned to full-time planning duties if qualified civilian personnel can be found.

The police planner may report directly to the chief of police, or may be responsible to a senior staff officer, such as the commander of the administrative services division. Regardless of his organizational location, the police planner should be regarded as a resource to the entire police operation. Planning assistance should be made available to all elements of the police organization in solving problems and developing more efficient operating methods.

Planning Functions   Planning can be used in many ways to improve the quality and level of police services. Planning may be divided into a number of functional areas, including:

1. *Management Planning.* Management planning includes such matters as policy formulation and development, budget preparation, accounting procedures, fiscal management, personnel administration, and the development of organizational goals and objectives.
2. *Operational Planning.* Operational planning relates to the day-to-day operations of the police department. Operational planning might include, for example, the development of work schedules and assignments; devising enforcement strategies and tactics; analyzing crime trends and methods of operations and developing appropriate response measures; and defining needs in terms of personnel and equipment.
3. *Procedural Planning.* Procedural planning involves the development of appropriate methods for responding to anticipated contingencies. Procedures are necessary to ensure that police operations are conducted in a uniform manner. Procedures may be developed to ensure uniformity in reporting systems and methods; dispatching procedures; arrest, interrogation, and custody practices; and so on.
4. *Tactical Planning.* Tactical planning usually relates to the development of methods of operation for dealing with certain emergency situations, such as jail breaks; natural catastrophes; civil disorders; robberies in progress; and the like.[3]

Research

Law enforcement has become a research oriented profession. For the better part of its existence, American policing has operated under a number of assumptions, with little or no research being conducted to test the validity of those assumptions. As a result, many police policies, procedures, and programs were conducted with no valid measures of their reliability. Research has been introduced into the police profession to fill this information gap.

In 1967, the President's Commission on Law Enforcement and Administration of Justice emphasized that "the greatest need is the need to know."[4] The same commission recommended a major effort to develop research, development, test, and evaluation (RDT&E) programs in policing at the local, state, and federal level, with the federal government playing a key role in stimulating such efforts through financial assistance to local police agencies. On June 19, 1968, Public Law 90-351 was signed. This law, commonly known as the Omnibus Crime Control and Safe Streets Act, effectively revolutionized American law enforcement and did much to foster an increased interest in criminal justice research. As a result, hundreds of thousands of dollars are spent each year on research into a variety of law enforcement and criminal justice related problem areas.

The act created the Law Enforcement Assistance Administration within the Department of Justice, and gave it the responsibility of administering the law enforcement assistance program. The act also created the National Institute of Law Enforcement and Criminal Justice (NILECJ), as the research arm of the Law Enforcement Assistance Administration, and called for "research and development directed toward the improvement of law enforcement and the development of new methods for the prevention and reduction of crime. . . ."[5] With the passage of the Omnibus Crime Control Act, the federal government became an active participant in a comprehensive program of research and development to improve the quality and effectiveness of law enforcement in the United States. At the same time, it effectively promoted the development of research as a necessary element of police administration and management.

Research in Police Organizations   Police authorities have discovered that the problems of law enforcement in modern society cannot be solved by traditional methods and procedures. The evolving nature of our society and the increased demands being placed upon the police require that new techniques be developed, tested, and

Courtesy of the Metropolitan Police Department, Washington, D.C.

Planning and research has become an integral function of modern law enforcement.

implemented by police agencies. Much more must be known about the causes of crime and social disorder and effective police methods for dealing with them. New laws require the police to develop more sophisticated and sensitive ways of dealing with such matters as individual privacy and human rights. As a result, research has become an integral component of police operations.

The ready availability of state and federal funds for conducting research into police related problems has stirred the imagination and enthusiasm of police administrators. Colleges, universities, research institutions, public interest groups, and police departments themselves have undertaken a variety of research projects designed to answer many of the problems that have plagued police operations for years. Research has been conducted into such diverse problem areas as the application of computer technology to police problem solving, the effects of various types of crime prevention programs and enforcement tactics on crime and citizen attitudes toward law enforcement, the nature and causes of assaults on police officers, the effectiveness of non-punitive diversionary tactics for dealing with youthful offenders; and many more. The preventive patrol experiment conducted by the Kansas City, Missouri, Police Department, with the assistance and support of the Police Foundation, is a notable example of a comprehensive research project designed to add to the growing body of knowledge about police operations.[6]

Unfortunately, the potential for applying research methods to police problems has not yet been fully realized. In many instances, police practioners are still skeptical of the value of scientific research. Social and behavioral scientists, with little or no practical knowledge of police operations, are often viewed with suspicion by members of the police community. All too often, police administrators are more concerned about increasing the size of their patrol force or acquiring new gadgetry and equipment than with devising new methods for solving problems.

If police administrators are to respond effectively to the new and complex problems confronting them in modern society, they must become more research oriented. They must recognize that old ways must be replaced by new approaches and that experimentation and innovation have a role to play in modern law enforcement. Research and development can help to provide the answers that many police practitioners have been seeking for years.

Evaluation

As police departments recognize the need to develop new operating techniques and methods, they must also recognize that some systematic method must be developed to assess the effectiveness of new programs and procedures. In the past, police departments have undertaken new programs with little regard to determining their effectiveness. In some cases, changes have been initiated merely because they were new and different. While innovation and experimentation is necessary and desirable, the impact of new programs on their intended objectives must be carefully evaluated.

Evaluation Defined

Evaluation, simply stated, is the process of determining whether a particular program or activity accomplishes the goals and objectives for which it was created. Evaluation ususally focuses on measures of effectiveness and efficiency. Effectiveness is the degree to which a program or activity achieves a desired state or condition. For example, does a high visibility police patrol program have an observable effect on the rate of residential burglaries? Or, does a program emphasizing diversionary techniques instead of punitive ones substantially reduce juvenile delinquency recidivism? These are typical questions that might be asked in the attempt to evaluate the effectiveness of a new program or procedure.

The efficiency of a program should also be determined. Efficiency may be defined as the extent to which the resources of a program are used in a manner designed to maximize cost-effectiveness. Evaluation seeks to determine whether personnel and materials are being used in a well managed and systematic manner, with a minimum of waste and duplication of effort. Efficiency is a measure of how well a program was conducted, regardless of the outcomes it produces.

A program may be quite effective, in that it accomplishes the goals and objectives it was created to attain, and still be inefficient, in that program resources are not utilized to their maximum. Similarly, an efficient program may not necessarily be an effective one. Most evaluation efforts should focus on both the efficiency of a program (i.e., process) and the effectiveness of a program (i.e., outcome).

The Need for Evaluation

Police operations consist of a series of interrelated programs and activities designed and implemented to accomplish certain established goals and objectives. In some cases, goals and objectives are neither clearly identified nor formally stated. In other instances, the manner in which programs and activities are intended to accomplish goals and objectives is not fully understood. The exact relationship between programs and activities and goals and objectives often rests on assumptions and speculation rather than on hard fact and empirical evidence. This relationship can be strengthened through systematic evaluation.

Evaluation is an aid to rational and logical decision making. In the police service, evaluation can be used for a number of purposes. As Maltz indicates, evaluation can be used to "determine whether to continue, stop, or modify a program; to determine whether local funds should be used to support the program after its experimental phase; or to decide whether the program should be promoted in other jurisdictions. Information obtained from evaluations can lead to general principles and guidelines to assist local administrators in setting their priorities for testing and implementing new programs."[7]

Law enforcement is an expensive public service. Indeed, police protection is perhaps the most expensive public service that a municipality can offer to its citizens. Members of the community have a right to expect that their tax dollars are being spent wisely, particularly in times of rising costs and shrinking incomes.

Millions of dollars are spent annually to develop new programs for the reduction and control of crime and the improvement of police services. In many instances, new programs are designed and implemented with little thought given to determining their effectiveness. In other cases, new programs are developed, tested, and then discarded before any real attempt has been made to determine whether or not they work.

As a result of this seeming confusion, waste, and inefficiency, citizens and their elected representatives have begun to question the wisdom of increased spending in these areas. The remarks of Congresswomen Florence P. Dwyer (R., N.J.) are characteristic of this growing concern:

> It is becoming increasingly clear that much of our investment in such areas as education, health, poverty, jobs, housing, urban development, transportation and the like is not returning adequate dividends in terms of results. Without for a moment lessening our commitment to provide for these pressing human needs, one of Congress' major, though oft-delayed, challenges must be to reassess our multitude of social programs, concentrate (indeed, expand) resources on programs that *work* where the needs are greatest, and reduce or eliminate the remainder. We no longer have the time nor the money to fritter away on non-essentials which won't produce the needed visible impact on problems.[8]

**The Process of
Evaluation**

Evaluation applies the principles of scientific research to the practical problems of law enforcement. While evaluation utilizes the scientific methods of research design, data collection, measurement, and analysis, it can be distinguished from pure scientific research in that it is not conducted in the sterility of the scientific laboratory. Rather, evaluation may be characterized as applied research, in that scientific methods are applied to the practical problems of the everyday world.

Because evaluation is not conducted in the carefully controlled surroundings of a scientific laboratory, more latitude is often required in the interpretation of research results. For this reason, evaluation is more imprecise than most types of purely scientific research.[9] For example, it may be difficult to determine exactly the precise effect that a particular type of crime control program has on the crime rate due to a number of extraneous variables that may also effect the rate of crime.

In order for a program to be properly evaluated, certain operating assumptions must be established. These assumptions should (1) define the parameters of the program; (2) establish the relationship between the resources required to implement the program and the intended results; (3) determine the manner in which the program will be implemented; and (4) define the nature of the program impact upon the problem being attacked. These conditions must be met if the evaluation effort is to be successful.

Evaluation Planning

Careful planning is necessary to ensure a successful program evaluation. All too often, evaluation is an afterthought, undertaken only after a program has been initiated and is well underway. By this time, it may be difficult to adequately assess the results of the program. To be entirely successful, evaluation should be planned as an integral component of any new program or activity. Indeed, many police projects established through state or federal grants require that some form of evaluation component be included in the original grant application.

Evaluation planning consists of five sequential steps, as follows:[10]

1. **Identify goals and objectives.** Every program should have clearly identified goals and objectives. These goals and objectives should be developed through the program planning stage. Each goal should describe the long-range impact of the program, while the supporting objectives should provide mea-

surable criteria by which progress toward the goal can be monitored. Program objectives should, wherever possible, be stated in quantitative terms, such as numbers, ratios, and percentages. For example:

- *Program Goal*—Improve the level of police officer training.
- *Program Objective 1*—Provide 40 hours of in-service training to all officers annually.
- *Program Objective 2*—Provide all police supervisory personnel with eighty hours of supervisory training within six months of appointment.

2. Establish relationships between goals and objectives. The relationships between program goals and objectives must be clearly established. That is, there must be some logical connection between what is to be done in a particular program and its intended goal. Using the example cited above, it is logical to assume that increasing the number of in-service training hours provided to each officer will necessarily raise the overall training level of the department.

3. Develop evaluation measures. Evaluation measures are the means whereby the effectiveness of a program can be determined. Evaluation measures should include both effectiveness and efficiency criteria.

Measures of efficiency indicate how well a program is executed in terms of expenditures of time, personnel, and resources. Examples of efficiency measures might include (a) per capita cost to train officers; (b) percent of total resources devoted to in-service training programs; and (c) the relative costs of various training methods (i.e., lecture, seminar, class participation, etc.).

Measures of effectiveness should be developed to determine the impact of a program on the problem. Effectiveness measures are results-oriented, rather than means-oriented, and are concerned with outcomes. Effectiveness measures might include (a) pre-training and post-training test scores; (b) supervisory ratings of personnel before and after a training program; and (c) student evaluations of training methods, subject matter, instructional staff, and so on.

4. Identify data needs. The fourth step in the process of evaluation planning is the identification of data requirements. The type of data needed, the sources of the data, and the means by which the data will be collected, should be known beforehand. In some cases, existing sources of data may be utilized, while in other instances new sources of data may need to be developed. This information should be known and incorporated into the initial program planning. Several contingencies should be recognized when developing data needs.

- *Data Sources.* The sources of the data that will later be needed for analysis and evaluation need to be identified during the program planning stages. If new data sources are required, appropriate data collection instruments must be developed. If existing data sources are to be used, the methods for obtaining the data should be known.
- *Data Constraints.* There may be limitations on the amount and type of data that can be collected. Some data may be readily available, while others may be more difficult to obtain. Compromises may be necessary in collecting the data necessary to conduct a successful evaluation. For example, probability sampling may be required to reduce the amount of data collected.
- *Data Collection.* Data collection techniques should be as simple as possible. Too often, elaborate data collection procedures are developed that consume an inordinate share of the resources available within the constraints of the program. Data collection may be facilitated by:

  1. designing simple data collection instruments and procedures;
  2. using existing sources of data whenever possible, providing the reliability of the data can be ensured;
  3. training persons responsible for data collection in proper data collection procedures;
  4. establishing an effective data management system that will ensure the timely and accurate collection, storage, maintenance, and processing of the data.

- *Data Validity.* Care should be taken to ensure that the data collected for analysis is reliable. Auditing procedures should be established to verify the accuracy of the data. Periodic spot checks should be implemented to continually monitor the validity and reliability of the data collected.

5. Data Analysis. The final step of evaluation planning is the determination of the methods that will be used when analyzing the collected data. The analytical techniques employed will depend upon the nature of the program being evaluated and the type of data available for analysis. The analytic techniques used to measure the effectiveness of crime control programs will undoubtedly be different than those used to evaluate an in-service training program.[11]

Improving Productivity

State and local government is the fastest growing industry in the United States today. Between 1960 and 1970, local government expenditures increased by 135 percent. Today, one out of every six workers in the United States is employed by an agency of government, and 80 percent of all government employees work at the state and local level.[12]

While the scope of local government has been increasing, the costs of maintaining government services has risen even more dramatically. State and local government budgets are growing by billions of dollars each year. The point has been reached where taxpayers have become weary of seeing an ever-increasing portion of their income being devoted to government. At the same time, citizens have become skeptical of the seeming inefficiency of government and its inability to provide an adequate level of public services. When taxes rise and the level and quality of public services decrease, there is good reason for the average citizen to complain about governmental productivity.

Historical Perspective   In order to better understand the reason for the growing concern over governmental productivity, it is helpful to examine the background of the current problem. Since the Industrial Revolution, the United States has been a world leader in industrial productivity. For years, productivity in American industry has been closely associated with the well-being of the nation. Between 1950 and 1970, for example, productivity in the United States increased by 3.1 percent, and real income rose at the same rate. In 1969 and 1970, however, productivity in this country increased by less than one percent, representing the worst performance in 16 years. This sudden reversal in the trend in productivity improvement was accompanied by rising prices, high unemployment, and a rapidly declining foreign trade surplus.

In 1970, President Nixon recognized the alarming trend in the productivity rate and appointed a National Commission on Productivity and charged it with seeking new ways in which national productivity levels could be raised in order to improve the quality of life in the United States.

During its deliberations, the commission immediately recognized that one of its most important tasks was to find ways to improve productivity in the public sector, including police services. In 1973 the commission established an Advisory Group on Productivity in Law Enforcement, composed of representatives of a broad cross-section of law enforcement groups.

At the conclusion of the advisory group's efforts, the commission published a report intended to provide guidelines for police administrators and public officials to follow in their attempts to improve productivity in the police service.[13] Since its initial report, the commission has issued a number of supplemental publications intended to expand the growing body of knowledge concerning productivity improvement in both the private and the public sector.[14] In addition, the work of the commission has stimulated a number of research projects and the interest of several public interest groups in the entire productivity issue.[15]

Law enforcement is one of the most expensive services offered by government. It is estimated that it may cost as much as $80,000 annually to place one police officer on the street twenty-four hours a day.[16] Like other governmental expenditures, the costs of maintaining police services have risen dramatically in recent years. Municipal police expenditures increased by 70 percent—from $2.1 billion to $3.5 billion—between 1967 and 1971.[17] For this reason, it has become more important than ever before for law enforcement practioners and public officials to direct their attention toward the development of new methods for improving productivity in the police service.

The Meaning of Productivity

Many authorities argue over the exact meaning of the term *productivity*. Generally, productivity may be defined as the relationship between the resources used and the results produced in any program or activity. Accordingly, *productivity improvement* may be described as the effort to obtain more and better results from the resources consumed, or

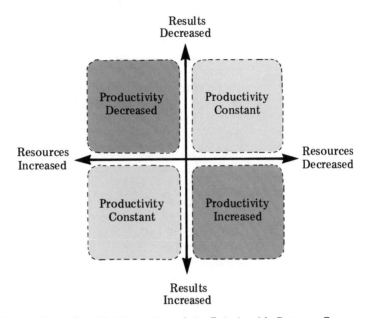

Figure 10-1. Graphic Illustration of the Relationship Between Resources and Results in the Concept of Productivity.

using fewer resources to maintain a constant level of output.[18] The relationship between results and resources in the context of productivity is illustrated in Figure 10–1.

Productivity in Law Enforcement

Due to the complex nature of law enforcement and the intangible nature of the services provided by the police, it is relatively difficult to measure police productivity. Is one police department, for example, more productive because it makes more arrests? Or, should the productivity of a police department be measured by the number of cases it clears, or the value of stolen property it recovers, or the number of felony cases it successfully prosecutes? In the past, a number of variables have been used to assess police productivity (or performance), but the validity of many of these criteria is questionable in light of our present understanding of the police mission and role. There are, however, several ways in which police productivity can be improved.[19]

First the efficiency of police operations can be improved. Police administrators and public officials are constantly seeking ways in which efficiency can be improved. Outmoded procedures and record-keeping practices, duplication of effort, and inadequate equipment and facilities all contribute to a loss of efficiency and productivity. Second, priorities must be established that will assist decision makers in allocating limited resources to those efforts that are likely to produce greater results. For example, traffic enforcement programs should be directed toward those violations, and at those times and locations, which are likely to contribute to the greatest number of traffic accidents. Issuing a large number of traffic citations is not really productive if the enforcement effort has little overall impact upon the frequency of traffic accidents. (Refer to Chapter for a discussion of selective traffic enforcement.) Third, law enforcement can become more results oriented. That is, police practitioners should examine existing practices and procedures to ensure that there is a clearly established purpose for their existence. In addition, there should be a logical relationship between goals and objectives, efforts, and results. Another term for this is *Management by Objective*. Fourth, police administrators can endeavor to get the most out of the personnel under their command. Too often, the unique skills, interests, and capabilities of individuals are lost or ignored in the semi-military, highly structured environment in which the police operate. Individuals are routinely assigned to duties, classes, or positions with little thought given to their potential ability to contribute meaningfully toward the goals and objectives of the organization. Improved training programs, individual career development plans, a more flexible organizational structure, and decentralization of the decision-making processes can lead to greater productivity by individual members of the police organization.

Implementing Productivity Improvement

Productivity improvement is not a particularly unique or revolutionary concept. Indeed, public officials and government leaders are continually seeking means to improve the quality and level of services while maintaining constant the efforts required to produce those services. In most cases, however, these efforts are not part of an overall, systematic plan of action, and are somewhat fragmented and disjointed. A formalized productivity program, however, can help to ensure that greater organizational emphasis is given to productivity improvement at all levels uniformly, and that such efforts are undertaken in a logical and systematic manner.

A formalized productivity program should include several elements.

1. Goals and objectives. A police department needs goals and objectives to establish direction and purpose and to set priorities. Goals and objectives must be the focal point of any productivity improvement program, and should provide the framework within which productivity can be measured and evaluated.

2. Analysis and evaluation. A systematic program should be developed to analyze and evaluate productivity improvement efforts. Performance targets should be established, along with a series of performance indicators, to indicate whether or not goals and objectives are being achieved. A number of cities have developed comprehensive programs by which progress toward goals and objectives can be continually monitored. One such program is shown in Figure 10-2.

3. Research and development. The productivity improvement program should be based on a philosophy that is committed to seeking new and improved ways of doing things. Police administrators should be receptive to new ideas and must be willing to experiment with untried methods, even at the risk of occasional failure.

4. Change orientation. Finally, police administrators must endeavor to develop a change oriented environment within the police organization. Only through change will new ideas and concepts emerge. Police departments, like other bureaucratic institutions, typically resist change in order to protect internal stability and establish traditions. Resistance to change must be overcome if productivity improvement is to be a viable concept within the police profession.

Measures of Police Productivity

As indicated earlier, police performance is difficult to measure, since the police typically deal with people and actions, rather than with inanimate objects. Public safety, domestic tran-

PROTECTING PEOPLE'S RIGHTS AND PROPERTY

Protection from Criminal Attack

All "Comparative Data %" show improvement trends if the figures are less than 100 except (1)% of Patrol Force assigned to Patrol Duty, (2) Clearance Rates, and (3)% of Stolen Property Recovered.

*AAL = Anticipated Activity Level

Activity Measure	MONTH		Fiscal YTD		This Mo Actual / AAL	% Met This Mo / Last Mo	This Mo / Same Mo Last Yr	This Mo / Last Mo	This YTD / Last YTD
	AAL*	Actual	AAL*	Actual					
Reported Crimes: Part I	1838	1998	18,380	19,036	109	100	103	100	123
Part II	320	429	3,200	3,481	134	102	134	102	126
Part I Crimes/1,000 Population	6.8	7.5	68	70	110	101	98	101	115
Population Served Per:									
Patrol Officer	745	881	745	745	118	112	-	112	97
Sworn Officer	512	624	512	692	122	95	-	95	99
Police Employee	344	434	344	480	126	95	-	95	100
Mean Man-Min. Spent Per:									
Crime Service Call	56	51	56	71	91	113	-	113	97
Non-Crime Service Call	88	35	88	48	40	87	-	87	98
% of Patrol Force Assigned to Patrol Duty	60	60	60	-	100	95	-	95	-
Average Response Time Per:									
Priority Call (min.)	5	5.7	5	5.7	114	102	-	102	100
Non-Priority Call (min.)	15	16.0	15	15.1	107	107	-	107	100
Clearance Rate: Murder	76	80	76	112	105	40	-	40	122
Rape	60	0	60	61	0	0	-	0	92
Robbery	22	43	22	27	195	110	-	110	104
Aggravated Assault	70	69	70	64	99	105	-	105	101
Burglaries	17	15	17	15	88	63	-	63	100
Larcenies	20	23	20	21	115	128	-	128	100
Auto Theft	50	41	50	56	82	62	-	62	97
% of Stolen Property Recovered (Excl. Autos)	8	16	8	11	200	53	-	200	110
% of Stolen Autos Recovered	88	36	88	83	41	51	-	41	94

Header spanning: PROTECTION FROM CRIMINAL ATTACK | Comparative Data %

Source: Management Improvement Department, *Public Services Evaluation Report, October, 1974*, City of St. Petersburg, Florida.

Figure 10-2. Example of the Public Services Evaluation Report System Employed by the City of St. Petersburg, Florida.

quility, and equitable justice under the law defy adequate definition and measurement, unlike other goods and services that can be counted and measured according to established economic formulas.

Nevertheless, a few crude attempts have been made to develop measures of police effectiveness and efficiency. Crime rates, conviction records, arrests, per capita expenditures on police service, and officer-to-population ratios are often used as rough indicators for determining the adequacy of the level and quality of police services.

Nearly forty years ago Ridley and Simon published a handbook in which a number of criteria were suggested for measuring the efficacy of a variety of municipal services.[20] One chapter of this text dealt with the police. Among the measures proposed were the following: (1) crime rates; (2) cases cleared by arrest; (3) the percentage of stolen goods recovered; (4) the conviction rate of persons arrested by the police; and (5) the number of traffic accidents, injuries and fatalities per inhabitants and registered motor vehicles.[21] To a great extent, these measures of police performance are still used today.

The advent of the Uniform Crime Reporting system during the 1930s stimulated interest in comparing and evaluating crime rates and trends as measures of police performance. Unfortunately, crime rates have proven to be generally unreliable, and their validity as police performance measures has been frequently challenged. An early critic suggested that since crime is largely beyond the capability of the police to control, crime rates are not reliable measures of police success or failure.[22] On the other hand, it may be perfectly realistic to use such factors as crime clearance rates and property recovery rates as indicators of police effectiveness.

Another early attempt to measure police productivity (or performance, as the terms are used here interchangeably) was developed by Parratt. Parratt proposed an objective rating technique by which a consensus of expert opinion could be derived to determine the effectiveness of particular police methods and procedures. Based upon this consensus, a municipality could be evaluated on the extent to which universal police methods were employed.[23]

In his proposal, Parratt argued that any attempt to measure police effectiveness must take into consideration standards of public approval (or disapproval) of police practices. In other words, according to Parratt, police effectiveness should be determined, at least to a degree, by the extent to which the community is satisfied with the level and quality of services provided by the police. Parratt's concept, though given little attention by the law enforcement community, was unique in several respects. First, it provided for qualitative, as well as quantitative, measures of police effectiveness. Second, it called for the development of objective criteria of police performance, as determined by expert opinion. Third, and most important, it recognized that public acceptance should be a primary consideration in determining the extent to which the police achieve their stated goals and objectives.[24]

Despite some of these early attempts to develop a systematic method for assessing police effectiveness, relatively little has been accomplished in this respect. The concept of measuring and improving police productivity has generated renewed enthusiasm and interest, but most of the problems that impeded the early efforts to develop systems of police performance measurement remain unsolved today.

Suggested Measures of Police Productivity

As police departments become more sensitive to the need to respond effectively to the public, they should begin to recognize that productivity improvement is a concept that deserves increased attention. Citizens have a right to expect that the monies appropriated for police services will be utilized efficiently, with maximum benefit to the public. Accordingly, it is incumbent upon the police to develop new criteria by which police efforts can be meaningfully evaluated. In some instances, the data required to measure police productivity may be readily available in the files of the police agency. In other cases, it may be necessary to develop new sources of data and reporting systems to generate the information needed to measure police productivity. For example, citizen surveys may be conducted to assess community attitudes toward the police and the adequacy of police services. In most cases, police departments will not have access to such data. New techniques may need to be developed for the collection and analysis of such data.

Suggested measures of police productivity are described in Figure 10-3. These are but a few examples of the many measures that might be developed to enable police administrators and public officials to better determine the adequacy of existing services. Experimentation and innovation could lead to the development of many more such measures.

Objective	Performance Measure	Data Source
Crime Prevention	1. Number of security hazards (i.e., open/unlocked doors, windows, etc.) discovered by patrol officers. 2. Percent of crimes committed through forced entry. 3. Percent of domestic quarrels and disturbances which do not require second or third response within stated period of time.	1. Officer Activity Logs 2. Offense Reports 3. Complaint Cards; Activity Summaries
Criminal Investigation	1. Percent of all criminal cases cleared through investigation and arrest. 2. Percent of all crimes cleared with given period of time after being reported to police. 3. Percent of stolen property recovered through police action.	1. Arrest and Offense Reports 2. Case Clearance Records 3. Offense Reports; Investigative Summaries
Criminal Apprehension	1. Percent of officer-initiated field checks which result in arrest and/or case clearance. 2. Percent of all Index offenses cleared through officer-initiated activity.	1. Arrest Reports; Case Clearance Records 2. Arrest and Offense Reports
Citizen Satisfaction	1. Citizen attitudes toward police and police services. 2. Percent of all emergency calls responded to within three minutes and non-emergency calls responded to within five minutes.	1. Telephone interviews; Follow-up contacts; Mailed questionnaires 2. Complaint Cards
Traffic Safety	1. Ratio of convictions for moving violations to traffic injuries and fatalities. 2. Percent of traffic arrests which result in conviction.	1. Court dispositions; Traffic Accident Reports; Enforcement Summaries 2. Court dispositions

Figure 10-3. Suggested Measures of Police Productivity and Performance.

Each police department is unique with respect to the social, economic, cultural, and political characteristics of the community it serves. Therefore, no single method of measuring police productivity can be developed and universally applied to all police agencies. Rather, the particular circumstances and problems of the individual police agency and the community it serves must be taken into consideration when developing a productivity measurement system. Similarly, efforts to improve police productivity must be tailored to meet the needs and requirements of the individual police agency. There are no standard techniques or formulas that can be applied universally to all jurisdictions.

Management by Objective

Management by Objective (MBO), or Management by Results, as it is sometimes called, is not a particularly new concept in management literature. In fact, the idea of managing by objectives has been around since the 1930s, but it has only recently gained widespread attention. For the most part, MBO has received its most enthusiastic support in private industry, and has been applied only sparingly in the public sector. One reason for this is the erroneous assumption that MBO must be tied to a profit motive. Nothing could be further from the truth.

As McConkey points out, nonprofit institutions (both public and private) have just as much reason to be concerned with maximizing results and utilziing resources wisely as do profit-making organizations.[25] The difference between the two is simply that success or failure in a private organization is usually measured in terms of profits and losses, while in the public organization results are much less tangible. Nevertheless, as the costs of government soar, and as public administrators are faced with the dual problems of shrinking financial resources and escalating service demands, they must be even more conscious of the need to maximize results.

McConkey also notes that we are rapidly becoming a service oriented society in which government may one day overshadow private industry in terms of its impact upon the economy.[26] If that is true, there is even more reason for public managers to develop management skills and techniques designed to improve the efficiency of their organizations. Management by Objectives is one such technique.

MBO Defined   The underlying rationale of MBO is simply that the better a manager understands what he hopes to accomplish (the better he knows his objectives), the greater will be his chances for success. In one sense, MBO provides the manager with a blueprint which guides him toward the objectives he has set for himself or his organization. As Brady has suggested, ". . . if one knows where he is going, he finds it easier to get there, he can get there faster, and he will know when he arrives."[27]

Management by Objectives is a technique designed to predict and influence future events through the planned, logical, and orderly control and direction of programs and activities. Management by Objectives differs from other, more traditional, styles of management in that it is proactive rather than reactive.

Management by Objective is results oriented and places emphasis on accomplishments rather than on process. It is more than a management technique; rather, it is a system of management which embraces the allied functions of planning, organizing, directing, evaluating, problem solving, and decision making. As a management system, MBO brings together separate and distinct programs and activities within an organization and combines them into a total, integrated, unified effort.

Elements of MBO   Management by Objective consists of an orderly series of elements.

1. **Assessment of activities.** The activities of the organization should be clearly defined in functional terms (i.e., patrol, criminal investigation, recordkeeping, prisoner processing, etc.). In the police organization, a number of distinct activities will be identified.

2. **Formulation of goals and objectives.** This is one of the most important elements of MBO. When formulating goals and objectives, several things must be considered—

- Goals and objectives should be complementary, integrated, and coordinated.

- Goals and objectives should be ones that cannot be too easily achieved. An organization that consistently reaches all the goals it sets for itself probably is setting its sights too low.
- Priorities should be established in the goal-setting process. Some goals should take precedence over others. Some will have to be accomplished before others can be undertaken.
- Goal setting should be a participative exercise, involving the collective thinking of representatives of all command echelons and units in the organization. Without this element of participation, the entire MBO process may not succeed.[28] (Refer to Chapter 3 for a discussion of participative management.)

3. **Development of work plan.** Once goals and objectives have been established and priorities assigned to them, it will be necessary to develop a work plan. The work plan simply describes how the goals and objectives are to be accomplished. It should establish a logical relationship between goals and objectives, efforts, and intended results. The work plan should specify the resources required and level of effort necessary to achieve the goals. In addition, it should delineate the actions required, by whom, and in what general sequence they will need to be executed. Costs, if known, should also be identified.

4. **Feedback.** Upon implementing the work plan, the system should be continually monitored to ensure that it is operating as planned. Defects in the system, if any, should be identified and corrected. This requires the development of:

- Performance indicators, guides, or measuring criteria by which progress toward stated goals and objectives can be evaluated. The performance measurement system used by the City of St. Petersburg, Florida, provides such guides. (Refer to Figure 10-2.)
- An information system which will ensure the delivery of timely, accurate, and complete information by which management can evaluate progress toward stated goals and objectives.

5. **Remedial action.** No system is fail safe. Under MBO, a continuous effort should be made to detect weaknesses

in the system and to develop alternative, more satisfactory, methods of goal accomplishment. Trial and error is a fundamental ingredient in the MBO process.

MBO Requirements

Management by Objective has been implemented successfully in a great many organizations, both public and private. It is not, however, without its share of failures. Experience has shown that several factors are necessary for the MBO system to function effectively. These include—

1. Sufficient time must be allowed for the system to work. Three to five years may be necessary before MBO can be fully implemented.
2. Total commitment to the MBO process must be obtained from top and middle management.
3. There must be decentralization of management authority and responsibility, coupled with individual accountability.
4. MBO requires the careful selection of key management and administrative personnel.
5. MBO requires extensive training (and ocassional retraining) of management personnel in MBO concepts and processes.
6. MBO must be tailored to the particular conditions, problems, and circumstances of the organization. A predesigned MBO system cannot be superimposed upon an organization and expected to work without some modifications.
7. For MBO to be successful, the organization must have a structure which facilitates the free flow of communications among all functional units. This expedites decision-making and problem solving.
8. Restrictive rules and regulations (i.e., civil service rules) which limit individual accountability and initiative must be eased or eliminated. Emphasis should be placed on results rather than effort.

Obstacles to MBO

Management by Objective systems fail for many reasons. Stein conducted a study in which the attitudes of lower-level and mid-level management personnel working in organizations (both public and private) employing MBO were examined. The results of the study revealed a number of problems associated with implementing and maintaining an MBO system. The three most important problems discovered were—[29]

1. difficulty in defining objectives which were both meaningful and measurable;
2. insufficient follow-up, monitoring, and updating of the program;
3. lack of commitment by management to the purposes and concepts of MBO.

For too long, the police have functioned without clearly identified goals and objectives. Moreover, once goals and objectives have been identified, many police departments fail to initiate carefully designed programs directed toward goal accomplishment. Whether MBO is suitable to a particular police organization is problematic. What is more important is that the entire police mission and role can be better understood, and more easily accomplished, if it is conducted within the framework of a systematic approach to defined goals and objectives.

Summary

Police departments must be constantly alert to methods for the improvement of the quality and level of services provided to the public. This chapter has examined several such methods. The functions of planning, research, evaluation, and productivity improvement have been outlined generally. It is hoped that the student will recognize the tremendous potential that exists for continually improving the efficiency and effectiveness of police operations. No single program or method of improving efficiency and effectiveness can be sufficient. Rather, it must be an on going process, whereby existing operational strategies are continually monitored and evaluated and new methods developed and tested. This should be a primary concern of the modern police administrator.

Discussion Questions

1. *Describe several ways in which planning should be integrated into the management of police operations.*

2. *Identify the four types of planning described in the chapter and give examples of each.*

3. *Describe several subject areas in which scientific research may make a meaningful contribution to the resolution of problems affecting law enforcement.*

4. *Why has research not yet been utilized to its full potential in the field of law enforcement?*

5. *Define evaluation.*

6. *Describe the difference between efficiency and effectiveness.*

7. *Describe the five sequential steps involved in evaluation planning.*

8. *In general, how is productivity related to the national economy?*

9. *Define productivity and productivity improvement.*

10. *Describe several ways in which productivity in the police service can be improved. Give examples of each.*

11. *Describe the relationship between resources and results in the context of productivity.*

12. *List several suggested measures of police productivity and describe their relative advantages over commonly used measures.*

13. *Describe several elements necessary for an effective MBO system and discuss how they apply to the police organization.*

References

1. National Advisory Commission on Criminal Justice Standards and Goals, *Police* (Washington, D.C.: U.S. Government Printing Office, 1973), p. 101.

2. See Chapter 3 for a discussion of the planning process.

3. Raymond T. Galvin and J. L. LeGrande, "Planning and Research," in George D. Eastman and Esther M. Eastman, eds., *Municipal Police Administration*, 6th Ed. (Washington, D.C.: International City Management Association, 1969), p. 214.

4. President's Commission on Law Enforcement and Administration of Justice,

The Challenge of Crime in a Free Society (Washington, D.C.: U.S. Government Printing Office, 1967), p. 273.

5. *Omnibus Crime Control and Safe Streets Act of 1968* (PL 90–351), Title I, Declarations and Purpose.

6. George E. Kelling, Tony Pate, Duane Dieckman, and Charles E. Brown, *The Kansas City Preventive Patrol Experiment: A Summary Report* (Washington, D.C.: Police Foundation, 1974).

7. Michael D. Maltz, *Evaluation of Crime Control Programs* (Washington, D.C.: U.S. Department of Justice, Law Enforcement Assistance Administration, National Institute of Law Enforcement and Criminal Justice, 1972), p. 1.

8. Rep. Florence P. Dwyer, *Report to the People*, 12th District, New Jersey, 14 (January 22, 1970), as cited in Carol H. Weiss, *Evaluation Research: Methods for Assessing Program Effectiveness* (Englewood Cliffs, New Jersey: Prentice-Hall, Inc., 1972), p. 3.

9. David T. Stanley, "How Safe the Streets, How Good the Grant?" *Public Administration Review*, 34 (July-August, 1974), pp. 380-89; David Glaser, "National Goals and Indicators for the Reduction of Crime and Delinquency," *The Annals of the American Academy of Political and Social Science*, 371 (May, 1967), pp. 104-26.

10. Ellen Albright, et al., *Criminal Justice Research: Evaluation in Criminal Justice Programs: Guidelines and Examples* (Washington, D.C.: U.S. Department of Justice, Law Enforcement Assistance Administration, National Institute of Law Enforcement and Criminal Justice, 1973), pp. 5-10.

11. The evaluation of crime control programs is described in greater detail in Daniel Glaser, *Routinizing Evaluation: Getting Feedback on Effectiveness of Crime and Delinquency Programs* (Rockville, Md.: National Institute of Mental Health, Center for Studies of Crime and Delinquency, 1973).

12. J.M. Morgan, Jr. and R. Scott Fosler, "Police Productivity," *The Police Chief*, 41 (July, 1974), p. 28.

13. *Opportunities for Improving Productivity in Police Services* (Washington, D.C.: National Commission on Productivity, 1973).

14. *National Incentives to Improve State and Local Government Productivity* (Washington, D.C.: National Commission on Productivity and Work Quality, 1975).

15. See, for example, Joan L. Wolfle and John J. Heaphy, eds., *Readings on Productivity in Policing* (Washington, D.C.: Police Foundation, 1975).

16. *Opportunities for Improving Productivity in Police Services* (Washington, D.C.: National Commission on Productivity, 1973), p. 1.

17. Ibid.

18. George H. Kuper, "Productivity: A National Concern," in Wolfle and Heaphy, eds., *Readings on Productivity in Policing*, p. 2.

19. *Opportunities for Improving Productivity in Police Services* (Washington, D.C.: National Commission on Productivity, 1973), pp. 2-3.

20. Clarence E. Ridley and Herbert A. Simon, *Measuring Municipal Activities* (Chicago: International City Management Association, 1938).

21. Ibid., pp. 15-20.

22. Donald C. Stone, "Can Police Effectiveness Be Measured?" *Public Management*, 12 (September, 1930), pp. 465-71.

23. Spencer D. Parratt, "A Scale to Measure Effectiveness of Police Functioning," *Journal of Criminal Law and Criminology*, 28 (January-February, 1938), pp. 739-56.

24. Ridley and Simon, *Measuring Municipal Activities*, p. 19.

25. Dale D. McConkey, "Applying Management by Objectives to Nonprofit Corpora-

tions," *S.A.M. Advanced Management Journal*, 38 (January, 1973), pp. 10-20.

26. Ibid.

27. Rodney H. Brady, "MBO Goes to Work in the Public Sector," *Harvard Business Review*, 51 (March-April, 1973), pp. 65-74.

28. Bruce H. DeWoolfson, "Public Sector MBO and PPB: Cross Fertilization in Management Systems," *Public Administration Review*,

35 (July-August, 1975), pp. 387-95; Heinz Weihrich, "MBO: Appraisal With Transactional Analysis," *Personnel Journal*, 55 (April, 1976), pp. 173-75, ff.

29. Carrol D. Stein, "Objective Management Systems: Two to Five Years After Implementation," *Personnel Journal*, 54 (October, 1975), pp. 525, ff.

Appendix

Sources of Police Management Training

Many colleges, universities, and other institutions offer courses on police management, varying both in scope and duration. A few of the more widely recognized ones are listed here. Interested individuals are encouraged to write to the address indicated for further information about a particular course or institution.

Center for Criminal Justice
Gund Hall
Case Western Reserve Law School
Cleveland, Ohio 44106
(216) 369-3308

The center offers periodic courses in police management and supervision for lieutenants, captains, and chiefs of police. Courses are taught either at the center, or in the field, and range from 18 to 30 hours in duration. Course costs are from $75 to $100 per enrollee.

Center for Criminal Justice
California State University, Long Beach
1250 Bellflower Boulevard
Long Beach, California 90840
(213) 597-2505 or 498-4940

The center offers a variety of in-service police training courses, technical as well as managerial. The courses range from 24

340

hours to 120 hours with enrollment fees from $85 to $290. Upper division course credit is available through the university for all courses offered.

Center for Criminal Justice Training
School of Public and Environmental Affairs
Indiana University
400 East Seventh Street
Bloomington, Indiana   47401
(812) 337-2023

The center offers a two week introductory course and a one week advanced course on police management. Tuition for the introductory course is $375 and $245 for the advanced course. The center also conducts courses on police supervision, police records systems, police–community relations, and other topics.

Federal Bureau of Investigation
U.S. Department of Justice
Washington, D.C.   20535
(202) 324-3000

The Bureau conducts four 11-week National Academy sessions annually at its training complex located at Marine Corps Base, Quantico, Virginia. Applicants must be full-time law enforcement officers with five years continuous experience, between twenty-five and fifty years of age, and nominated by the head of their agency. Courses cover such diverse fields as management science, behavioral science, forensic science, and communication arts. There is no charge to agencies or their participants. Graduates receive up to 16 undergraduate or 8 graduate college units upon completion of training.

Florida Institute for Law Enforcement
St. Petersburg Junior College
P.O. Box 13489
St. Petersburg, Florida   33733
(813) 546-0011

The institute offers several courses for police administrators and law enforcement practioners, including courses on budgeting, police supervision, executive development, police leadership, management, and investigative skills. Courses range from 5 to 10 days in length.

International Association of Chiefs of Police
Professional Standards Division
Eleven Firstfield Road
Gaithersburg, Maryland   20760
(301) 948-0922

The Professional Standards Division offers a variety of training programs and seminars, ranging from police intelligence management to management of police training. Most courses last five days and are held in major cities throughout the United States. Fees of $275 per person include all books and materials, but do not include transportation, meals, or lodging.

International City Management Association
Institute for Training in Municipal Administration
1140 Connecticut Avenue, N.W.
Washington, D.C.   20036
(202) 293-2200

The institute offers a series of home study courses for municipal officials engaged in a variety of public administration fields, including police administration. A maximum of one year is allowed for course completion, but students are allowed to set their own pace. The average length of time required to complete one lesson is three to four hours. Completed assignments are sent directly by the student to his or her individual instructor. Enrollment, which includes materials, costs $150. Group rates are also available.

Massachusetts Institute of Technology
Alfred P. Sloan School of Management
50 Memorial Drive
Cambridge, Massachusetts   02139

The school of management conducts periodic 4-week schools designed for urban administrators, including city managers, administrative assistants, and police and fire executives. Primary emphasis is on management and technology concepts. Successful applicants are awarded a scholarship grant of $1,000 to partially defray the total program cost of $2,600, which covers tuition, meals, accommodations, and all teaching materials.

The New England Institute of Law Enforcement Management
Babson College, Drawer E
Babson Park, Massachusetts   02517
(617) 235-1200

The Institute conducts a Command Training Institute, consisting of ten 3-week sessions annually, designed for supervisory police personnel; and the Management Training Institute, which includes eight 1-week courses available to senior officers. There is no charge to participating agencies.

The Pennsylvania State University
College of Human Development
Law Enforcement and Corrections Services
Human Development Building
University Park, Pennsylvania   16802
(814) 865-1336

The university offers a series of 4-week police executive development institutes each year. Classes are limited to thirty-two senior police officers, lieutenants and above. Courses are held at the University Park campus. A single fee of $760 covers tuition and instructional materials.

Police Training Institute
359 Armory Building
Champaign, Illinois   61820
(217) 333-2337

The Institute conducts several 2-week courses in police supervision and management, along with a variety of other training schools, annually. Enrollment fees average $250 per student and include room and board.

Southern Police Institute
School of Police Administration
University of Louisville
Louisville, Kentucky 40208
(502) 636-4534

The Institute offers two 14-week administrative officers courses each year, in addition to other seminars and training programs. Preference is given to police officers in commanding, supervisory, or administrative positions when considering applications for the administrative officers course. Fifteen semester hours of college credit are awarded upon successful completion of the program.

The Traffic Institute
Northwestern University
405 Church Street
Evanston, Illinois   60204
(312) 492-7245

The institute conducts a variety of courses relating to highway transportation and traffic law administration. Its courses in law enforcement include police supervision, administration, and management, as well as units focusing on the principles and techniques of traffic accident investigation and traffic law enforcement. Courses range from three days to nine months. Course fee includes tuition and study materials. Living accommodations, meals, and transportation are not included. College credit, from 3 to 30 semester hours, may be awarded upon successful course completion.

University of Wisconsin—Extension
Institute of Governmental Affairs
Criminal Justice Education
610 Langdon Street
Madison, Wisconsin   53706
(608) 262-7769

The Institute conducts several college level semester courses in criminal justice management each year. Most courses are offered at several satellite campuses in Milwaukee, Wausau, Eau Claire, Beloit, and Oshkosh, as well as the main campus at Madison. Tuition ranges from $135 to $165 per semester.

Bibliography

Aboud, Antone and Grace Sterrett Aboud.
The Right to Strike in Public Employment.
Ithaca, N.Y.: School of Industrial and
Labor Relations, Cornell University, 1974.

Ahern, James F. *Police in Trouble: Our Frightening Crisis in Law Enforcement.* New
York: Hawthorne Books, 1972.

Albert, Rory Judd, *A Time For Reform:
A Case Study of the Interaction Between
the Commissioner of the Boston Police
Department and the Boston Police Patrol-
men's Association;* Technical Report
No. 12-75. Cambridge, Mass.: Operations
Research Center, Massachusetts Institute
of Technology, 1975.

Albright, Ellen, et al. *Criminal Justice Research: Evaluation in Criminal Justice
Programs: Guidelines and Examples.* Washington, D.C.: U.S. Department of Justice,
Law Enforcement Assistance Administration, National Institute of Law Enforcement and Criminal Justice, 1973.

Allen, William A., "Four-Day Work Week:
Another Approach," *The Police Chief.*
January 1973, pp. 48-49.

Anderson, Arvid and Hugh D. Jascourt,
eds. *Trends in Public Sector Labor Relations: An Information and Reference
Guide for the Future.* Chicago: International Personnel Management Association
and Public Employment Relations Research
Institute, 1975.

Angell, John E., "Toward an Alternative to
Classical Police Organizational Arrange-
ments: A Democratic Model," *Criminology.*
August-November 1971, pp. 185-206.

Applewhite, Philip B., *Organizational Behavior.*
Englewood Cliffs, N.J.: Prentice-Hall, 1965.

Argyris, Chris, "The Individual and Organization: Some Problems of Mutual Adjustment," *Administrative Science Quarterly.*
June 1957, pp. 1-24.

Argyris, Chris, "Personality and Organization
Theory Revisited," *Administrative Science
Quarterly.* June 1973, pp. 141-167.

Arondon, Albert H., "The Duke Power Com-
pany Case, *"Public Employment Practices
Bulletin No. 1.* Chicago: Public Personnel
Association, 1971.

Aronson, J. Richard and Eli Schwartz, eds.
*Management Policies in Local Govern-
ment Finance.* Washington, D.C.: International City Management Association
(in cooperation with Municipal Finance
Officers Association), 1975.

Ash, Phillip. *Meeting Civil Rights Require-
ments in Your Selection Program.* Chicago:
International Personnel Management
Association, 1974.

Baehr, Melany E., John E. Furcon, and
Ernest C.Froemel. *Psychological Assess-
ment of Patrolman Qualifications in
Relation to Field Performance.* Washing-
ton, D.C.: U.S. Government Printing
Office, 1968.

Barrett, Raymond J. . "Management in
The Public Sector," *New Jersey Municipalities.* December 1975, pp. 8-9, ff.

Bartholomew, Paul C. *Public Administration*, 3d ed. Totowa, N.J.: Littlefield, Adams, and Co., 1972.

Bergsman, Ilene. *Police Unions*, Management Information Service Report, Vol. 8, No. 3. Washington, D.C.: International City Management Association, 1976.

Berkley, George E. *The Democratic Policeman*. Boston, Mass.: Beacon Press, 1969.

Biddle, Richard E. "Discrimination: What Does It Mean?" *Public Employment Practices Bulletin No. 5*. Chicago: International Personnel Management Association, 1973.

Blake, Robert R. and Jane S. Mouton. "Managerial Facades" *Advanced Management Journal*. July 1966, pp. 30-37.

Blau, Peter M. and W. Richard Scott. *Formal Organizations*. San Francisco: Chandler Publishing Co., 1962.

Bloch, Peter, Deborah Anderson and Pamela Gervais. *Policewomen on Patrol—Major Findings: First Report, Volume I*. Washington, D.C.: Police Foundation, 1973.

Blum, Richard, ed. *Police Selection*. Springfield, Illinois: Charles C. Thomas, 1964.

Blumin, Deborah. *Victims: A Study of Crime in a Boston Housing Project*. Boston: Mayor's Safe Streets Act Advisory Committee, 1973.

Bopp, William J. *Police Personnel Administration*. Boston: Holbrook Press, 1974.

Bowers, Mollie H. "Police Administrators and the Labor Relations Process," *The Police Chief*. January, 1975, pp. 52-59.

Boyer, Jacque K. and Edward Griggs. *Equal Employment Opportunity Program Development Manual*. Washington, D.C.: Office of Civil Rights Compliance, Law Enforcement Assistance Administration, U.S. Department of Justice, 1974.

Brady, Rodney H. "MBO Goes to Work in the Public Sector," *Harvard Business Review*. March-April 1973, pp. 65-74.

Bristow, Allen P. *Effective Police Manpower Utilization*. Springfield, Ill.: Charles C. Thomas, 1969.

Brown, Donna. "The UCR Program: Development of a Standardized Audit," *The Police Chief*. December 1974, pp. 34-38.

Buren, R. Michael. "A Police Management Training Program: Efficient Use of Man and Money?" *Journal of Police Science and Administration*. September 1973, pp. 294-302.

Bussell, Horace G. "Results-Oriented Affirmative Action," *The Municipal Year Book 1975*. Washington, D.C.: International City Management Association, 1975, pp. 163-170.

Byham, William C. and Carl Wettengel. "Assessment Centers for Supervisors and Managers: An Introduction and Overview," *Public Personnel Management*. September-October, 1974, pp. 352-364.

Caldwell, James D. and James M. Nehe. "Implementing Unit Beat Policing: Patrol Distribution in Arlington County" *The Police Chief*. September 1974, pp. 47-49.

Cann, William. " Our 4/40 Basic Team Concept," *The Police Chief*. December 1972, pp. 56-64.

Capozzola, John M. "Productivity Bargaining: Problems and Prospects," *National Civic Review*. April 1976, pp. 176-86.

Chaiken, Jan M. *The Criminal Investigation Process, Volume II: Survey of Municipal and County Police Departments*. Santa Monica: The Rand Corporation, 1975.

Chambliss, William J., ed. *Crime and the Legal Process*. New York: McGraw-Hill, 1969.

Chapman, Samuel G., ed. *Police Patrol Readings*, 2d ed. Springfield, Ill.: Charles C. Thomas, 1970.

Chapman, Samuel G., et. al. *Perspectives of Assaults in the South Central United States, Vol. I*. Norman, Okla.: The University of Oklahoma, 1974.

Clark, Donald E. and Samuel G. Chapman. *A Forward Step: Educational Backgrounds for Policemen.* Springfield, Ill.: Charles C. Thomas, 1966.

Clarren, Sumner N. and Alfred I. Schwartz. *An Evaluation of Cincinnati's Team Policing Program.* Working Paper: 3006-11. Washington, D.C.: The Urban Institute, October 8, 1974.

Clawson, Calvin. "A Theoretical Approach to the Allocation of Police Preventive Patrol," *The Police Chief.* July 1973, pp. 53-59.

Cohen, Bernard and Jan M. Chaiken. *Police Background Characteristics and Performance—Report Prepared for the National Institute of Law Enforcement and Criminal Justice.* New York: The Rand Institute, 1972.

Colton, Dennis and Larry T. Hoover. "Role of Law Enforcement Training Commissions in the United States," *Journal of Criminal Justice.* Winter 1973, pp. 347-352.

Cordrey, John B. "Crime Rates, Victims, Offenders: A Victimization Study," *Journal of Police Science and Administration.* March 1975, pp. 100-110

Corwin, Ronald G. "Patterns of Organizational Conflict," *Administrative Science Quarterly.* December 1969, pp. 507-520.

Couturier, Jean L. "The Quiet Revolution in Public Personnel Laws," *Public Personnel Management.* May-June 1976, pp. 150-67.

Craft, James A. "Notes on the Administration of Collective Bargaining Agreements," *Personnel Administration/Public Personnel Review.* July-August 1972, pp. 30-33.

Crime in the Nation's Five Largest Cities: Crime Panel Surveys of Chicago, Detroit, Los Angeles, New York and Philadelphia—Advance Report. Washington, D.C.: U.S. Department of Justice, Law Enforcement Assistance Administration, National Criminal Justice Information and Statistics Service, April, 1974.

Crimes and Victims: A Report on the Dayton-San Jose Pilot Survey of Victimization. Washington, D.C.: United States Department of Justice, Law Enforcement Assistance Administration, National Criminal Justice Information and Statistics Service, June, 1974.

Criminal Justice Monograph: Innovation in Law Enforcement. Washington, D.C.: U.S. Department of Justice, Law Enforcement Assistance Administration, National Institute of Law Enforcement and Criminal Justice, 1973.

Criminal Victimization Surveys in 13 American Cities: National Crime Panel Surveys of Boston, Buffalo, Cincinnati, Houston, Miami, Milwaukee, Minneapolis, New Orleans, Oakland, Pittsburg, San Diego, San Francisco, and Washington, D.C.. Washington, D.C.: U.S. Department of Justice, Law Enforcement Assistance Administration, National Criminal Justice Information and Statistics Service, June 1975.

Cummings, Paul W. "Does Herzberg's Theory Really Work?" *The Personnel Administrator.* October 1974, pp. 19-22.

Dalton, Melville. "Conflict Between Staff and Line Managerial Officers," in Amitai Etzioni, ed., *Complex Organizations: A Sociological Reader.* New York: Holt, Rinehart and Winston, 1961, pp. 212-21.

Damos, James P., Peter Richman, and Eldon Miller, "P·R·E·W·A·R·N·S. . .A Police Response Early Warning System," *The Police Chief.* August 1973, pp. 24-27.

Danielson, William F. "Should Policemen and Firemen Get The Same Salary?" *Public Personnel Report No. 641.* Chicago: Public Personnel Association, 1964.

D'Arcy, Paul F. "Assessment Center Program Helps to Test Managerial Competence," *The Police Chief.* December 1974, pp. 52-53, ff.

Davis, Keith. *Human Relations at Work: The Dynamics of Organizational Behavior,* 3d ed. New York: McGraw-Hill, 1967.

———. "Evolving Models of Organizational Behavior," *Academy of Management Journal*. March 1968, pp. 27–38.

Deladurantey, Joseph C. and Lyle Knowles. "The New Management Team," *The Police Chief*. October 1973, pp. 18–23.

Dewoolfson, Bruce H. "Public Sector MBO and PPB: Cross Fertilization in Management Systems," *Public Administration Review*. July-August 1975, pp. 387–95.

Dimock, Marshall E. "The Meaning and Scope of Public Administration," in John M. Gaus, Leonard D. White, and Marshall E. Dimock, *The Frontiers of Public Administration*. Chicago: The University of Chicago Press, 1936, pp. 1–12.

Dowson, Robert Macgregor. "The Civil Service is Different," in Donald C. Rowat, ed., *Basic Issues in Public Administration*. New York: The Macmillan Company, 1961, pp. 23–26.

Drucker, Peter F. *Management: Tasks, Responsibilities, Practices*. New York: Harper & Row, 1973.

Dwyer, Rep. Florence P. *Report to the People*, 12th District, New Jersey, January 22, 1970.

Dyment, Robert. "A Case for the Foot Patrolman," in Samuel G. Chapman, ed., *Police Patrol Readings*, 2d ed. Springfield, Ill.: Charles C. Thomas, 1970, pp. 186–88.

Eastman, George D. and Esther M. Eastman, eds. *Municipal Police Administration*, 6th ed. Washington, D.C.: International City Management Association, 1969.

Etzioni, Amitai. *Modern Organizations*. Englewood Cliffs, N.J.: Prentice-Hall, 1964.

Fayol, Henri. *General and Industrial Management*, trans. Constance Storrs. London: Sir Isaac Pitman and Sons, Ltd., 1949.

Fear, Richard A. *The Evaluation Interview*, 2d ed. New York: McGraw-Hill, 1973.

Federal Bureau of Investigation. *Crime In the United States 1974*. Washington, D.C.:

U.S. Government Printing Office, 1975.

Federal Bureau of Investigation. *Manual of Police Records*. Washington, D.C.: U.S. Department of Justice.

Federal Bureau of Investigation. *Uniform Crime Reporting Handbook*. Washington, D.C.: U.S. Department of Justice, 1974.

Feld, Lipman G.. "Fifteen Questions You Dare Not Ask Job Applicants," *Management Review*. November 1974, pp. 34–36.

Finckenhauer, James O. "Higher Education and Police Discretion." *Journal of Police Science and Administration*. December 1975, pp. 450–57.

Fosdick, Raymond B. *American Police Systems*. New York: The Century Company, 1920.

Fowler, Robert Booth. "Normative Aspects of Public Employee Strikes," *Public Personnel Management*. March-April 1974, pp. 129–37.

"Fringe Benefits For Public Employees," *Public Management*. October 1973, entire issue.

Galvin, Raymond T. and J.L. LeGrande. "Planning and Research," in George D. Eastman and Esther M. Eastman, eds., *Municipal Police Administration*, 6th ed. Washington, D.C.: International City Management Association, 1969, pp. 208–16.

Gammage, Allen Z. and Stanley L. Sachs. *Police Unions*. Springfield, Ill.: Charles C. Thomas, 1972.

Gardiner, John A. *Traffic and the Police: Variations in Law Enforcement Policy*. Cambridge, Mass.: Harvard University Press, 1969.

Gaus, John M., Leonard D. White, and Marshall E. Dimock. *The Frontiers of Public Administration*. Chicago: The University of Chicago Press, 1936.

Gavin, James F. and John W. Hamilton. "Selecting Police Using Assessment Center Methodology," *Journal of Police*

Science and Administration. June 1975, pp. 166–76.

Gawthrop, Louis C., ed. *The Administrative Process and Democratic Theory.* Boston: Houghton Mifflin, 1970.

Germann, A.C., Frank D. Day and Robert R.J. Gallati. *Introduction to Law Enforcement and Criminal Justice.* Rev. 19th Printing, Springfield, Ill.: Charles C. Thomas, 1973.

Gilroy, Thomas P. and Anthony C. Russo. "Bargaining Unit Issues: Problems, Criteria, and Tactics," in Arvid Anderson and Hugh D. Jascourt, eds., *Trends in Public Sector Labor Relations: An Information and Reference Guide for the Future.* Chicago: International Personnel Management Association and Public Employment Relations Research Institute, 1975, pp. 67–70.

Gladden, E.N. *The Essentials of Public Administration.* London: Staples Press, 1953.

Glaser, Daniel. "National Goals and Indicators for the Reduction of Crime and Delinquency," *The Annals of the American Academy of Political and Social Science.* May 1971, pp. 104–26.

———. *Routinizing Evaluation: Getting Feedback on Effectiveness of Crime and Delinquency Programs.* Rockville, Md.: National Institute of Mental Health, Center for Studies of Crime and Delinquency, 1973.

Godfrey, E. Drexel, Jr., and Don R. Harris. *Basic Elements of Intelligence.* Washington, D.C.: U.S. Department of Justice, Law Enforcement Assistance Administration, Office of Criminal Justice Assistance, Technical Assistance Division, 1971.

Gomez, Luiz R. and Stephen J. Mussio. "An Application of Job Enrichment in a Civil Service Setting: A Demonstration Study," *Public Personnel Management.* January-February 1975, pp. 49–54.

Goodin, Carl V. "Effective Personalized Patrol." *The Police Chief.* November, 1972, pp. 18–19, ff.

Goodnow, Frank J. *Politics and Administration.* New York: The Macmillan Company, 1900.

Greenwood, Peter W., Jan M. Chaiken, Joan Petersilia, and Linda Pursoff. *The Criminal Investigation Process, Volume III: Observations and Analysis.* Santa Monica: The Rand Corporation, 1975.

———. and Joan Petersilia. *The Criminal Investigation Process, Volume I: Summary and Policy Implications.* Santa Monica: The Rand Corporation, 1975.

Grimes, John A. "The Police, the Union, and the Productivity Imperative," in Joan L. Wolfle and John F. Heaphy, eds., *Readings on Productivity in Policing.* Washington, D.C.: Police Foundation, 1975, pp. 47–85.

Gulick, Luther, and Lyndall F. Urwick, eds. *Papers on the Science of Administration.* New York: Institute of Public Administration, 1937.

Gulick, Luther. "Next Steps in Public Administration." *Public Administration Review.* Spring 1955, pp. 73–76.

———. "Science, Values, and Public Administration," in Luther Gulick and Lyndall F. Urwick, eds., *Papers on the Science of Administration.* New York: Institute of Public Administration, 1937, pp. 191–95.

Guthrie, C. Robert and Paul M. Whisenand. "The Use of Helicopters in Routine Police Patrol Operations: A Summary of Recommendations," in S.I. Cohn, ed., *Law Enforcement Science and Technology II.* Chicago: ITT Research Institute, 1968, pp. 551–55.

Haire, Mason, ed. *Organization Theory in Industrial Practice.* New York: John Wiley & Sons, 1962.

Hale, Charles D. *Police-Community Relations.* Albany, N.Y.: Delmar Publishers, 1974.

Halpern, Stephen C. *Police-Association and Department Leaders: The Politics of Co-Optation.* Lexington, Mass.: Lexington Books, D.C. Heath Co., 1974.

Hampton, Robert E. "Rededicating Ourselves to Merit Principles," *Personnel Administration/Public Personnel Review*. July-August 1972, pp. 57-59.

"The Hatch Act: Civil Servants Watching For A Break," *Congressional Quarterly Weekly Report*. September 9, 1972, pp. 2296-2299.

Herzberg, Frederick, Bernard Mausner, and Barbara Bloch Snyderman. *The Motivation to Work*, 2d. ed. New York: John Wiley & Sons, 1959.

Heydebrand, Wolf V. and James J. Noell. "Task Structure and Innovation in Professional Organizations," in Wolf V. Heydebrand, ed., *Comparative Organizations*. Englewood Cliffs, N.J.: Prentice-Hall, 1973, pp. 294-322.

Hillgren, James S. and L.W. Spradlin. "A Positive Disciplinary System for the Dallas Police Department," *The Police Chief*. July 1975, pp. 65-67.

Huntley, Gene. "Diminishing Reality of Management Rights," *Public Personnel Management*. May-June 1976, pp. 174-80.

"ICMA Statement on Management/Labor Relations," *Public Management*. March, 1975, pp. 18-19.

Igleburger, Robert M. and John E. Angell. "Dealing With Police Unions," *The Police Chief*. May 1971, pp. 50-55.

Igleburger, Robert M., John E. Angell, and Gary Pence. "Changing Urban Police: Practitioner's Views," *Criminal Justice Monograph: Innovation in Law Enforcement*. Washington, D.C.: U.S. Department of Justice, Law Enforcement Assistance Administration, National Institute of Law Enforcement and Criminal Justice, 1973, pp. 76-114.

Juris, Hervey A. and Peter Feuille, "Employee Organizations," in O. Glenn Stahl and Richard A. Stauffenberger, eds., *Police Personnel Administration*. Washington, D.C.: Police Foundation, 1974, pp. 203-26.

———. *The Impact of Police Unions—Sum-*

mary Report. Washington, D.C. U.S. Department of Justice, Law Enforcement Assistance Administration, National Institute of Law Enforcement and Criminal Justice, 1973.

Kassoff, Norman C. *Organizational Concepts*. Washington, D.C.: International Association of Chiefs of Police, 1967.

Kearney, William J. and Desmond D. Martin, "The Assessment Center: A Tool for Promotion Decisions," *The Police Chief*. January 1975, pp. 31-33.

Kelling, George E., Tony Pate, Duane Dieckman, and Charles E. Brown. *The Kansas City Preventive Patrol Experiment: A Summary Report*. Washington, D.C.: Police Foundation, 1974.

Kenney, John P. *Police Administration*. Springfield, Ill.: Charles C. Thomas, 1972.

———. *Police Administration*, rev. 3d. Printing. Springfield, Ill.: Charles C. Thomas, 1975.

Kenney, John P., George T. Felkenes, Carl Bloom, and Michael O'Neil. "Field Patrolman Work Load in California: Cities with 25,000 to 100,000 Population," *Journal of California Law Enforcement*. January 1970, pp. 124-31.

Kimble, Joseph. "Recruitment," in Richard Blum, ed., *Police Selection*. Springfield, Ill.: Charles C. Thomas, 1964, pp. 71-84.

Koontz, Harold and Cyril O'Donnell. *Principles of Management: An Analysis of Managerial Functions*, 4th ed. New York: McGraw-Hill, 1968.

Kroes, William H., Bruce L. Margolis, and Joseph H. Hurrell, Jr. "Job Stress in Policemen," *Journal of Police Science and Administration*. June 1974, pp. 145-55.

Kulus, Joseph C., Robert A. Lorinskas and Rebecca Byrne, eds. *Psychology and the Police: A Bibliography and Summary of Findings*. Chicago: The Chicago Police Academy, 1972.

Kuper, George H. "Productivity: A National

Concern," in Joan L. Wolfle and John F. Heaphy, eds. *Readings on Productivity in Policing*. Washington, D.C.: Police Foundation, 1975, pp. 1–10.

Kuykendall, Jack and Armand P. Hernandez. "A University's Administration of Justice Program," *Journal of Police Science and Administration*. September 1974, pp. 297–307.

Labor Relations for Supervisors: A Manual for Day to Day Living With Employee Organizations. Washington, D.C.: Labor Management Relations Service.

Landy, Frank J. and Carl V. Goodin. "Performance Appraisal," in O. Glenn Stahl and Richard A. Staufenberger, eds., *Police Personnel Administration*. Washington, D.C.: Police Foundation, 1974, pp. 165–84.

Leonard, V.A. *The Police Detective Function*. Springfield, Ill.: Charles C. Thomas, 1970.

———. *Police Personnel Administration*. Springfield, Ill.: Charles C. Thomas, 1970.

———. *The Police Records System*. Springfield, Ill.: Charles C. Thomas, 1970.

Lesieur, Fred G., ed. *The Scanlon Plan: A Frontier in Labor Management Cooperation*. Cambridge, Mass.: The MIT Press, 1958.

Lesieur, Fred G. and Elbridge S. Puckett. "The Scanlon Plan Has Proved Itself," *Harvard Business Review*. September–October 1969, pp. 109–18.

Levitan, David M. "Political Ends and Administrative Means," in Louis C. Gawthrop, ed., *The Administrative Process and Democratic Theory*. Boston: Houghton Mifflin Co. 1970, pp. 427–36.

Lewin, David. "Wage Parity and the Supply of Police and Firemen," *Industrial Relations*. February 1973, pp. 77–85.

Lewis, Carlton. "State Regulation of Local Government Labor Relations," *Public Management*. February 1975, pp. 7–9.

"Lifelong Learning," *The Royal Bank of Canada Monthly Letter*. December 1974.

Likert, Rensis. *New Patterns of Management*. New York: McGraw-Hill, 1961.

———. *The Human Organization: Its Management and Value*. New York: McGraw-Hill, 1967.

Lindholm, Richard W., David S. Arnold, and Richard R. Herbert. "The Budgetary Process," in J. Richard Aronson and Eli Schwartz, eds., *Management Policies in Local Government Finance*. Washington, D.C.: International City Management Association (in cooperation with Municipal Finance Officers Association), 1975, pp. 63–92.

Lloyd, Lewis E. "Origins and Objectives of Organizations," in Mason Haire, ed., *Organization Theory in Industrial Practice*. New York: John Wiley & Sons, 1962, pp. 28–47.

Longenecker, Justin G. *Principles of Management and Organizational Behavior*, 2d. ed. Columbus, Ohio: Charles E. Merrill Publishing Co., 1969.

Loveridge, Ronald O. *City Managers in Legislative Politics*. Indianapolis: Bobbs-Merrill Co., Inc., 1971.

Luthans, Fred. *Organizational Behavior: A Modern Behavioral Approach to Management*. New York: McGraw-Hill, 1973.

Lutz, Carl F., and James P. Morgan. "Jobs and Rank," in O. Glenn Stahl and Richard A. Staufenberger, eds., *Police Personnel Administration*. Washington, D.C.: Police Foundation, 1974, pp. 17–44.

McConkey, Dale D. "Applying Management by Objectives to Nonprofit Corporations," *S.A.M. Advanced Management Journal*. January 1973, pp. 10–20.

McCutcheon, James T. "Should Police and Fire Salaries Be Equal?" *The Tax Journal*. 4th Quarter 1974, pp. 111–13, ff.

McGinnis, William H. "Small Department Duty Schedule," *The Police Chief.* July 1974, pp. 61-62.

McGregor, Douglas. *The Human Side of Enterprise.* New York: McGraw-Hill, 1960.

Maltz, Michael D. *Evaluation of Crime Control Programs.* Washington, D.C.: U.S. Department of Justice, Law Enforcement Assistance Administration, National Institute of Law Enforcement and Criminal Justice, 1972.

Mansfield, W. Ed. "An Affirmative Action Program Proposal," *Public Employment Practices Bulletin No. 6.* Chicago: International Personnel Management Association, 1974.

Margolis, Richard J. *Who Will Wear the Badge?* Washington, D.C.: U.S. Civil Service Commission, 1971.

Martin, Edward A. "Central Issues in Police and Fire Negotiations: A City Manager's Viewpoint," *Arizona Review.* April 1976, pp. 2-8.

Martin, Phillip L. "The Hatch Act: The Current Movement for Reform," *Public Personnel Management.* May-June 1974, pp. 180-84.

Maslow, Abraham H. *Motivation and Personality*, 2d ed. New York: Harper & Row, 1970.

Mayo, Elton. *The Human Problems of an Industrial Civilization.* New York: The Macmillan Co., 1933.

Michels, Robert. "Oligarchy," in Oscar Grusky and George A. Miller, eds., *The Sociology of Organizations.* New York: The Free Press, 1970, pp. 25-43.

Miewald, Robert D. "Conflict and Harmony in the Public Service," *Public Personnel Management.* November-December, 1974, pp. 531-35.

Mooney, James D. *The Principles of Organization.* rev. ed. New York: Harper & Row, 1970.

Morgan, J.M. Jr., and R. Scott Fosler. "Police Productivity," *The Police Chief.* July 1974, p. 28.

Morris, Norval and Gordon Hawkins. *The Honest Politician's Guide to Crime Control.* Chicago: The University of Chicago Press, 1970.

Morse, Mureil M. "Shall We Bargain Away the Merit System?" in Kenneth O. Warner, ed., *Developments in Public Employee Relations: Legislative, Judicial, Administrative.* Chicago: Public Personnel Association, 1965, pp. 154-61.

Mosher, Frederick C. *Democracy and the Public Service.* New York: Oxford University Press, 1968.

"Municipal Worker Fringe Benefits Grow Faster Than Pay Scales," *Nation's Cities.* February 1965, p. 27.

The Municipal Year Book 1975. Washington, D.C.: International City Management Association, 1975.

National Advisory Commission on Criminal Justice Standards and Goals. *Police.* Washington, D.C.: U.S. Government Printing Office, 1973.

National Civil Service League. *Judicial Mandates for Affirmative Action.* Washington, D.C.: National Civil Service League, 1973.

National Incentives to Improve State and Local Government Productivity. Washington, D.C.: National Commission on Productivity and Work Quality, 1975.

Newland, Chester A. "Collective Bargaining Concepts: Applications in Governments," *Public Administration Review.* March-April 1968, pp. 117-26.

Nigro, Felix A. *Modern Public Administration*, 2d ed. New York: Harper & Row, 1970.

Omnibus Crime Control and Safe Streets Act of 1968 (PL 90-351).

Opportunities for Improving Productivity in Police Services. Washington, D.C.: National Commission on Productivity, 1973.

Parratt, Spencer D. "A Scale to Measure Effectiveness of Police Functioning," *Journal of Criminal Law and Criminology*. January-February 1938, pp. 739–56.

Paul, William J., Keith B. Robertson, and Frederick Herzberg. "Job Enrichment Pays Off," *Harvard Business Review*. March-April 1969, pp. 61–78.

Paulionis, A.N. "The Value of Practical Promotional Standards in the Police and Fire Ranks," *Public Personnel Management*. May-June 1973, pp. 179–81.

Pigeon, Carol A. "Personnel, Compensation, and Expenditures in Police, Fire, and Refuse Collection and Disposal Departments," *Urban Data Service Reports*. Washington, D.C.: International City Management Association, April 1975.

Police Training and Performance Study. Washington, D.C.: U.S. Department of Justice, Law Enforcement Assistance Administration, National Institute of Law Enforcement and Criminal Justice, 1970.

Prentice-Hall. *Public Personnel Administration Bulletin* December 17, 1974.

President's Commission on Law Enforcement and Administration of Justice. *Task Force Report: Assessment of Crime*. Washington, D.C.: U.S. Government Printing Office, 1967.

————. *Task Force Report: Organized Crime*. Washington, D.C.: U.S. Government Printing Office, 1967.

————. *Task Force Report: The Police*. Washington, D.C.: U.S. Government Printing Office, 1967.

————. *The Challenge of Crime in a Free Society*. Washington, D.C.: U.S. Government Printing Office, 1967.

Price, James L. *Organizational Effectiveness: An Inventory of Propositions*. Homewood, Ill.: Richard D. Irwin, Inc., 1968.

Redford, Emmette S., *Democracy in the Administrative State*. New York: Oxford University Press, 1969.

————. *Ideal and Practice in Public Administration*. Birmingham: University of Alabama Press, 1958.

Reiser, Martin. "Some Occupational Stresses on Policemen." *Journal of Police Science and Administration*. June 1974, pp. 156–59.

Report of the National Advisory Commission on Civil Disorders. New York: Bantam Books, 1968.

Ridley, Clarence E. and Herbert A. Simon. *Measuring Municipal Activities*. Chicago: International City Management Association,1938.

Roethlisberger, F.J. and W.J. Dickson. *Management and the Worker*. Cambridge, Mass.: Harvard University Press, 1939.

Rosenbloom, Daniel H. "Citizenship Rights and Civil Service: An Old Issue in a New Phase," *Public Personnel Review*. July 1970, pp. 180–84.

Rowat, Donald C., ed. *Basic Issues in Public Administration*. New York: The Macmillan Company, 1961.

Royster, Paul H. and Harry J. Patterson. "The Computer As a Collective Bargaining Tool." *Public Management*. April 1975, pp. 13–14.

Ruddock, Robert L. "Recruit Training: Stress v. Nonstress," *The Police Chief*. November 1974, pp. 47–49.

Saso, Carmen D. and Earl P. Tanis. *Selection and Classification of Eligibles: A Survey of Policies and Practices*. Chicago: International Personnel Management Association, 1974.

Schein, Edgar H. *Organizational Psychology*. Englewood Cliffs, N.J.: Prentice-Hall, 1965.

Schmidt, Emerson P. *Union Power and the Public Interest*. Los Angeles: Nash Publishing Corp., 1973.

Schur, Edwin M. *Crimes Without Victims: Deviant Behavior and Public Policy*. Englewood Cliffs, N.J.: Prentice-Hall, 1965.

Schwartz, Alfred I. and Sumner N. Clarren. *Evaluation of Cincinnati's Community Sector Team Policing Program, A Progress Report: The First Six Months, Summary of Major Findings*, working paper: 3006-4. Washington, D.C.: The Urban Institute, July 30, 1974.

Second National Survey of Employee Benefits for Full-Time Personnel of U.S. Municipalities. Washington, D.C.: Labor Management Relations Service, National League of Cities, U.S. Conference of Mayors, and National Association of Counties, 1974.

Selznick, Phillip. "Foundation of the Theory of Organization," in Amitai Etzioni, ed., *Complex Organizations: A Sociological Reader.* New York: Holt, Rinehart and Winston, 1961.

Sheehe, Gordon H. "Police Traffic Supervison," in George D. Eastman and Esther M. Eastman, eds., *Municipal Police Administration*, 6th ed. Washington, D.C.: International City Management Association, 1969, pp. 104-28.

Shepard, George H. "Youth Services Systems: An Innovative Concept in Prevention," *The Police Chief.* February 1973, pp. 48-53.

Sherman, Lawrence W., Catherine H. Milton, and Thomas V. Kelly. *Team Policing: Seven Case Studies.* Washington, D.C.: Police Foundation, 1973.

Sikula, Andrew F. *Management and Administration.* Columbus, Ohio: Charles E. Merrill Publishing Co., 1973.

Simon, H.A., D.W. Smithburg, and V.A. Thompson. "The Universality of Administration," in Donald C. Rowat, ed., *Basic Issues in Public Administration.* New York: The Macmillan Company, 1961, pp. 18-23.

Skolnick, Jerome H. *Justice Without Trial: Law Enforcement in Democratic Society.* New York: John Wiley & Sons, 1966.

Smith, David H. and Ezra Stotland. "A New Look at Police Officer Selection," in John R. Snibbe and Homa M. Snibbe, eds., *The Urban Policeman in Transition: A Psychological and Sociological Review.* Springfield, Ill.: Charles C. Thomas, 1973, pp. 5-24.

Snibbe, John R. and Homa M. Snibbe, eds. *The Urban Policeman in Transition: A Psychological and Sociological Review.* Springfield, Ill.: Charles C. Thomas, 1973.

Stahl, O. Glenn. *Public Personnel Administration*, 6th ed. New York: Harper & Row, 1962.

Stahl, O. Glenn and Richard A. Staufenberger, eds. *Police Personnel Administration.* Washington, D.C.: Police Foundation, 1974.

Stanley, David T. "How Safe the Streets, How Good the Grant?" *Public Administration Review.* July-August, 1974, pp. 380-89.

———. "What Are Unions Doing to Merit Systems?" *Public Personnel Review.* April 1970, pp. 108-13.

Stead, Philip John. "The Humanism of Command," *The Police Chief.* January 1974, pp. 26-28.

Stein, Carrol D. "Objective Management Systems: Two to Five Years After Implementation," *Personnel Journal.* October 1975, pp. 525-28, ff.

Sterling, James W. "The College Level Entry Requirement: A Real Or Imagined Cure-All," *The Police Chief.* August, 1974, pp. 28-31.

Stone, Donald C. "Can Police Effectiveness Be Measured?" *Public Management.* September 1930, pp. 465-71.

Sweeney, Thomas J. and William Ellingsworth. *Issues in Police Patrol: A Book of Readings.* Kansas City, Mo.: Kansas City Police Department, 1973.

Taylor, Frederick W. *The Principles of Scientific Management.* New York: Harper & Brothers, 1911.

The Traffic Institute. *Position Statement: Uniform Traffic Law Enforcement.* Evanston, Ill.: Northwestern University Press.

Urban Data Service, Laurie S. Frankel. *Personnel Practices in Municipal Police Departments*. Washington, D.C.: International City Management Association, November, 1973.

Urwick, L. *The Elements of Administration*. New York: Harper & Brothers, 1943.

Urwick, L. and E.F.L. Brech. *The Making of Scientific Management, Vol. I: Thirteen Pioneers*. London: Management Publications Trust, 1949.

U.S. Bureau of Labor Statistics. *Handbook of Labor Statistics 1973*. Washington, D.C.: U.S. Government Printing Office, 1973.

Vollmer, August and Albert Schneider. "The School for Police As Planned at Berkeley," *Journal of the American Institute of Criminal Law and Criminology*. March 1917, pp. 877-98.

Wahlrobe, Thomas E. "The Cafeteria Approach to Employee Benefits," *Administrative Management*. December 1974, pp. 48-52.

Walton, Richard E., John M. Dutton, and Thomas P. Cafferty. "Organizational Context and Interdepartmental Conflict," *Administrative Science Quarterly*. December 1969, pp. 522-42.

Ward, Steven M. *Individual Technical Assistance Report in Response to a Request for Technical Assistance by the Augusta, Georgia, Police Department*. Chicago: Public Administration Service, 1974.

Warner, Kenneth O., ed. *Developments in Public Employee Relations: Legislative, Judicial, Administrative*. Chicago: Public Personnel Association, 1965.

Webb, Donald G. and Gene F. Westergren. "The Detraining Syndrome," *The Police Chief*. November 1973, pp. 36, ff.

Weihrich, Heinz, "MBO: Appraisal With Transactional Analysis," *Personnel Journal*. April 1976, pp. 173-75.

Weiss, Carol H. *Evaluation Research: Methods for Assessing Program Effectiveness*. Englewood Cliffs, N.J.: Prentice-Hall, 1972.

Wellington, Harry H. and Ralph K. Winter, Jr. *The Unions and the Cities*. Washington, D.C.: The Brookings Institution, 1971.

What You Need to Know About Labor Relations: Guidelines for Elected and Appointed Officials. Washington, D.C.: Labor Management Relations Service, 1975.

Whisenand, Paul M., George M. Medak, and Bradley L. Gates, "The Four-day—Forty-Hour Workweek," in *Criminal Justice Monograph: Innovation in Law Enforcement*. Washington, D.C.: U.S. Department of Justice, Law Enforcement Assistance Administration, National Institute of Law Enforcement and Criminal Justice, 1973, pp. 143-63.

Wilson, O.W. "Problems in Police Personnel Administration," *Journal of Criminal Law, Criminology, and Police Science*. March-April 1953, pp. 840-47.

Wilson, O.W. and Roy C. McLaren. *Police Administration*, 3d ed. New York: McGraw-Hill, 1972.

Wilson, Woodrow, "The Study of Administration" *Political Science Quarterly*. June, 1887, pp. 197-222.

Witherford, David K. *Speed Enforcement Policies and Procedures*. Saugatuck, Conn.: Eno Foundation for Transportation, 1970.

Wolfle, Joan L. and John F. Heaphy, eds. *Readings on Productivity in Policing*. Washington, D.C.: Police Foundation, 1975.

Wurf, Jerry. "Merit: A Union View," *Public Administration Review*. September-October 1974, pp. 431-34.

Your Employment Application: Bridge or Barrier to Public Employment. Washington, D.C.: Bureau of Intergovernmental Programs, U.S. Civil Service Commission, 1975.

Zurcher, James C., Dale Miller, and Jay C. Rounds. "Selecting Effective Police Sergeants," *The Police Chief*. January 1975, pp. 28-30.

Index